The Country Life Book of

ROYAL PALACES CASTLES & HOMES

*Including Vanished Palaces and Historic Houses
with Royal Connections*

by Patrick Montague-Smith and Hugh Montgomery-Massingberd

Country Life Books

First published by Country Life Books, 1981
ISBN 0 600 36808 4

Created and produced by Antler Books, London
Designed by Paul Watkins
Picture research by Tom Williams

Published by Country Life Books
and distributed for them by
The Hamlyn Publishing Group Ltd
London.New York.Sydney.Toronto
Astronaut House, Feltham, Middlesex, England

Typesetting by Input Typesetting Limited, London
Colour separations and printing by
New Interlitho SPA Milan

We should like to thank Patrick Montague-Smith and
Hugh Montgomery-Massingberd not only for their
contributions but also for their help and advice. In their
turn they have asked us to express their appreciation for
the co-operation which they received from a large number
of libraries and individuals. In particular we want to
thank Lt Col Sir John Johnston, Peter Hartley, Marcus
Bishop and Charles Noble of the Lord Chamberlain's
office, without whose co-operation this book could
not have been published. Apart from those who supplied
the illustrations (acknowledged elsewhere) we also want to
say thank-you to the following:
Capt Alastair Aird, Vice-Admiral Sir Peter Ashmore,
John Barratt, Linda Bell, Mark Bence-Jones, Lt Col
Simon Bland, Major Shane Blewitt, Noelle Brown, the
Duke of Buccleuch and Queensberry, Lt Commander
Richard Buckley, John Caiger, Francis Cornish, Frances
Dimond, Rosalind Fisher, Desmond Green, Liz Gregory,
Carron Greig, Joanna Hickson, Maureen Jones, Laurie
Keeler, Mary Killen, Steve Lawrence, Major N S
Lawson, Mona Mitchell, Jane Oliver, Robert Owen,
Amanda Parry-Williams, John Phillips, Capt Mark
Phillips, Patricia Pierce, Hon George Plumptre, J L
Pollard, Hon Jane Roberts, Kenneth Robertson, Michael
Sayer, Michael Shea, Richard Tilbrooke, Hugo Vickers,
Anne Wall, David Wrench, the Provost and Fellows of
Worcester College, Oxford, the County Archivists of
Gloucestershire and Northamptonshire.
Robert Dudley, John Stidolph
Antler Books, London, July 1981

ROYAL PALACES
CASTLES & HOMES

Contents

Preface

The title and subtitle of this book give a clear idea of what the reader can expect to find between its covers. The very large number of buildings associated with the Royal Family over the centuries has made the task of editorial selection a crucial one, so it may be helpful to give some pointers to the way in which the choice was made.

Royal Palaces, Castles and Homes is not designed to be a tourist guide-book, peering over the wall at the private lives of the Royal Family. The emphasis is much more on the historical and architectural significance of the palaces and homes, and on the part they played in the unfolding pageantry of our monarchy. Private houses are included, such as Gatcombe Park, Nether Lypiatt Manor and Highgrove: these are places of considerable interest in themselves. Readers looking for descriptions of the holiday hideaways of the Royal Family will be disappointed. There are none such in this book.

There may be disagreement as to the merits of the final selection. Some may miss Audley End, Rotherhithe Palace or Guildford Castle, but we have tried to include those buildings most closely associated with the monarchy over the longest period or those which, for some historical reason, have an unusual claim on our attention. The list of possible homes is a very long one however, and space is limited. Over the centuries the kings and queens of England and their families built and lived in many more castles, palaces and homes than we could hope to include in this volume. Learned advice was taken before the final selection was made and we hope that all readers will find much that is new, as well as some that is happily familiar, in the pages that follow.

Kew Palace, now called the Dutch House, seen here in a watercolour from the Queen's collection, epitomises the buildings described in this book. Once the home of George III and Queen Charlotte, the house is now unoccupied but remains a royal palace. It stands in historic Kew Gardens, the site of several other royal palaces and homes, now vanished, which witnessed dramatic events in the lives of our monarchs and their families during the eighteenth and nineteenth centuries

BUCKINGHAM PALACE

At the beginning of the seventeenth century the site where Buckingham Palace now stands was covered with 30,000 mulberry trees by James I who was keen on producing raw silk and was under the impression that silkworms enjoy tucking into black mulberries. Unfortunately silkworms actually prefer white mulberries for their daily diet so the scheme was not a success. By the middle of the century the Mulberry Garden had become a public pleasure ground and booths were established among the trees for the sale of refreshments.

The lease of the garden had been acquired in 1633 by Lord Goring who built Goring House nearby. He was a Royalist commander in the Civil War, being created Earl of Norwich, and although some of his fellow cavaliers looked askance at his heavy drinking, none doubted the ardency of his support for the Stuarts. "Had I millions of crowns or scores of sons," he once told his wife, "the King and his cause should have them all".

After the Restoration Goring House was acquired by the black-plastered Henry Bennet, first Earl of Arlington (the first 'A' in Charles II's 'Cabal'), who later rebuilt it after a fire and added extensively to the grounds. The grander new building was called Arlington House but it too suffered a fire when being occupied by the Duke of Devonshire as a tenant of Lord Arlington's daughter Isabella. This heiress married one of Charles II's bastards, the Duke of Grafton, and eventually sold Arlington House to John Sheffield, who was created Duke of Buckingham in 1703. Sheffield (an ancestor, incidentally, of one of the present Prince of Wales' former girlfriends, Miss Davina Sheffield) was an old friend of Queen Anne who gave him some of St James's Park to enlarge his estate.

In the year that he became a Duke, Buckingham demolished the fire-damaged Arlington House and built Buckingham House in its stead to the designs of William Talman and Captain William Winde, a Dutch architect. Like many an overmighty subject before him, the Duke overreached himself. Queen Anne took a dim view of his building the house so that it looked down the Mall. With its spacious grounds, more like a country house park than a town garden, Buckingham House was the finest private house in London. The Duke was delighted with his creation, taking a special pride in the staircase 'with eight and forty steps ten feet broad, each step of one entire Portland stone'.

Upon the Duke's death in 1721, Buckingham House passed to his widow, a bastard daughter of James II by his mistress Catherine Sedley and inordinately proud of her

Opposite: The view over the Queen Victoria Memorial from the Centre Room and the Balcony from where the Royal Family wave to the crowds on ceremonial occasions

Previous page: The procession for the wedding of the Princess Royal in 1858 showing Buckingham Palace, St James's Palace, Lancaster House, Clarence House and York House

Stuart blood. Her staff wore Stuart livery and she was known to her contemporaries as 'Princess Buckingham'. The Buckinghams and the Hanoverians had little time for each other; when George II expressed an interest in buying Buckingham House the Duchess asked for as much as £60,000 and the deal was not proceeded with. She remained there until her death in 1742 when a bastard son of her husband came into the place. Finally, twenty years later George III bought the house and grounds for under half what his grandfather had been asked to pay by the Jacobite Duchess.

Buckingham House at this time was not as grand as all that – certainly not on the scale of a European royal palace. Ironically, if it had been, it would not have appealed to the homely George III. He saw the place as a pleasant retreat from the formality of ceremonial life at St James's and renamed it 'The Queen's House'. Various building alterations and extensions were made to the garden front and the King's most notable addition to the house was his important Library, much admired by Doctor Johnson. There was a celebrated 'house-warming' when the improvements had been made, with the grounds being illuminated by 4,000 coloured lamps and a vast picture of George III showing this unlikely figure dispensing peace to all the world.

By the time that great royal builder George IV inherited Buckingham House, Parliament was on its guard against granting any more money for his grandiose schemes, which had already involved excessive sums for Carlton House, Windsor and Brighton. None the less, the King extracted some £200,000 for 'a repair and improvement of Buckingham House'. In fact, he spent about three times as much as that in turning it into a palace large enough for royal entertaining.

It was not so much 'a repair and improvement' as a rebuilding. John Nash built the new palace, or 'The King's House in Pimlico' as it was called at one stage, round a three-sided courtyard, the open side facing the Mall and approached through a triumphal arch. Nash's principal front of golden Bath stone, incorporating the shell of the original house, overlooked the gardens which were landscaped by William Aiton. The painted staircase in the old house and its other interiors were not preserved, though the style of Nash's new state apartments recalled the sumptuousness of Carlton House demolished in 1827.

George IV died in 1830 before the New Palace, as it also had been called, was completed. William IV was not keen to live there, suggesting that it might be used as the Houses of Parliament (following the fire at Westminster of 1834) or as a barracks. The building was eventually finished by Edward Blore who removed Nash's much-derided dome and in 1847 this architect provided rooms for Queen Victoria's growing family by enclosing the courtyard with a rather dull range in Caen stone facing the Mall. Nash's

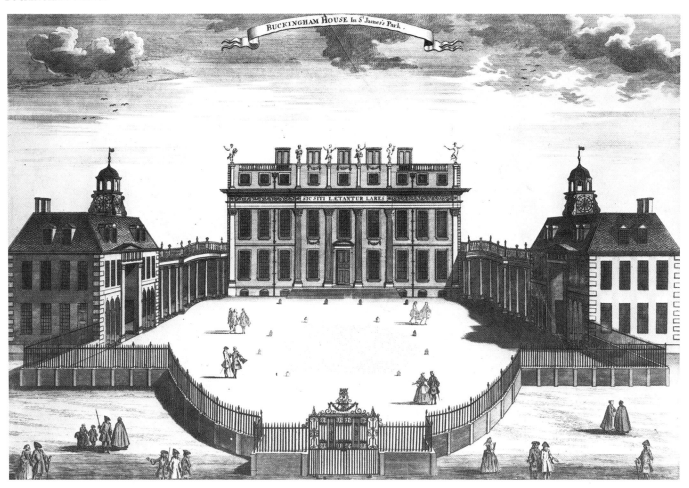

BUCKINGHAM HOUSE In St James's Park.

SIC SITI LÆTANTUR LARES

*Above: An early 18th-century view of Buckingham House,
described at the time as the finest private house in London.
We see it again (left) when it was known as the Queen's
Palace, Pimlico before the addition of Blore's east front. In
1851 Nash's triumphal arch was moved to its present position
at Marble Arch*
*Bottom left: The King's Library, built by George III, was
that monarch's most important contribution to the house*
*Opposite top: A ball held in the Ballroom on 17 June 1896,
from a painting by Louis Haghe, and the same painter's view
of a banquet in the Picture Gallery in 1893 (below)*

triumphal arch was banished in 1851 to Tyburn where it
became familiar to later generations of Londoners as the
Marble Arch.

Blore was replaced by Sir James Pennethorne, a nephew
and a pupil of John Nash, who added the south wing which
contains the State Supper Room and the enormous Ballroom. Pennethorne's work was finished in 1855, but six
years later occurred the death of Prince Albert and the
palace was deserted for much of Queen Victoria's long
widowhood. In 1873 it was lent to the Shah of Persia for
his state visit and there were some bizarre goings-on.
Apparently the Shah took his meals on the floor, was re-
luctant to avail himself of the palace's lavatories and organ-
ized a boxing match in the garden. It has even been
suggested that he had one of his staff executed with a
bowstring and buried in the grounds. Such a happening
would have been in keeping with the story of how when
visiting an English prison on a later state visit, he was
shown the gallows and asked whether he could see it in use;
on being told that there was nobody who was to be hanged,
he said, "Take one of my suite!"

Buckingham Palace can be said not really to have come into its own until virtually within living memory when it was the setting for the brilliant receptions and Court balls held by Edward VII and Queen Alexandra. Edward was born and died here. George V and Queen Mary thought about returning to Kensington Palace, but after they had dropped this idea the last major alterations were made to the palace in 1913 by Sir Aston Webb. He refaced Blore's shabby east front with a facade of Portland stone looking out on to the newly-erected Victoria Memorial.

It is this not particularly inspiring grey front that signifies Buckingham Palace for countless millions, but the fortunate thousands who have been invited to one of the frequent royal garden parties know that Nash's garden front is much

Left: A garden party at Buckingham Palace in 1897. It is interesting to see the spectators assembled on the roof of the palace. We see the gardens less busy (below) looking across the lake at Nash's west front

the nicer. Even if now overlooked by the monstrous skyscrapers which were allowed to disfigure London in the 1960s, the Buckingham Palace gardens, with a lake, form a wonderful oasis in the centre of the metropolis. Although visitors can sign their names as a gesture of loyal greeting at the Privy Purse Door (on the right of the Mall front), the palace itself is not open to the public.

The ornamental gates at the front of the palace have ironwork designed by members of the Bromsgrove Guild. Through the central entrance from the forecourt one penetrates to the quadrangle where Nash's elegant entrance portico is revealed on the west side. Under this is, in effect, the front door of the palace. The Grand Hall is lower in height than one might expect, though with fine Carrara marble columns and an excellent chimneypiece. The white and gold colouring of the hall dates from the time of C H Bessant who redecorated much of the palace in the Frenchified Edwardian taste in 1902.

On the left of the hall, facing the south end of the palace, is the Grand Staircase which splits into three flights. Straight ahead leads to the East Gallery, the State Supper Room and the Ballroom whereas the other two flights converge at the entrance to the Guard Room in between portraits of William IV and Queen Adelaide. The Guard Room is an ante-room to the Green Drawing Room, formerly Nash's Saloon, which is itself a glorified ante-room to the 60 ft long Throne Room. Finished after George IV's death in 1830, the Throne Room's ceiling and most of the sculptural decoration followed the designs of Nash. The frieze showing events of the Wars of the Roses was provided by E H Baily in 1828. The best sculptures in the room are Bernasconi's winged Victories; the carved trophies on either side of the throne dais were designed by Henry Holland and are said to have come from the Throne Room of Carlton House. Another item to have come from there is the superb chimneypiece supported by bronze and ormolu caryatids in the Royal Closet – probably the best chimneypiece in the palace.

From a secret door in the Royal Closet one gains access to the White Drawing Room whose five large windows overlook the gardens and lake. This room was finished in 1831 and has a ceiling decorated with reliefs by William Pitts showing the 'sports of boys'. Next along the first floor of the west front comes Nash's Music Room with its bold reliefs of putti in the spandrels of the domed ceiling. Underneath the Savonnerie carpet is an inlaid floor by George Seddon. The Blue Drawing Room is another example of Nash's surviving designs; until Pennethorne's addition of the 1850s this used to be the Ballroom. There are portraits of Edward and Queen Alexandra, as well of James I's egregious favourite George Villiers, Duke of Buckingham. An astronomical clock on the chimneypiece records the lunar changes.

The State Dining Room is one of Edward Blore's efforts and the pictures include a portrait of George IV by Sir Thomas Lawrence and others by Gainsborough of his parents. The West Gallery leads to Pennethorne's Ballroom, the largest of all the state apartments, which was redecorated by Bessant in Edwardian times. Here investitures are held. The throne canopy was designed by Lutyens out of the Imperial Shimiama used at the Delhi Durbar of 1911. Occasionally the great chamber comes into its own for state banquets and balls.

The highly impressive Picture Gallery is 155 ft long and occupies the whole of the central area of the first floor on the west side of the palace with an arched glass ceiling. It houses some of the finest pictures in the royal art collections including works by Rembrandt, Hals, Cuyp, Van Dyck and Poussin. Early in her reign Queen Victoria salvaged many of these paintings collected by George IV from store, where they had been placed after the destruction of Carlton House, and hung them four deep in the Picture Gallery. The hanging arrangements were no less of a muddle in Queen Mary's time, though today the old masters are sensitively arranged against a newly painted peachy background.

Down the Ministers' Staircase (where there is a group of Eskimo art) are the semi-state apartments on the ground floor. These include the Household Breakfast Room (where members of the household are fed); the 1855 Room (commemorating the occupation by Napoleon III and the Empress Eugènie); the Bow Room (through which the 20,000 garden-party guests a year make their way to the lawn); the

1844 Room (named because of it occupation by Emperor Nicholas of Russia); and the Belgian Suite where Edward VII used to live. Prince Andrew was born in the Orléans Bedroom here. The Garden Entrance on the north front of the palace is the one used by the Queen and her family.

The ground floor of the north wing is given over to the offices of the Duke of Edinburgh and the Privy Purse. In the centre of the quadrangle front Nash formed the King's Entrance. The chinoiserie chimneypiece in the King's Waiting Room was originally in the Chinese Drawing Room in Carlton House. The Chinese Dining Room in the northeast angle of the east front facing the Mall is the most exotic room in Buckingham Palace. It is a colourful confection of Blore's and Cubitt's made up from parts of the Music and Banqueting Rooms at Brighton Pavilion from which Queen Victoria and Prince Albert decamped in 1847. The old Queen enjoyed lunching in the room, though in modern times it has tended to be used more for meetings. This extraordinary corner room has just recently been comprehensively restored, recapturing all its vivid, not to say overwhelming, effect.

The first floor of the east front is known at the palace as the 'principal floor'. Along it are such rooms as the Yellow Drawing Room (with a fantastic Chinese chimneypiece) and the Blue Sitting Room. Also decorated in the Chinese taste is the Centre Room from which the Royal Family emerge on to the balcony overlooking the forecourt. It is a surprisingly small room; somehow one had always imagined a larger 'backstage' area.

The Chapel at Buckingham Palace was gutted by the strips of bombs that fell across Buckingham Palace on 13 September 1940. Queen Elizabeth, the present Queen Mother, said she was glad that the palace had suffered bomb damage because it meant that she could look the blitzed East End in the face. In 1959 her daughter the Queen decided to create an art gallery on part of the bombed site so that the public could see masterpieces from the royal collection. Three years later a spectacular exhibition opened 'the Queen's Gallery', as it was called, and ever since there has been a rotating series of shows that are musts for anyone with an interest in paintings.

Also open to the public is the Royal Mews which displays the collection of coaches, including Sir William Chambers's ravishing rococo State Coach first used for the opening of Parliament in 1762. This is now the coach for coronations; the Irish State Coach is used for the Opening of Parliament and the Glass State Coach for royal weddings. The old Carriage House in the Mews has a frieze showing the coronation of William IV. Numerous other coaches, landaus, barouches, broughams, phaetons and sociables can be inspected, together with the Windsor greys themselves, state saddlery and other horsy tackle.

Every morning at half past eleven the guard is changed at Buckingham Palace. When the Queen is in residence, her standard flying, there is a guard of four sentries, otherwise only two. For herself and the family firm 'Buck House' is the London office, but the inside is much more cheerful and interesting than one might imagine gazing in from the outside. The gardens, which run to nearly 40 acres, are a special delight. In the south-west corner can be found one of the mulberry trees that James I planted in 1609. **HMM**

Top: The Queen's Audience Room. The family photographs indicate that this is a semi-private room unlike the White Drawing Room (below) where the Royal Family assemble before state functions, through a door disguised as a mirror

PALATIVM REGIVM EDINENSE
quod & Cænobium S. Crucis
The royal palace of holy rood hous. by I. G

THE PALACE OF HOLYROODHOUSE

One alone among the ancient royal palaces of Scotland has continued to be the abode of her kings and queens down to the present time, though it was deserted for long periods in the past. This, of course, is Holyrood, crouching below the cliffs of that brooding, extinct volcano, Arthur's Seat, at the opposite end of Edinburgh to the Castle.

Here in 1128 David I of Scotland established a house of Augustinian canons, presenting the community with a reliquary containing a fragment of the True Cross; in consequence the abbey was dedicated to the Holy Cross or Holy Rood. Like other religious houses, Holyrood was used by the kings of Scotland, though their Edinburgh stronghold remained the castle. None the less, Robert the Bruce and Edward Baliol held parliaments here and in the guest house, which was adapted as a royal residence, James II was born in 1430.

Of the medieval abbey itself all that remains now are the ruined nave of the church and the foundations of its transepts and quire. The guest house, west of the main monastic building, was altered and enlarged by James IV, who was determined to make Edinburgh the undisputed capital of Scotland and to give it a suitably magnificent royal palace. After his ill-fated expedition south of the Border had ended at Flodden, his young son James V carried on the building work at Holyrood and the Great Tower (of 1529–32) survives from this period. The tower contained lodgings for the King and for his two French Queens, Madeleine de Valois and Marie de Lorraine.

Holyroodhouse suffered considerable damage at the hands of Henry VIII's marauding raiders. The English King's nose was put out of joint by the spurning of his son Edward as a prospective husband for the future Mary Queen of Scots, James V's baby daughter. Henry was even

Opposite top: Holyrood Palace as it appeared in the time of Mary Queen of Scots (from a drawing by Gordon of Rothiemay) and an isometric projection of its appearance in the 19th century (above). By then its name had changed to The Palace of Holyroodhouse, but not its spectacular setting (opposite bottom) with the backdrop of Salisbury Crag and Arthur's Seat

less pleased when Mary was betrothed to the French Dauphin instead.

After thirteen years' absence in France, Mary Queen of Scots returned as the widow of Francois II in 1561 to a much changed country. The 'Auld Alliance' with France was broken, the Reformation had triumphed over the old religion to which Mary adhered and the monastery at Holyrood no longer existed. She did her best to promote civil and religious harmony, granting several interviews in her lodging at Holyroodhouse to the reformer John Knox, author of the *First Blast of the Trumpet against the Monstrous Regiment of Women*. Needless to say, the bearded little bigot did most of the talking.

Mary's time at Holyrood is overshadowed by the tragic drama that unfolded after her marriage to Darnley. The latter suspected Mary of being the lover of her secretary David Rizzio. The political influence of this Piedmontese upstart was taken amiss by the Protestant lords whose conspiracy was readily joined by Mary's jealous husband. On 9 March 1566 Darnley and some confederates entered the Cabinet where the Queen and her secretary were partaking of a light supper. The intruders asked for a word with Rizzio, then dragged him away to be messily murdered in the Queen's Outer Chamber. Within a year the pox-ridden Darnley was found dead outside the blown-up Kirk o' Field and Mary subsequently married his reputed murderer Bothwell before being forced to abdicate.

Her son James VI came to live at Holyrood in 1578 at the age of twelve and spent more time here than any other monarch; but after travelling south to become King James I of England he only returned once, in 1617, when some repairs and improvements were carried out to the palace. Holyroodhouse ceased to have regular occupation for nearly 200 years.

During the Civil War Cromwell's soldiers were quartered here after the Battle of Dunbar when the palace caught fire. After the Restoration drastic change came to Holyroodhouse; in works lasting from 1671 to 1680, the great sixteenth-century tower was remodelled and the rest of the palace was rebuilt. Sir William Bruce and Robert Mylne produced a new quadrangle in an austere style, though the plain walls were relieved in places by typically Scottish turrets. Inside, however, were rich furnishings and tapestries; the Gallery was adorned with 100 fanciful portraits of Scottish kings, painted at £2 a head by an enterprising artist called Jacob de Wit. The series claims a ludicrously extended lineage for the Stuarts going back to the fourth century BC. However, in spite of these elaborate preparations Charles II never turned up, though his brother James was packed off here when it was convenient to keep him out of London during the struggle over the Exclusion Bill.

James's grandson, Bonnie Prince Charlie (the 'Young Pretender') arrived in 1745 during the victorious part of his campaign and held court here for five weeks. He touched for the 'Kings Evil', dined publicly and gave a state ball, but it was all founded on sadly unrealistic hopes. The following year the Duke of Cumberland dropped in at Holyroodhouse on his way to Culloden. Bonnie Prince Charlie and the Butcher stayed in the rooms of the Dukes of Hamilton, Hereditary Keepers of Holyroodhouse who, with other noblemen occupied much of the palace in the long years of royal absence. In 1795 the witty Duc d'Artois, fleeing from the French Revolution, was granted asylum at Holyrood and he came back again as the exiled Charles X after the 'July Revolution' of 1830.

Meanwhile, at long last, interest in the palace had been revived by George IV's popular visit to Scotland in 1822. Inspired by Sir Walter Scott, the ample George donned a kilt, wearing flesh-coloured tights to preserve his modesty. The King revelled in it all, being cheered to the echo by crowds estimated at a million as he drove in state to and from Holyrood, where some 2000 people were presented to him at a levée. Scott, who acted as master of ceremonies, reported that 'the visit of the King to Edinburgh . . . was like the awaking of Abou Hassan to a dream of Sovereignty'. Possibly overcome with emotion, George IV stumbled on the staircase at Holyrood but was saved from a nasty fall by the shoulders of a stout baronet.

The success of this adventure can be seen as a prologue to Queen Victoria's attachment to Scotland and to its remaining intact as a royal palace. The Queen was fond of driving round Arthur's Seat, where the impression of being far away from it all in the Highlands (although still on the edge of a city) is just as striking today as it was then. The route has become known as 'The Queen's Drive'. The Queen started the custom, continued by her successors, of occupying Holyrood for a brief period every year. This has helped to give a lasting vitality to one of the most interesting buildings in Scotland.

As early as the 1850s Queen Victoria ordered that the royal apartments should be open to the public. The Outer Court has a Victorian copy of the Linlithgow fountain and the main entrance leads into the west arcade of the Inner Court. The principal floor above the arcades contained the apartments intended for Charles II and his Queen, Catherine of Braganza; while above on three sides there were lodgings for the Court. The West Drawing Room, used by the Queen today, has a fine moulded ceiling of the 1670s. The Royal Family use the Old Guard Hall as their dining room; formerly it was fitted up as a throne room. The Privy Chamber, which has superb Caroline decoration (ceiling, woodwork and chimneypiece are all original), was used by Queen Victoria as her sitting room and is now the Morning Drawing Room. Similarly the Ante Chamber, among the semi-state apartments, has some intact plasterwork and woodwork of the 1670s. The private rooms of the present Royal Family are on the second floor.

The spacious Gallery, extending along the whole northern range of the rebuilt palace, joined Charles II's Great Apartment to the Old Apartment (the Great Tower and adjoining range of James V). Mary Queen of Scots' old bedroom on the second floor has been carefully restored to its original condition. Rizzio's gruesome murder comes vividly to life when one sees where it all happened. The Cabinet where the fateful supper party was held is a remarkably tiny little room. The timber ceiling of the Outer Chamber was probably ordained by Marie de Lorraine to commemorate the marriage of her daughter Mary Queen of Scots to the Dauphin.

George V and Queen Mary took a particular interest in all the matters affecting the palace, authorizing large works of redecoration and renovation, particularly the oak panelling of several state rooms. Queen Mary also played a leading part in the appropriate refurnishing. In addition to much eighteenth-century furniture, a collection of French and Flemish tapestries is on show and there is a noted exhibition of arms and armour. The modern royal portraits include an excellent likeness of Queen Mary by a relation of Mick Jagger.

Holyroodhouse remains the official residence of the Queen when she comes to Edinburgh every year. There is a garden party and other state occasions take place here, enhanced by the presence of the Queen's Body Guard, the Royal Company of Archers, in their picturesque green uniforms. State visits have been paid to Scotland in recent years by the Kings of Norway and Sweden when the special character of the palace was seen at its best. For all its somewhat forbidding appearance, Holyroodhouse is one of the most fascinating of royal palaces; little changed from the time of Charles II and with a combination of intimacy and grandeur that is particularly Scottish. **HMM**

A painting of the Prince Consort in the West Drawing Room Opposite top: The west front with the fountain copied from Linlithgow and (below) the gardens showing the ruined nave of Holyrood Abbey

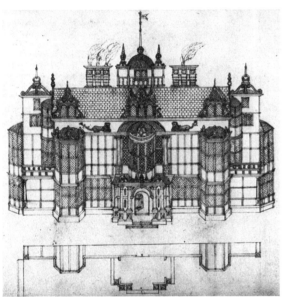

KENSINGTON PALACE

Kensington Palace, a gracious royal home of mellow red brick, is prettily situated in one of London's green oases in Kensington Gardens. Though today Kensington is one of the busiest parts of London, until the nineteenth century it was a country village, popularly known as 'the Court suburb' from its royal associations.

Since 1689 Kensington Palace has belonged to the Crown, and from then until the death of George II, it was the most loved home of our kings and queens. It is noteworthy as the birthplace of Queen Victoria and Queen Mary, and throughout the last two centuries has been the home of several members of the Royal Family including, at present, the Prince and Princess of Wales, Princess Margaret, and Prince and Princess Michael of Kent.

When William III and his Queen, Mary Stuart, our only joint sovereigns, looked round at the beginning of their reign, for a convenient home close to London, they turned to Kensington. The King suffered acutely from asthma, and the river mists which hung over Whitehall Palace made him gasp for air. Hampton Court Palace, though suitable in the summer, was too far from London. Having inspected and turned down Holland House, he purchased nearby Nottingham House, (as Kensington Palace was then called), for 18,000 guineas. It was then a small country retreat, which had been built in 1605 by Sir George Coppin, James I's Clerk to the Crown. The architect is thought to have been John Thorpe, whose book of drawings, now at the Soane Museum, London, includes a plan of the ground floor, showing the Great Hall extending the whole length of the house from south to north.

Fifteen years later the house was sold to Sir Heneage Finch, Speaker of the House of Commons in Charles I's Parliament. The change of name to Nottingham House occurred in 1681 when his son was created Earl of Nottingham. When the King and Queen purchased the estate however, the name reverted to Kensington.

Alterations started immediately, but as the Court was required to move in by Christmas of that year, the house was not entirely rebuilt. Sir Christopher Wren skilfully extended it by building four pavilions at the corners of the main block, and followed the traditional pattern of royal residences by preparing the King's apartments on the right and the Queen's on the left.

Top: An 18th-century view of the gardens showing the parterres which reminded George I of the Herrenhausen in Hanover
Centre left: John Thorpe's drawing of the original house, later called Nottingham House
Centre right: The Queen's Gallery was built by Sir Christopher Wren for William and Mary in 1690–91. The painting by Stephanoff shows the view looking towards the Queen's Staircase
Bottom: The south front in the 19th century. The view remains substantially unchanged today

The State Entrance was positioned on the west side, where an archway, surmounted by a clock tower and weather vane, led into a large courtyard, Clock Court, with two-storeyed wings attached to the new pavilions. To the north were the kitchens, and beyond were two irregular small courtyards, Green Cloth Court to the west, (so called from the board of that name who dealt with the Royal Household accounts), and Pump Court to the east, adjoining the Queen's apartments.

To the south of Clock Court a long ground floor corridor, the Stone Gallery, was constructed. This led from a colonnaded portico, which faced Palace Green on the west, to the south-west pavilion, containing the King's Staircase, Chapel and Guardroom. The two eastern pavilions formed the King's apartments, and the north-west pavilion, together with the old Great Hall, was allotted to the Queen.

In 1790 Wren built the Queen's Gallery, 84 ft in length, running northwards from the north-west pavilion along the first floor. At the northern end is the delightful staircase with oak balusters, through which the public gain access to the state apartments. In Pump Court, adjacent to the Queen's Gallery, were the panelled apartments on three floors of the Maids of Honour, which have survived to form No 10 Kensington Palace. A communicating door, still to be seen, led to the Queen's apartments.

In the early hours of a November morning 1691, the King and Queen were awakened by the sound of musket shots. Fire had broken out in the Long Gallery above the Stone Gallery in Clock Court. The Queen's ladies rushed out into the gardens in their nightgowns, screaming. Defoe commented that:

> The Queen was a little surprised at first, apprehending some Treasons, but King William a Stranger to Feare, smil'd at the suggestion, chear'd Her Majesty up, and being soon dress'd they both walked out into the Garden, and stood there some Hours till they perceived the Fire by the help that came in, and by the Diligence of the Foot Guards, was gotten under Foot.

The south side of Clock Court was gutted, and the south-west pavilion was subsequently rebuilt as a two-storeyed guardroom. The King's Staircase, which had resembled the Queen's, was replaced by a larger and more imposing one in three wide flights of steps of black Irish marble, with fine wrought iron balustrading by Jean Tijou.

Though dour and undemonstrative, King William had real affection for Mary; and when she died at Kensington in 1694, he abandoned his plan entirely to rebuild Hampton Court. The completion of Wren's finest work at Kensington, dates from this period. In 1695 he ordered the completion of the King's Gallery, which he and Queen Mary had planned five years previously. This formed the upper part of a new range of buildings, across the two south pavilions. William III died at Kensington Palace on 3 March 1702 from a fever which followed his fall from a horse at Hampton Court a few days earlier.

Above left: The south front with its statue of William of Orange, given by the Emperor of Germany
Above: The view from the east showing the Clock Tower, the apartments of which were occupied by the late Princess Alice
Opposite: Kent's famous staircase showing the simulated marble balustrade and the painted groups of his contemporaries apparently looking down the steps
Below: Maids of Honour House in Princesses' Court, the home given to Princess Margaret after her marriage to Lord Snowdon

Queen Anne, Mary's younger sister, who then succeeded, came also to love Kensington. She never liked William, and uprooted his Dutch gardens of 'tiresome uniformity,' according to Thomas Faulkner, in his *History and Antiquities of Kensington*, 1820. In 1704–5 she built the stately Orangery on the north side of the palace. This is generally attributed to Nicholas Hawksmoor. As sovereign, Queen Anne occupied the King's side of the palace, and her dull husband, Prince George of Denmark, lived in the Queen's side, which was thereafter known as 'the Denmark Wing'. At Kensington came the final rupture in the friendship between the Queen and Sarah, Duchess of Marlborough. Their last interview took place on 6 April 1710 in one of the little closets beyond the Queen's Gallery. Bitter words were spoken, and the humiliated Duchess emerged weeping. Queen Anne, our last Stuart monarch, died at Kensington Palace in 1714, making way for George I, who came over from Hanover to be King.

Selfish, unimaginative and immoral, King George was, without doubt, the most unattractive of our sovereigns, but he liked Kensington, which reminded him of the Herrenhausen in Hanover. He decided to reconstruct the house into a palace suitable for a king's residence. In the year of his accession he dismissed Wren, whose undistinguished successor as Surveyor General, William Benson, made considerable alterations. After Nicholas Hawksmoor's survey in 1718, which showed that the original Nottingham House was 'very ruinous and out of repair,' Benson demolished the old building, and built in its place the three new state rooms, the Cupola Room, the King's Drawing Room and the Privy Chamber which were all superbly decorated by William Kent. The Cupola Room, in the centre of the old house, is the principal reception room in the palace. The ceiling is formed of four great coves, surmounted in blue and gold with octagonal coffers meeting in a panel above, also octagonal, which is painted with the Star of the Order of the Garter. The shallow dome appears to rise to a great height, thanks to Kent's clever use of perspective.

In 1724 Kent painted the ceiling of the third of Benson's new rooms, the Privy Chamber, and also Wren's Presence Chamber, which adjoins it. In the following year he painted the King's Drawing Room. The most interesting of his decorative paintings are those for the King's Staircase which, in its final form, dates from the 1720's. In four bays, three on the north wall and one on the east, he painted an arcaded gallery with a marble balustrade, behind which various court contemporaries look out over the stairs. Some of these can be identified, such as George's two Turkish *valets de chambre*, and Peter the Wild Boy, who had been discovered as a child of about thirteen years, walking on his hands and feet in the woods of Hanover, 'with the agility of a squirrel'. On the ceiling, Kent painted a self portrait, and 'a beautiful actress', with whom, according to Faulkner, 'he lived on terms of intimacy'.

So badly built were Benson's State Rooms that in 1724 £1,925 had to be spent repairing them. The two smaller courts, the Prince of Wales' Court, (formerly Green Cloth Court), probably re-named after George II's son Frederick, Prince of Wales, to the west and the Princesses' Court, (previously known as Pump Court) to the east, were rebuilt with arcaded cloisters.

As George I had no Queen to accompany him, the apartments previously assigned to the Maids of Honour, were occupied by the three eldest of the King's grandchildren, Anne, Amelia (or Emily) and Caroline. A new apartment (now Apartment 8), in the north range of the western court, also decorated by Kent, was occupied by the King's ugly German mistress, the Duchess of Kendal, whom he used to visit between five and eight o'clock in the evening.

Two of George I's gardeners, Henry Wise and Charles Bridgeman, laid out Broad Walk and parterres reminiscent of the Herrenhausen. Wise had already done much work for Queen Anne. He laid out the Upper Garden which, unhappily, has not survived. About 1705 he prepared a plan which shows the future Round Pond as an oblong pool and the Serpentine as a series of separate basins. Most of this work however did not take place until the reign of George II whose wife, Queen Caroline had a passion for landscape gardening. The Round Pond was ready to be filled with water in 1728, and the Serpentine was begun in 1730.

George II, the palace's next occupant was never a popular king. Fortunately his wife, Caroline of Anspach was a woman of great culture. She had a passion for landscape gardening and was an art enthusiast. She it was who discovered in a cabinet (still to be seen in the Queen's Bedroom) the books of Holbein sketches which are today in the Royal Collection. When she lay dying at Kensington Palace in 1737 the unfaithful George II was heartbroken. She begged him to remarry. "Non," he stammered, "J'aurai des maîtresses." The lady he had in mind was Madame Walmoden with whom he was wont to dally in Hanover. Walpole, the Prime Minister, for his own political purposes now brought the German over to England saying "I was for the Queen against the mistress, but I will be for the mistress against the daughters". The daughters to whom he was referring were the five princesses who had lived at Kensington Palace since early childhood days when their grandfather was King and who gave their name to Princesses' Court.

George III and Queen Charlotte had an enormous family, of whom thirteen children lived to adulthood and Kensington Palace was to become useful to house some of them. In 1799 the King gave an apartment to his fourth son, Prince Edward, Duke of Kent, but as he was usually with his French mistress, Madame de St Laurent, they principally lived 'unofficially' in a house in nearby Knightsbridge when in London.

In 1807 another brother, the bookish Prince Augustus, Duke of Sussex, was given the south range of Clock Court. His 50,000 books were housed in the Long Gallery and 5,000 bibles in what became known as the Divinity Room. He also had a large collection of watches and clocks whose ticking disconcerted visitors.

Nine months before the old King, George III died, the Duke of Kent was back at Kensington Palace with his new wife. After the death in 1817 of Princess Charlotte, the Regent's only child, his younger brothers scrambled to take part in the 'succession stakes' and accordingly had to leave their mistresses and marry. The Duke of Kent chose Victoire of Coburg, Dowager Princess of Leiningen. When she became pregnant they were in Germany with many pressing debts which delayed their urgent desire to return to Britain for the birth of their offspring. At last, in his wife's eighth month, the Kents were back in England and the Prince Regent allowed them to occupy a suite on the east side of Kensington Palace. Here, on 24 May 1819 their daughter, Princess Victoria was born in the bedroom on the northeast corner. She was christened in the ornate Cupola Room by the Archbishop of Canterbury in the midst of a row

between the Prince Regent and the baby's parents over her christian names.

The Duke of Kent died eight months later but his widow and daughter continued to live at Kensington. The Duchess was dominated by the evil Sir John Conroy, her Comptroller, who managed to defraud her out of large sums of money. Princess Victoria grew up under Conroy's 'Kensington system,' by which he planned to isolate her both from the Royal Family and from the Coburgs, making her entirely dependent on her mother, who was under his control. Victoria was never allowed to be alone for one minute. As she grew up, Kensington Palace became the battleground between the Duchess and Conroy on the one hand and on the other the Princess and her governess, Baroness Lehzen, both of whom loathed Conroy. A less spirited princess would have succumbed to his ambition.

In May 1837 Princess Victoria came of age on her eighteenth birthday. She now knew that if she could hold out until the King's death and her own accession, she would escape from Conroy's influence. Early on the morning of the following 20 June when asleep in the King's State Bed Chamber she was aroused by her mother. She recorded in her diary that:

> I was awoke at 6 o'clock by Mamma who told me that the Archbishop of Canterbury and Lord Conyngham were here and wished to see me. I got out of bed and went into the sitting room (only in my dressing gown and alone) and saw them. Lord Conyngham then acquainted me that my poor uncle, the King, was no more and had expired at 12 minutes past 2 this morning and consequently that I am Queen.

Queen Victoria was the last sovereign to have lived in the palace. Two of her daughters, Princess Louise, Duchess of Argyll, and Princess Beatrice, and three of her grandchildren made their homes there. The late Princess Alice, daughter of the Duke of Albany, took over her mother's apartment of Clock House in 1922. She married Queen Mary's brother, the Earl of Athlone. When she died at the beginning of 1981 she was the oldest member of the Royal Family in our annals, linking the reign of Queen Victoria to our own time. The other two children were both Battenbergs. Prince Philip's grandmother, the Dowager Marchioness of Milford Haven, came to Kensington in 1921 on the death of her husband, formerly Prince Louis of Battenberg. Her grandson, as a young wartime naval officer, spent some of his leaves with her and he was at Kensington for his last night as a bachelor before his marriage in 1947 to the Queen. Lord Carisbrooke, son of Princess Beatrice and Prince Henry of Battenberg, lived in Maids of Honour House in Princesses' Court until his death in 1960. This apartment was granted to Princess Margaret on her marriage, but she later moved into a larger one on the south side of Clock Court which had been Princess Louise's.

An apartment in Clock Court has been the home of two aunts of the Queen. Princess Marina, Duchess of Kent, died there in 1968 and Princess Alice, Duchess of Gloucester, has made her home there after the death of her husband in 1974. Princess Marina's younger son, Prince Michael of Kent also lives at Kensington Palace with his wife Princess Michael and their two children.

The Prince and Princess of Wales have their London home at 8/9 Kensington Palace. This is on three floors and has been converted into one apartment. **PMS**

Opposite: The great gateway to St James's Palace built by Henry VIII. This is all that remains of the original palace started by him in 1532

ST JAMES'S PALACE

After the burning of Whitehall in 1698, St James's became what it still officially is: the metropolitan palace of the sovereign. Even now it is to the Court of St James's that ambassadors are accredited, though the palace itself is of fairly modest dimensions.

It was another fire that first led Henry VIII to acquire the place for, after the partial destruction of the Palace of Westminster, he felt the monarchy needed another establishment in the metropolis in addition to Whitehall. In exchange for lands in Suffolk, the King secured the Convent of St James the Less from its custodians, Eton College. The convent had been founded in the fourteenth century for 'fourteen leprous maiden sisters, living chastely and honestly in divine service'. The hospital enjoyed the right to hold a May fair in the neighbouring fields – the origin of Mayfair.

Of the palace Henry built here, little now remains save the gateway facing up St James's Street, which bears the cyphers of the King and Anne Boleyn and thus dates the structure to the early 1530s when that lady was still in favour. Some of the decoration inside the palace was executed by Holbein. However, following another sort of execution on Tower Green, when Anne Boleyn's 'little neck' was chopped, Henry VIII neglected St James's.

His daughter Mary used it quite frequently for entertaining visiting Spaniards and held sung masses here. During the Wyatt rebellion against popery she took refuge inside while the rebels fought a skirmish without. As every schoolboy knows, Mary died with 'Calais' written on her heart, at St James's in 1558. Elizabeth's principal association with the palace was during the year of the Armada; it was from here that she set out to inspect her troops at Tilbury.

It was described in Elizabethan times as being:

> of a quadrate forme, erected of brick, the exterior shape whereof, although it appears without any sumptuous or superfluous devices, yet is the spot very princelye, and the same with art contrived within and without. It standeth from other buyldinges about two furlongs, having a farme house opposite to its north gate. But the situation is pleasant, indued with a good ayre and pleasant prospects. On the east London offereth itself in view; in the south, the stately buyldings of Westminster with the pleasant park, and the delights thereof; in the north, the green fields.

With the arrival of the Stuarts, St James's became the official residence of James I's eldest son, Henry, Prince of Wales. This brilliant figure gave the palace a stylish air and the tragedy of his early death deprived the monarchy of an expansive patron of the arts. He succumbed to what was probably typhus at the age of eighteen, dying at St James's, despite (or perhaps because of) such primitive remedies as pigeons pecking the soles of his feet, in 1612.

Under the next occupant, Charles I, St James's was popularly supposed by the Puritans to be a den of papists. Queen Henrietta Maria, was given the exquisite Chapel designed by Inigo Jones in 1623 for her own use and mass was said daily there by priests. It is notable for its royal pews. Henrietta Maria was deeply attached to St James's, bearing several of her children here, including Charles II. Puritan priests eventually obliged Charles I to send his Queen's French retinue and his mother-in-law packing. One of the latter's attendants reported that St James's was:

> very magnificent and extremely convenient. It is built with brick, according to the fashion of the country, having the roof covered with lead, in form of a floor surrounded all sides with battlements which serve for an ornament to the whole body of the building . . .

He found it impossible to describe 'the great number of chambers, all covered with tapestry, and superbly garnished with all sort of furniture'. Certainly Charles and Henrietta Maria had some fine collections here before the rude interruption of the Parliamentarians in the Civil War.

The palace was then used as a prison for the royal children, though Princess Henrietta effected an escape dressed as a boy urchin and her brother, the future James II, did likewise in drag. There was no escape, though, for their sad father who spent his last night at St James's before walking across the park to have his head cut off at Whitehall. His splendid works of art were sold off and the palace suffered the indignity of becoming a military prison.

Charles II restored some glamour to his birthplace, commissioning Wren to enlarge the state apartments towards the park where he became such a legendary figure feeding the ducks and exercising his dogs. These apartments were later embellished by William Kent and, though some eighteenth-century grandees considered them unworthy of being the headquarters of the Court, they have an admirably quiet dignity and comfortable proportions. A pleasantly English effect is achieved through portraits and tapestries rather than elaborate ornamentation.

It was under Queen Anne that 'Our Court of St James's'

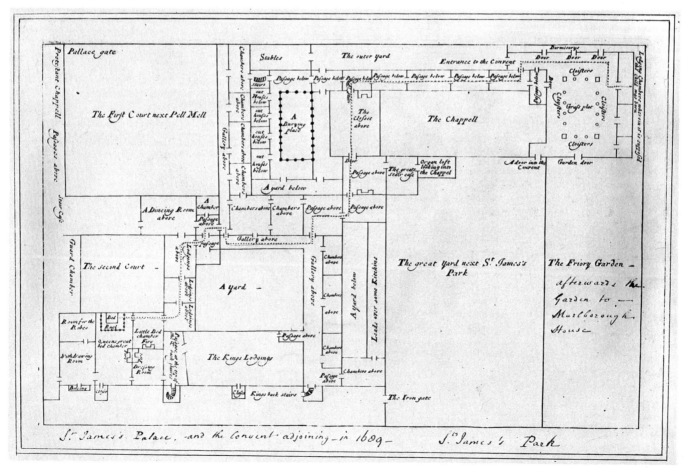

St James's Palace, and the Convent adjoining in 1689. St James's Park

Opposite top: An 18th-century view of St James's Palace and the Mall looking east towards the City. The early 17th-century plan (below) indicates a few of the changes
Above: A detachment of the Queen's Guard leaving Friary Court and (below) the interior of the Chapel Royal, scene of royal weddings and christenings

was formally established; a fairly stuffy Court it was too by all accounts, though the Queen happily indulged her passion for playing cards between official gatherings. The most significant event to take place at St James's during her reign was the completion of the Act of Union between England and Scotland.

Later in the eighteenth century the palace had witnessed two of the corking rows that played havoc with the family harmony of the Hanoverians. Following an unseemly altercation with his father, George I, at a family christening, the future George II was ordered out of St James's by nightfall, having first been confined to his quarters. History was repeated when George II expelled his own son 'Poor Fred' from the palace following a farcical dash from Hampton Court with his pregnant wife. The object of this exercise was to escape from the prying eyes of George II's Queen, Caroline, who was not exactly Fred's staunchest admirer (her last words on the subject were to express relief that she would 'never see that monster again'). The acidulous Lord Hervey recorded the scene:

> Notwithstanding all the handkerchiefs that had been thrust one after another up Her Royal Highness's petticoats in the coach, her clothes were in such a condition with the filthy inundations which attend these circumstances that when the coach stopped at St James's the Prince ordered all the lights to be put out that

the people might not have the nasty ocular evidence which would otherwise have been exhibited to them of his folly and her distress . . . Her Royal Highness was put to bed between two tablecloths. At a quarter before eleven she was delivered of a little rat of a girl, about the bigness of a good large tooth-pick case.

Despite these alarums and excursions, George II maintained a dignified Court at St James's, holding frequent receptions and balls. George III was married here, but preferred to spend the time in London at the newly acquired Buckingham House. State functions continued to take place at St James's though, and at one levée a bowing Scots colonel's kilt rode up his back causing George III to cry out, "Keep the ladies in front. Keep the ladies in front". A fire in 1809 revealed more flesh at the palace when the inhabitants were seen 'issuing in all directions from their apartments half-naked, and every effort was made to save the furniture and effects'.

The future George IV, who employed Nash to do some restoration work at the palace, was married to the wretched Caroline in the Chapel Royal, duly fortified with brandy. Some happier nuptials were celebrated in 1840 between Victoria and Albert, after the Chapel had been much altered. Queen Victoria moved most of the Court ceremonies to Buckingham Palace, but levées continued to be held at St James's right up to the last season of peace before the Second World War.

The tradition of Garter King of Arms proclaiming the new sovereign from the balcony of Henry VIII's lovely old Friary Court at St James's has carried on. In 1936 Edward VIII caused a stir by watching his own proclamation from an upper room in the palace in the company of Wallis Simpson. When the ceremony was over Mrs Simpson said to the King: "It was all very moving. But it has also made me realize how different your life is going to be". As Prince of Wales the King had lived in York House on the north side of Ambassadors Court in the palace. Today York House is the London residence of the Duke and Duchess of Kent.

The rest of the palace is now mainly occupied by those living in grace and favour apartments and by the offices of various royal functionaries such as the Lord Chamberlain's Department and the Central Chancery of the Orders of Knighthood. Every year at the Festival of the Epiphany (6 January) two of Her Majesty's Gentleman Ushers make an offering of gold, frankincense and myrrh on behalf of the Queen at Holy Communion in the Chapel Royal.

Clarence House Although Clarence House is physically attached to St James's Palace, it is somehow separate, being the London home of Queen Elizabeth the Queen Mother. Its origins were as a sort of outbuilding to St James's in the seventeenth century. At the end of the eighteenth century it was occupied by George III's third son, the Duke of Clarence. As a bachelor this somewhat eccentric, earthy sailor was content to reside in the small and far from elaborate dwelling, but after his marriage to Princess Adelaide he complained to his brother George IV about its 'inconvenience and unfitness' and of 'the wretched state and dirt of our apartments'. John Nash was accordingly authorized to rebuild Clarence House, between work on Buckingham Palace and Brighton Pavilion, in 1825.

Opposite top: Wild's painting of the Queen's Levée Room in St James's Palace
Below: The Drawing Room in York House in 1901 when it was the home of the future George V and Queen Mary

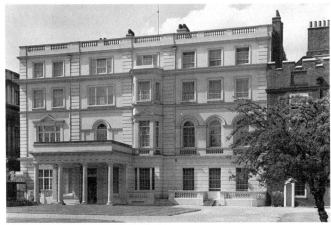

The south front of Clarence House, (top) as it was in the 19th century before the addition of the wing in 1873 and (bottom) as it is today

Five years later, George IV died and the Duke of Clarence succeeded to the throne as William IV. He lived in St James's Palace for a spell, but in the end decided to return to Clarence House. After the death of the bluff 'Sailor King', Clarence House reverted to its position as a lesser royal residence. Queen Victoria's mother, the Duchess of Kent, lived here and in 1866 it was given to Victoria's second son 'Affie', the Duke of Edinburgh. The appearance of the house today dates from this period. In 1873 it was linked to St James's Palace by the addition of a wing on the south front. The windows on the first floor were arched and the windows on the same floor of the original house were altered to conform with them – except for the pedimented window on the south front. A set of bay windows was also added to the south front where the wing joins the original part of the house. The entrance was switched from the west to the south, with a balcony placed in the old entrance in Clarence Gate; and a new Tuscan portico, entrance gate and lodges were added on the south front. Finally, a fourth storey was added in place of Nash's sloping roof and attics.

Queen Victoria's youngest son, the Duke of Connaught, a godson of the great Duke of Wellington, succeeded his brother here in 1900, staying on until his death over 40 years later. After a spell as the headquarters of the Red Cross, Clarence House then became the first married home of Princess Elizabeth and her husband. Their second child, Princess Anne, was born here in 1950.

The Queen Mother has redecorated the interior with her customary *élan* and eclectic taste. Her Majesty is a noted

connoisseur, with collections of Chelsea and Worcester porcelain and a stylish range of pictures by artists such as Stubbs, Monet, Sickert, Augustus John, Duncan Grant, Paul Nash, Graham Sutherland, John Bratby and even her friend Sir Noël Coward. The Lancaster Room, which was redecorated in the 1960s, houses John Piper's wartime impression of Windsor. The Dining Room has a ceiling of about 1825, though the walls were decorated in the 'Adam' style fashionable at the beginning of this century; the marble chimneypiece of 1770 has recently been inserted. The attractive Garden Room was formed out of two sitting rooms in the 1960s. Similarly on the first floor, the Drawing Room was also formed out of two rooms but at a much earlier date. The ceiling and chimneypieces are from Nash's time and the furniture is English, though mainly in the French style, of the late eighteenth century. The house, which is not open to the public, has a delightful atmosphere owing much to that immensely popular figure 'The Queen Mum' whose wartime activities alone ensure her a lasting place in the affections of the nation.

Marlborough House When he was deliberating where to live as King, William IV thought of moving into Marlborough House but, in the event, it was adapted for his widow, Queen Adelaide. It had been built, officially, for the victorious Duke of Marlborough by Sir Christopher Wren but the prime mover was, in fact, the Duke's formidable wife Sarah, a long-time favourite of Queen Anne. Sarah had apartments in St James's Palace itself but persuaded the Queen to grant her a lease of land on the eastern edge of St James's on the site of the old friary. The Duchess laid the foundation stone in 1709 and the house was finished two years later.

The rather simple plain design was probably drawn out by Wren's son and namesake; originally it was two storeys high. The main feature inside remains the series of historic paintings of the Duke's famous battles, by the appropriately named Laguerre, lining the walls of the Central Saloon and the staircases. Some years ago, incidentally, these paintings were restored and among those who worked on them was the celebrated faker Tom Keating. Shortly after the house was completed the termagant Sarah had a major bust-up with Queen Anne, storming out of St James's Palace leaving, a contemporary gossip claimed, her apartment 'in a state as if it had been sacked by a destructive enemy – the locks torn off the doors, marble slabs forced out, and looking-glasses and pictures rent from their panels'. She lived on at Marlborough House until her death in 1744; it remained in the Spencer-Churchill family until 1817 and Sir William Chambers did some remodelling in 1770s.

The house first came into royal occupation through the tenancy of Prince Leopold of Saxe-Coburg and Gotha, widower of George IV's daughter Princess Charlotte whose chances of becoming Queen were terminated by a careless doctor attending her in childbed. Leopold gave up Marlborough House in 1830 when the Belgians invited him to become their king. After the death of the next tenant, Queen Adelaide, it was settled on Albert Edward, Prince of Wales, who had extensive alterations made by Sir James Pennethorne. The building was heightened and the principal rooms were enlarged by knocking two, or sometimes even three, into one. The ground floor was extended some 30 ft on the north or entrance front. Other changes to provide extra accommodation in all directions can hardly be said to have improved Wren's original proportions.

Marlborough House was the focal point of the Edwardian age which began some years before the Victorian era drew officially to a close. The pleasure-loving and philistine circle that congregated around the Prince of Wales in the late nineteenth century came to be known as the 'Marlborough House set'. After Edward VII acceded to the throne, Marlborough House was allotted to the future George V and Queen Mary. Then, when George V became King, Edward's widow Queen Alexandra returned here; finally Queen Mary herself came back in 1936.

Above: The Conservatory, Marlborough House in 1912, replete with Edwardiana
Opposite: Lancaster House, showing the south front (top) and the lavish decor of the Hall and staircase (bottom)

The majestic figure of Queen Mary created a very different atmosphere at Marlborough House from the 'fast' world of her father-in-law. She filled the house with her legendary collection of *objets d'art*, gathered together, not to say solicited, over many years which included numerous items of antique furniture, gorgeous eighteenth-century English and European porcelain, portraits, snuff boxes and bottles, jades and enamels. The exhibition of her treasures at the Victoria and Albert Museum after her death was one of the memorable events of the 1950s. In 1959 Marlborough House became the Commonwealth Centre; the principle rooms are often open to the public.

Lancaster House Also under Government ownership is another building in the environs of St James's, Lancaster House, which is now used for conferences and as a 'hospitality centre'. It was built by the 'Grand Old' Duke of York, second son of George III, who bought the seventeenth-century Godolphin House on the site early in the nineteenth century and renamed it York House. The old building was pulled down, but by the time of the Duke of York's death in 1827 the new York House was unfinished. The Government bought out the mortgage and sold the lease to the Marquess of Stafford (later second Duke of Sutherland) who then renamed it Stafford House. Benjamin Wyatt had built the first two storeys for the Duke of York; and now Robert Smirke added a third and attic storey, with Charles Barry taking a hand in the striking colouring of the Staircase Hall. The exterior is of plain Bath stone with a Corinthian portico, but inside is an extravaganza of French decoration, all gilt and glitter, that invites the obvious comparison with Versailles.

Stafford House was often visited by Queen Victoria who was apparently wont to say to the Duchess of Sutherland: "I have come from my house to your palace". It was a Whig stronghold and the third Duke entertained Garibaldi here in 1864. It is, by the way, ironical that this Duke who carried out the most extensive of the Highland Clearances was such a liberal of advanced views – his methods caused terrible sufferings but were inspired by progressive economic theories and reforming zeal. In addition to political gatherings, Stafford House was also a noted place for musical evenings (Chopin played here before Queen Victoria in 1848) and an outpost of the 'Souls' – an intellectual group of Edwardians in marked contrast to the raffish Marlborough House set. In 1912 the fourth Duke of Sutherland sold the lease to the first Viscount Leverhulme, who renamed it (yet again) after his native county, the Royal Duchy of Lancaster.

Under the soap magnate's benevolent auspices Lancaster House became the home of the London Museum (later transferred to Kensington Palace and now in the Barbican). Today it is under the care of the Department of the Environment who do their best to present the building as it was in its Victorian heyday, though they are rather hampered in this endeavour by the impedimenta of modern conferences about the place. A high point in recent times was the banquet given by Sir Winston Churchill to the Queen on the Friday after her coronation.

Lancaster House stands in the south-west corner of the precinct of St James's Palace, facing Stable Yard. All in all, this well populated corner of royal London presents a fascinating variety of architecture and associations behind and around the old Tudor gatehouse with its familiar clock tower and sentry. **HMM**

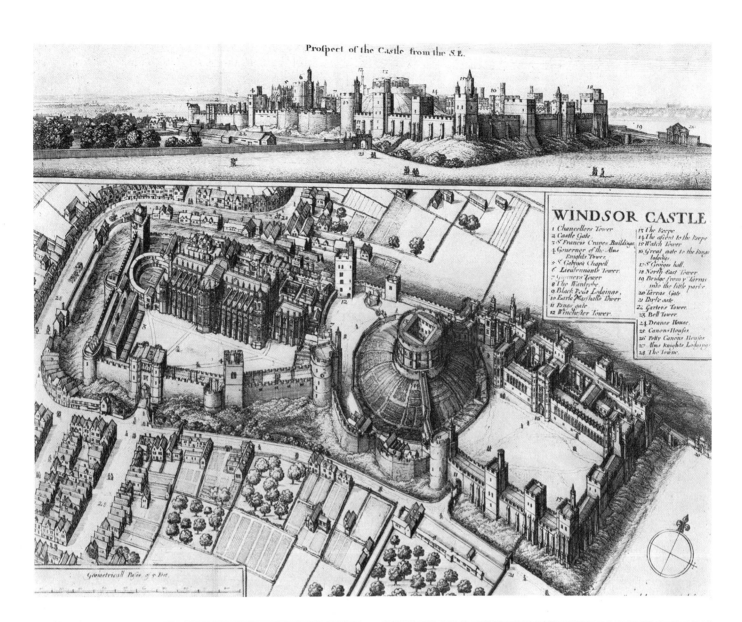

Prospect of the Castle from the S.E.

WINDSOR CASTLE

1 Chancellors Tower
2 Castle Gate
3 S.t Frances Cranes Buildings
4 Gouernor of the Alms
  Knights Tower
5 S.t Georges Chapell
6 Lieutennants Tower
7 Gunners Tower
8 The Wardrobe
9 Black Fryers Lodgings
10 Earle Marshalls Tower
11 Kings gate
12 Winchester Tower

13 The Keepe
14 The ascent to the Keepe
15 Watch Tower
16 Great gate to the Kings
   lodgings
17 S.t Georges hall
18 North East Tower
19 Bridge from y.e Tarras
   into the little parke
20 Tarras Gate
21 Darke gate
22 Garters Tower
23 Bell Tower
24 Deanes House
25 Canon Houses
26 Petty Canons Houses
27 Alms knights Lodgings
28 The Towne

Geometricall Pases of 5 Feet

34

WINDSOR

Of the three palaces that have continually been associated with the Crown throughout the past thousand years, Westminster, the Tower and Windsor, only the latter is still a royal residence. Windsor Castle was founded by William the Conqueror as one of a chain of fortresses designed to control the Thames Valley and the environs of London. At first it was a construction of earthwork and timber erected overlooking an old Saxon palace.

The Conqueror and his immediate successors moved from place to place as politics and the appetite of the Court required, for a medieval monarch could only stay in a particular place so long as the food supplies of the neighbourhood held out. However, Windsor gradually established itself as a favourite watering-hole. In addition to the significance of the River Thames as a thoroughfare, there was the pleasure of the chase. The strategic position of the fortress on the hill overhanging the river soon offset the greater comfort of the palace in the valley.

William Rufus, whose love of the chase resulted in his death in the New Forest in 1100 (a similar fate had befallen his brother Richard and one would have thought Rufus might have tried elsewhere), celebrated the Easter of 1097 at Windsor attended by the nobles 'both of England and Normandy with great fear and reverence'. His brother Henry I first held Court at the castle at Whitsuntide 1110, having built new lodgings which were probably timber-framed, and married his second Queen in the chapel here eleven years later. The familiar Round Tower, on top of the mound which the Conqueror had piled up, dates from the reign of the first Plantagenet monarch, Henry II, who began replacing the wooden defences of the castle with stone brought from Bagshot. By the time of his death in 1189 Henry II had made a start on a ring of stone around the castle, as well as building the Great Hall in the Lower Ward and the *Domus regis* in the Upper.

It was said of King John that he 'loved the Castle above all others', but there is little to show for his time at Windsor save for some damage done in a siege following Magna Carta in 1215. His son Henry III completed the circuit of stone walls and added 'D'-shaped towers, giving Windsor a stylish air that moved a chronicler to describe it as 'that very flourishing castle, than which, at that time, there was not another more splendid within the bounds of Europe'. Henry's remodelling marked the advance from just a fortress, but it was in the following century that Edward III made Windsor into a magnificent castle, carrying out an ambitious building programme with the help of William of Wykeham. Edward was not amused, however, when Wykeham had '*Hoc fecit Wykeham*' carved on the wall of a tower.

Opposite top: Hollar's engraving shows the castle before the extensive renovation made by George IV, so evident below

At Windsor Edward, as Holinshed recorded, 'took in hand to repair that place, the rather indeed because he was born there, and therefore he took great pleasure to bestow cost beautifying it with such buildings as may appear even unto this day'. Edward was a romantic, obsessed with chivalry, and in 1348 he founded the Order of the Garter intending it to embody the ideals of the Round Table. The original garter in question is traditionally believed to have dropped from the leg of the 'Fair Maid of Kent' at a dance, whereupon the King picked it up, tied it round his own leg and said, "*Honi soit qui mal y pense.*" The ritual of the order still continues and every June, on the Monday of Ascot week, the two-dozen knights assemble, wearing their lovely blue velvet robes, in St George's Hall in the castle and then process down the hill for the service in St George's Chapel – a sight worth going a long way to see.

The decaying old chapel was replaced by Edward IV with what he wanted to be 'another and altogether more glorious building'. It is said that he wanted St George's to outshine the glories of his predecessor Henry VI's chapel across the river at Eton. Work began in 1472 and the final result was a most noble Gothic perpendicular edifice, with Henry VII being responsible for the nave and Henry VIII setting the choir roof. As it is the chapel of the Order of Garter, the banners of the knights are hung above their stalls. The royal pews can be seen and the sovereign's stall is marked by the Royal Standard. St George's contains the tombs of Henry VI, Edward IV, Henry VIII and his beloved Jane Seymour, Charles I, Edward VII and Queen Alexandra, George V and Queen Mary. George VI is buried in the memorial chapel named after him; whereas George III, Queen Charlotte, George IV and William IV are buried beneath the chapel at the east end of St George's which Queen Victoria restored in memory of Prince Albert.

The Albert Memorial Chapel was originally built by Henry VII in memory of Henry VI. Henry VIII rebuilt the entrance to the Lower Ward of the castle (the gatehouse is still named after him) and added the original wooden North Terrace overlooking what is now the Home Park in 1533. At Windsor the energetic young Hal 'exercised himself daily in shooting, singing, dancing, wrestling, casting of the bat, playing at the recorders, flute, virginals; in setting of songs and making of ballads'; but the years took their toll. His bed at Windsor was 11 ft square and eventually he had to be lifted up the stairs by a rope and pulley system.

His daughter Elizabeth rebuilt the North Terrace in stone in 1582 and made a pretty garden below, but the castle was too cold for her taste. For her indoor walks she built a long gallery (later adapted in the present Library) and she is said to have asked Shakespeare to write *The Merry Wives of Windsor*, reputedly first performed in the castle.

We have an idea of what Windsor was like in Elizabeth's reign from Paul Hentzner's *A Journey into England in the*

year 1598. Hentzner found the castle to be 'a town of proper extent, inexpugnable to any human force', with a view that embraced 'a valley extended every way, and chequered with arable lands and pasture, cloathed up and down with the groves and watered with that gentlest of rivers, the Thames'. James I preferred outdoor pursuits at Windsor, revelling in the chase through the vast deer forests, though he took a dim view of trespassers.

Inexpugnable or not, the royal occupancy of the castle came to an abrupt halt in 1642 when the Parliamentarians took possession after the Battle of Edgehill. Windsor remained the headquarters of Cromwell's army throughout the Civil War and reverted to one of its original functions as a prison. Among the prisoners here was none other than Charles I himself, ignominiously treated without 'the ceremonial of kingship' a few days before his execution and subsequent return to Windsor in a coffin amidst a snowstorm.

After the Restoration, the diarist John Evelyn recorded that the castle was 'exceedingly ragged and ruinous'. All this was to change with some splendour under the stylish Charles II. The King had spent much of his youth in France, forming plans to rival Versailles at Windsor, and the years of exile had increased his leanings towards the Baroque. He reconstructed the Sovereign Apartments to the design of Hugh May and, if the exterior was austerely classical in style, with only an enormous Garter Star for decoration, the interior was a riot of lavish magnificence.

There was an abundance of exuberant wood carvings by Philipps and the great Grinling Gibbons. Evelyn was suitably impressed by the latter; his work was 'stupendous and beyond all description incomparable'. Twenty vast painted ceilings were executed by Antonio Verrio, though sadly only three of these survived the redecoration by Wyatville for George IV.

Then, in 1684, Charles II set about constructing a grand avenue stretching away from the south front of the castle right up to the top of Snow Hill three miles away in the Great Park. This was the beginning of the Long Walk where, later, Queen Anne made a road for her chaise in which she would enjoy bowling along at a good lick, often in pursuit of a stag. The avenue which runs for another three miles through the park from Queen Anne's Gate to the Prince Consort's Gate at Windsor is still known as 'Queen Anne's Ride'. Rather than live in the castle itself, this ample Queen repaired to a little house by the rubbish gate which enjoyed the advantage of a water closet. George III followed her example, after the first two Hanoverian monarchs had shunned Windsor, but eventually found the

Above: The King's State Bedchamber; originally built for Charles II, this room was remodelled by Wyatville
Opposite top: The Queen's Audience Chamber, showing Verrio's ceiling and the carving by Gibbons
Bottom: St George's Chapel, dominating the Lower Ward of the Castle. The Royal Standard flies from the remodelled Round Tower

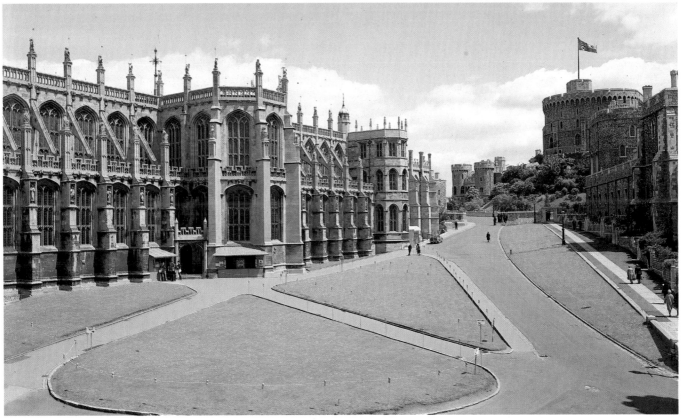

Queen's Lodge a less than satisfactory residence for a king.

With the help of his new Surveyor-General, James Wyatt, 'Farmer George' embarked, in a fairly modest manner, upon the Gothicizing of the castle. He had not got very far before succumbing to the horrible disease now believed to have been porphyria – a condition involving the swelling of glands which results in agonizing abdominal pain and bouts of mental disorder. At the time, of course, he was merely considered to be off his head. Incidents like the one observed by a page called Philip Withers in the Great Park tended to confirm people's worst suspicions. While out driving with the Queen, George III suddenly pulled the horses up, descended from the carriage and approached an oak tree, proceeding to shake it by one of the lower branches and carry on an earnest conversation with the oak under the impression it was the King of Prussia. Withers was glad to report, however, that 'His Majesty, though under a momentary dereliction of reason, evinced the most cordial attachment to freedom and the Protestant faith'. Sadly, the straitjacket was not long in being applied.

If George III was the first king to die at Windsor, the flamboyant George IV was the king to leave the biggest mark on the castle. This great builder transformed the place to how we see it today by restoring a medieval air to the castle. It was a tremendously ambitious enterprise undertaken by the nephew of James Wyatt (who had begun the

The Crimson Drawing Room (opposite) contains portraits of King George VI and Queen Elizabeth (now the Queen Mother)
Above: Wild's painting of St George's Hall in the 19th century, from the Queen's collection

replacement of the Baroque by the Gothic revival for George III), Jeffry Wyatville. His name was originally Wyatt but he had asked George IV if he could adopt this somewhat affected nomenclature to avoid confusion with the other architects in the family. "Veal or mutton, call yourself what you like," the King is said to have replied. Sir Jeffry (as he became) gave the Upper and Middle Wards a Gothic appearance by the romantic additions of curious windows, corbels and crenellations. Purists find much of his work at Windsor ugly and absurd but no one can deny that, at least from a distance, the overall picture is enchanting, indeed everything a castle should be.

Above all, over his sixteen years of work from 1824 onwards, Wyatville achieved a symmetry and a unity, giving the impression of a composite building. He also redesigned much of the interior. He doubled the length of St George's Hall by absorbing a former chapel; this handsome room rests on the fourteenth-century vaulting of Edward III's old palace, and it is interesting to note that the masonry of its walls remains unchanged from the days when the first Knights of the Garter feasted there. Wyatville also built the Grand Corridor (550 ft long) joining the east front to the south front. George IV was the first king to use the east front for his private apartments – a tradition actually begun by Queen Charlotte and continuing to this day – leaving the north front as the state apartments.

The best known of the state apartments is the Waterloo Chamber which the King planned towards the end of his reign to commemorate Wellington's mighty victory. The chamber was erected on the site of an open court in the centre of the north front which lies alongside parts of the castle inhabited by the sovereign from the earliest times, and much of the masonry of its walls dates from the first stone buildings put up by Henry II in the twelfth century. The Waterloo Chamber is sumptuously decorated and displays a stupendous series of portraits of the monarchs, soldiers and statesmen who contributed to the downfall of Napoleon; some 30 of them are by Sir Thomas Lawrence. The dining table seats 150 and the seamless carpet (80 ft by 40 ft) was woven by the prisoners of Agra. Every year a Waterloo Banquet is held here and, in addition to state occasions, it is used for concerts in the Windsor Festival.

George IV's other achievement at Windsor was the completion of the Long Walk. Hitherto a cluster of buildings had prevented the avenue from coming right up to the castle walls but the King razed these to the ground, including a house designed by his father. Perhaps to make up for this, he commissioned an imposing statue of George III, in the unlikely garb of a Roman emperor, astride a gigantic copper horse, which was placed as an eye-catcher at the far end of the Long Walk.

Although Windsor acquired its central place in the life of the British monarchy in the Victorian era, the Queen herself was not especially fond of the castle. 'Windsor always appears very melancholy to me,' she wrote at the beginning of her reign, 'and there are so many sad associations with it'. Her beloved Albert dying there did not improve matters. After his death the place became a gloomy shrine as the sad, not to say unfair, image of the 'Widow of Windsor' grew up.

Frogmore   Albert was buried in the Royal Mausoleum at Frogmore nearby. Originally part of the Crown lands at Windsor during the reign of Henry VIII, Frogmore became a royal retreat after George III's Queen, Charlotte, acquired the property in the 1790s. In the reign of William and Mary, William Aldworth, the tenant, replaced the old house with a new one built of brick in the Dutch style; a later inhabitant was George FitzRoy, Duke of Northumberland, the youngest of Charles II's bastards by Barbara Villiers. The Duke's second wife died at Frogmore aged 105 and, after a spell as a prison for the French Marshal Bellisle, it became the love nest of Sir Edward Walpole and the seamstress Dorothy Clement. Their daughter Maria ended up as the wife of William, Duke of Gloucester, who was George III's brother.

Queen Charlotte created a picturesque garden at Frogmore and James Wyatt converted the old brick house into the elegant cream mansion that survives today, adding a low central colonnade. Wyatt also designed a Grecian temple and some sham Gothic ruins in this rural paradise where the Queen escaped, in the manner of Marie Antoinette, from official life. Some notable *fêtes* were held here, including one for George III's Jubilee in 1809. Frogmore eventually passed to Queen Victoria's mother, the Duchess of Kent, who was the first person to be buried in the mausoleum planned by her son-in-law Prince Albert in conjunction with Ludwig Gruner and the future architect of Sandringham, A J Humbert. Albert also built a model dairy, beautifully hygienic and decorated with Minton tiles, not far away from Frogmore; but soon he was to join his mother-in-law at Frogmore in another mausoleum by Gruner and Humbert. Queen Victoria's own effigy was added to that of her husband in the mausoleum even though she was to live for nearly another 40 years. The Queen would visit Frogmore frequently, contemplating in the tea-house there or working at her papers under a tent, an Indian servant by her side.

Above: The Waterloo Chamber with its great table laid in preparation for the annual Waterloo Banquet
Opposite: Frogmore House, its gardens open to the public once a year, today stands empty. The picture below shows a painting by J Roberts of the Duchess of Kent's drawing room in 1897

The ill-fated Duke of Clarence was born at Frogmore in 1864; he had been engaged to Princess May, who subsequently married his brother the Duke of York, and the future Queen Mary always had a special affection for the place. The house has not been lived in since the last war but Frogmore remains a peaceful sanctuary for the Royal Family and, once a year, the public are allowed into this secret garden.

Fort Belvedere   Edward VIII abdicated at Windsor Castle but much of the dramatic saga was played out at his own retreat on the edge of the Great Park, Fort Belvedere. 'The Fort' was originally a gazebo built for the Duke of Cumberland (fourth son of George II) overlooking Virginia Water, a lake created for the Duke's pleasure by Thomas Sandby. Wyatville enlarged the structure, supposedly for one of George IV's favourites, giving it a tall tower which enhanced the effect of an old castle in a forest. In 1930 the dashing young Prince of Wales asked his father, George V, if he might live in this toy fort. "What could you possibly want that queer old place for?" enquired the King. "Those damn week-ends, I suppose". The Prince found a 'pseudo-Gothic hodge-podge' overgrown and untidy, but the half-buried beauty of the place appealed to him and he set to making it habitable with a will. In recent years Fort Belvedere was the home of his nephew Gerald Lascelles but has now passed out of the Royal Family.

Royal Lodge and Cumberland Lodge A year after George V consented to his elder son acquiring Fort Belvedere, the King offered Royal Lodge in the Great Park to the Duke and Duchess of York as their country home. Today it remains the much loved retreat of the Queen Mother who created an outstanding garden here with her late husband, George VI. Royal Lodge was formerly known as the Lower Lodge, a red-brick house in the manner of Queen Anne. Here in the middle of the eighteenth century lived Thomas Sandby, the Deputy Ranger of the Great Park whereas the Ranger himself, the Duke of Cumberland, lived in the Great Lodge (later known, in consequence, as Cumberland Lodge).

By 1811 Cumberland Lodge was empty and as the pleasure-loving Prince Regent needed a home close to Windsor and London, it was decided to fit it up accordingly. While the larger lodge was undergoing redecoration, the Prince Regent asked for the Lower Lodge to be made habitable. In the event, he settled in the latter, never making the move to Cumberland Lodge, and the Lower Lodge came to be known, sarcastically, as the 'King's Cottage'. John Nash was commissioned to convert the house into a fashionable thatched *cottage orné* of the time, but later Wyatville was called in to expand the building along more grandiose lines. The 'cottage' was now christened the Royal Lodge and by 1825 Wyatville had built a small chapel in one of the new plantations nearby.

In 1826 Sir Walter Scott paid the King a visit and recorded in his diary that though the 'kind of cottage' was too large 'perhaps for the style, but yet so managed that in the walks you can see only parts of it at once, and those

Opposite: The Royal Mausoleum, Frogmore, built by Queen Victoria for Prince Albert and herself; from a painting by Brewer in 1869
Below: Cumberland Lodge in 1880 when it was lived in by Princess Christian, Queen Victoria's third daughter

well composed, and grouping with the immense trees'. Within a year of George IV's death, his successor William IV caused most of it to be knocked down, save for Wyatville's new dining room and the conservatory. Prince Albert, however, took a sympathetic interest in the place, installing his secretary there and it remained a 'grace and favour' residence for members of the royal household until 1931.

At Royal Lodge the future George VI indulged his passion for rhododendrons with the help of Eric Savill (later knighted and commemorated by the marvellous Savill Gardens in the Great Park). In 1932 the small replica of a thatched Welsh cottage (*Y Bwthyn Bach*) was installed in the gardens here – a present from the people of Wales to Princesses Elizabeth and Margaret. When Queen Mary came to see her two granddaughters, she found that she could not stand up inside.

The little Welsh cottage is a rural complement to Queen Mary's Dolls House in the castle itself which the eminent architect Sir Edwin Lutyens designed to the scale of one-twelfth. It is a wonderfully elaborate spoof, with the work of noted artists and writers of the day well represented in miniature, and is one of the most popular attractions for the public. The state apartments are open regularly, affording a glimpse of the rich variety of paintings, furniture, armoury, china and other treasures that form part of the fabulous royal heritage.

If Buckingham Palace is the office, Windsor is very much the week-end home of the Royal Family who enjoy the equestrian pleasures available in the expanse of park. Ascot Week is the high point of the royal year at Windsor and now that the royal cousinage is too big to be accommodated at Sandringham, Christmas is also celebrated at Windsor. The extent to which our Royal Family identifies with Windsor, respecting its long royal tradition, is crystallized by the fact that since 1917 they have taken their surname from the place. **HMM**

Opposite and above: The Royal Lodge, Windsor is set in the south-east corner of Windsor Great Park. The Octagon Room is clearly seen above, the interior with the Queen Mother's desk is opposite

Below: The little thatched cottage, Y Bwthyn Bach, was given to Princess Elizabeth and Princess Margaret by the people of Wales in 1932 to mark our present Queen's 6th birthday

Royal Palaces and Fortresses No Longer

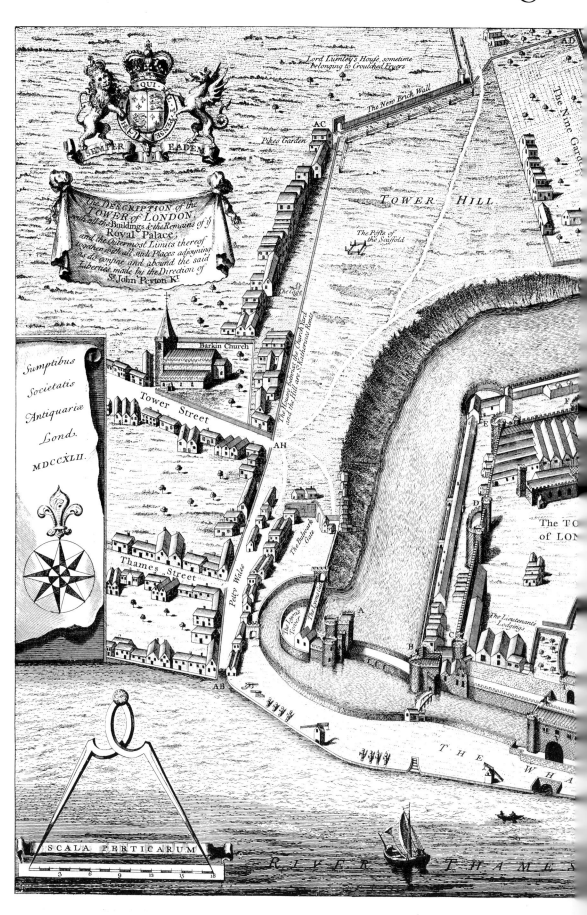

Lord Lumley's House, sometime belonging to Crouched Fryers

The New Brick Wall

The Nine Gardens

QUI EI SANCTA

SEMPER EADEM

Pikes Garden

AC

TOWER HILL

The Posts of the Scaffold

The DESCRIPTION of the TOWER of LONDON, with all the Buildings & the Remains of y Royal Palace, and the Outermost Limits thereof together with all such Places adjoyning as do confine and abound the said Liberties made by the Direction of S.r John Peyton K.t

The Cage

Barkin Church

The House beyond the Church yard and the Hill are S.t Katherines Rents

Sumptibus

Societatis

Antiquariæ

Lond.

MDCCXLII.

Tower Street

AH

The Tower of London

E

D

The Bulwork Gate

The Lyons Tower

The Byword

A

Thames Street

Petty Wales

The Lieutenants Lodgings

C

B

AB

THE WHA

SCALA PERTICARUM

3   6   12   15   18

RIVER THAMES

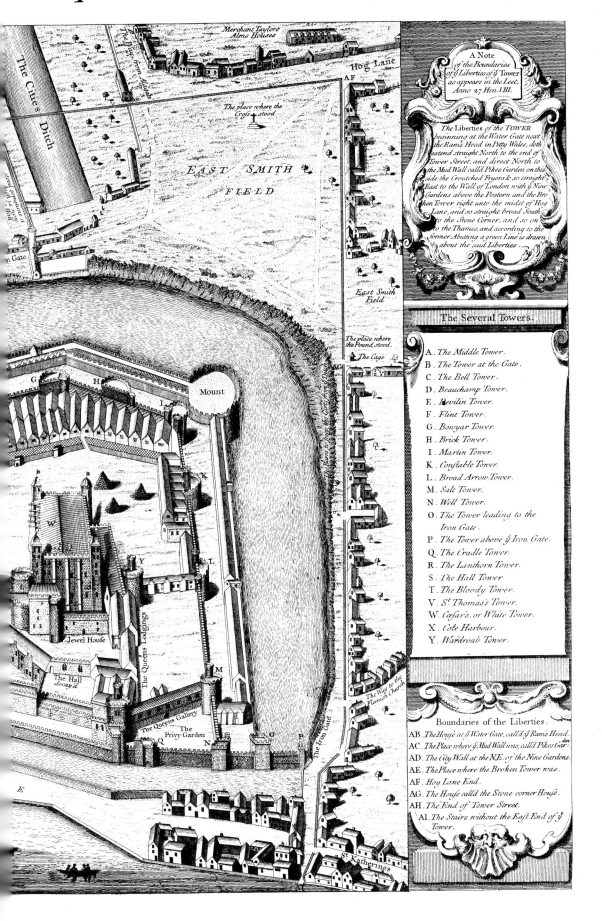

Merchant Taylors
Alms Houses

The Way from Aldgate

The Cities Ditch

Hog Lane
AF

The place where the
Cross stood

EAST SMITH
FIELD

East Smith
Field

The place where
the Pound stood

The Cage
AG

Mount

G
H
I

Brick Tower

K

Jewel House

The Queens Lodgings

Y

L

The Hall
decay'd

M

The Queens Gallery

The Privy Garden
Q   N   O   P

The Iron Gate

The Way to the
Flemish Church

E

St Katherines

A Note
of the Boundaries
of ỹ Liberties of ỹ Tower
as appears in the Leet,
Anno 27 Hen. VIII.

The Liberties of the TOWER
beginning at the Water Gate next
the Ram's Head in Petty Wales, doth
extend straight North to the end of
Tower Street, and direct North to
the Mud Wall call'd Pikes Garden on this
side the Croutched Fryers & so straight
East to the Wall of London with ỹ Nine
Gardens above the Postern and the Broken Tower right unto the midst of Hog
Lane, and so straight broad South
to the Stone Corner, and so on
to the Thames, and according to the
former. Abutting a green Line is drawn
about the said Liberties.

The Several Towers.

A. The Middle Tower.
B. The Tower at the Gate.
C. The Bell Tower.
D. Beauchamp Tower.
E. Devilin Tower.
F. Flint Tower.
G. Bowyar Tower.
H. Brick Tower.
I. Martin Tower.
K. Constable Tower.
L. Broad Arrow Tower.
M. Salt Tower.
N. Well Tower.
O. The Tower leading to the
   Iron Gate.
P. The Tower above ỹ Iron Gate.
Q. The Cradle Tower.
R. The Lanthorn Tower.
S. The Hall Tower
T. The Bloody Tower.
V. St Thomas's Tower.
W. Cæsar's, or White Tower.
X. Cole Harbour.
Y. Wardroab Tower.

Boundaries of the Liberties.

AB. The House at ỹ Water Gate, call'd ỹ Rams Head.
AC. The Place where ỹ Mud Wall was, call'd Pikes Garden.
AD. The City Wall at the NE. of the Nine Gardens.
AE. The Place where the Broken Tower was.
AF. Hog Lane End.
AG. The House call'd the Stone corner House.
AH. The End of Tower Street.
AI. The Stairs without the East End of ỹ
     Tower.

GREENWICH PALACE

From the tenth century onwards, the Crown leased the Manor of Greenwich on the south bank of the Thames to St Peter's Abbey in Ghent, but when Henry V suppressed the alien priories in England, his youngest brother Humphrey, Duke of Gloucester obtained the freehold. 'The Good Duke' Humphrey, who was a noted patron of the arts and a bibliophile, and whose library is now housed in the Bodleian at Oxford, built a riverside palace called Bella Court.

Humphrey, whose wife was accused of witchcraft, over-reached himself and was arrested for high treason, dying (supposedly murdered) while in prison in 1447. The manor reverted to the Crown and, just three weeks later, Henry VI's strong-willed Queen, Margaret of Anjou, had installed herself at Bella Court which she promptly rechristened

'Placentia' or 'Pleasaunce'. Margaret did it up in elaborate style, covering the floors with monogrammed terracotta tiles and the pillars and arcades with sculptured daisies, whereas the windows were filled with the novelty of glass.

The palace became a shuttlecock in the Wars of the Roses and further changes were made by Edward IV, Henry VI's adversary. Henry VII, the founder of the British navy, became particularly attached to Greenwich and it was one of his most regular residences. He carried out various improvements, refacing the palace in red brick. His Queen set out for her coronation from a water carnival here, joining up with the King at the Tower Wharf.

Their son Henry VIII also had a special affection for the riverside palace. Here he could hawk and hunt within easy water distance of London and was well placed for visiting the burgeoning shipyards at Woolwich and Deptford. He also built armouries and a tiltyard behind the river front of Greenwich Palace (as it was now known) and spent large sums of money on making it a 'pleasant, perfect and princely palace'. He created splendid gardens, built a banqueting hall and employed Holbein there at four shillings a day. From a view of it drawn in 1558 it appears to have consisted of several irregular ranges dominated by two groups of battlemented towers.

Above: The Queen's House, built by Inigo Jones, seen from the terrace of the Royal Observatory. Behind the house is the Royal Naval College and the Hospital for Seamen with the twin towers built by Wren

Previous page: An engraving showing the Tower of London as it looked in 1597

49

Many of the dramas of Henry VIII's life were played out at Greenwich. It was the scene of his marriage to Catherine of Aragon while their daughter Mary was born and betrothed (abortively, as it turned out) in some state to the Dauphin here. Henry and Anne Boleyn met at Greenwich in 1522; it was from here also that Anne processed up the river for her coronation 'while round it stood men . . . casting wild-fire and making hideous noises'. Elizabeth I was born at Greenwich and the *Te Deum* 'was sung incontinently'; but her mother was later indicted for incest and on this occasion her voyage up the Thames ended at the Tower. Henry's fourth marriage to the 'Flanders Mare' (or,

Above: Looking south in the early 17th century you could see the recently completed Queen's House in front of the ancient riverside palace of Placentia (below)

alternatively, 'Dutch Cow'), Anne of Cleves, was another Greenwich event.

Elizabeth I reviewed the City of London trained bands at Greenwich in the year of her accession, and fifteen years later revived the ancient custom of distributing Royal Maundy. This ceremony is still carried out by her successor in name every year on Maundy Thursday – for a long time it was only done at Westminster Abbey, but recently the scene has varied – even if some of the less salubrious aspects of the ceremonial have been dropped. Queen Elizabeth I, for instance, washed the feet of 39 pauper women and then kissed their big toes – it should be added, though, that the feet had been vigorously cleaned by royal lackeys beforehand. The feet could have been fairly muddy if the women had been walking along the Deptford to Woolwich road at the bottom of the garden; it was here that Walter Raleigh

is supposed to have thrown his cloak for the Queen to ford a 'plashy place'.

In James I's reign, it was decided to replace the old gatehouse over this road at the back of the palace with 'The House of Delight' (or Queen's House). Tradition has it that the King gave Greenwich to his Queen, Anne of Denmark, as a peace offering after he had scolded her too severely for accidentally shooting his favourite hound. Anne died in 1619 before this new 'curious device of Inigo Jones' was ready; it was later completed for her daughter-in-law, Charles I's Queen, Henrietta Maria.

Jones, England's first classical architect, had become Surveyor of the King's Works in 1615 and began work on the Queen's House the following year, not finishing the main structure until 1635 (the date carved on the north front), though even then there was some way to go. With its perfect classical proportions, its Ionic loggia, its painted ceilings by Jakob Jordaens and Orazio Gentileschi, its gilded decoration and its bust of Charles I by Bernini, it must have been the most elegant and sophisticated house in the England of its time – a testimony to Charles I's exquisite taste.

As built, the Queen's House consisted of two rectangular buildings, one facing the river, the other the park, which were linked by a single bridge (the 'middle bridge room') over the public road. The fine pictures, sculpture and furniture were removed during the Commonwealth. After the Restoration the house was enlarged to accommodate Charles II and his Queen, a further bridge being added at either end (the East and West Bridge Rooms) to form the present square structure. Jones's nephew, John Webb, was employed to do these enlargements.

The house is of brick, but the ground floor is faced in stone and the rest is rendered. The curving double staircase towards the river leads to a terrace from which three tall casement doorways used to lead into the Great Hall (before alterations in 1708). The Great Hall is the main room in the house – a magnificent cube of some 40 ft square by 40 ft high. The design of its striking black-and-white marble paving echoes the pattern of the ceiling above; the floor was completed by Nicholas Stone and Gabriel Stacey in 1637. Gentileschi's Muses and Arts painting on the ceiling was removed early in the eighteenth century to Marlborough House. The present painting is in the style of Thornhill. The gallery recalls the minstrel's gallery of a traditional English hall.

The Queen's Drawing Room has a richly decorated ceiling which (like the hall) is of pine and the blue colour matches traces of the original colouring detected in the course of restoration in the 1930s. Rubens was apparently to be employed here, but died before plans could come to fruition. The North-East Cabinet also retains its original carved ceiling by John Grove, later one of Wren's leading craftsmen in the City of London. Grove was also responsible for the plasterwork in the West Bridge Room.

The Queen's Bedroom remains, apart from the Great Hall, as the most splendid and best preserved apartment in the Queen's House. The broad curving cove of the ceiling is enriched with a highly coloured series of 'grotesques' (a fashion later revived at Kensington Palace by William Kent). Today the room is furnished as far as possible as it might have been when Henrietta Maria lived here.

Behind the Queen's House, the old royal park of Greenwich rises to the former Royal Observatory at Flamsteed House. Outside the Observatory is the celebrated Meridian Stone marking the zero of longitude. The park as we see it today was laid out by Le Nôtre for Charles II. There are lovely avenues of Spanish chestnuts and hawthorns and the stump of old Queen Elizabeth's oak under which Henry VIII is reputed to have danced with Anne Boleyn.

During the Civil War the old Tudor palace became a blot on the landscape and, on his Restoration, Charles II decided to replace it with an impressive Renaissance pile to be called 'The King's House' thus complementing Inigo Jones's exquisite Queen's House. Webb was given the commission but, as Pepys observed, progress went 'on slow'. At Charles's death, only the west wing was complete and that had cost £36,000.

The original idea was to form three sides of a square, with the river as the fourth, but Queen Mary II was determined that the view to the river from the Queen's House should not be closed when she gave the King's House over to be the Royal Hospital for Seamen after the Battle of La Hogue. Sir Christopher Wren executed the plans, erecting twin palaces flanking the much smaller Queen's House in the centre. The glory of the hospital inside was provided by Sir James Thornhill's decoration of the Painted Hall – a painting at £3 per yard which finally cost £6,085. In the eighteenth and early nineteenth centuries the hospital was full of naval wounded – some 2,700 pensioners were in residence around Nelson's time – but in 1869 it became the Royal Naval College.

The Queen's House became the official residence of the Governor of the Royal Hospital. The Hanoverian connections with Greenwich were fairly slight, though George I stepped ashore here in 1714 – a scene commemorated in Thornhill's painted ceiling in the hospital – and actually spent his first night in the Queen's House before his state entry into London. Similarly, Princess Augusta of Saxe-Gotha put up here on her way to marry 'Poor Fred'. The last Queen Consort to be associated with the Queen's House was George II's Queen Caroline. Later, some unruly servants at the Queen's House connived in making the place a centre of the smuggling trade, while the park became 'an Asylum for Rioters and a Receptacle for Whores and Rogues'.

From 1807 the Queen's House became a school for seamen's children and the flanking colonnades were added. A training ship was unsympathetically placed in front of the building. More serious were the drastic alterations made to the interior of the house before the school was moved to Suffolk in 1933. Fortunately the National Maritime Museum arrived on the scene and the formidable task of restoration was undertaken by the Office of Works (now the Department of the Environment).

An outstanding job has been done in recreating much of the detail and atmosphere of Inigo Jones's beautiful house and the museum authorities have done their best to provide appropriate furnishings, as well as concentrating in the building their most important historical paintings. It is highly satisfactory that the museum has maintained the naval and maritime associations of Greenwich that always gave it such appeal to our sovereigns.

The exhibits include Queen Mary II's 'Shallop' (a light, open boat) of 1689 and a state barge built for the Prince of Wales in 1732. It was at Greenwich that the Queen knighted the circumnavigator Sir Francis Chichester, and a descendant of the sea kings, Queen Margrethe of Denmark, began her state visit to these shores in 1974. The best view of this glorious riverside palace is, appropriately enough, from the water itself. **HMM**

HAMPTON COURT PALACE

Hampton Court is architecturally the finest palace which the British Crown possesses, the nearest equivalent to Versailles on this side of the Channel. However, it was abandoned in favour of Windsor by George III and has remained lamentably absent from the centre of the stage of state ever since.

In 1514 a butcher's son from Ipswich leased the site of Hampton Court on the River Thames for £50 a year from the Knights Hospitallers of St John of Jerusalem who had owned the manor from the beginning of the fourteenth century. The butcher's son was, of course, Thomas Wolsey, then Archbishop of York and approaching the zenith of his power. He wanted somewhere convenient for London and was attracted by the 'extraordinary salubrity' of the place. The house he built was nothing short of a palace, constructed around two large courtyards (the present Base and Clock Courts) and a number of small ones. There were reputed to be 1000 rooms and apartments for 280 guests; the Venetian ambassador reported that one had 'to traverse eight rooms' before reaching the Cardinal's audience chamber, 'and they are all hung with tapestry, which is changed every week'.

Wolsey entertained at Hampton Court in lavish style, specializing in enormous diplomatic parties. Inevitably all this grandeur from a commoner created envy and ill feelings. John Skelton asked:

Why come ye not to Courte?
To whyche Court
To the Kynges Courte,
Or to Hampton Court?

Henry VIII is traditionally supposed to have asked Wolsey why he had built such a magnificent house for himself and Wolsey is meant to have replied: 'To show how noble a palace a subject may offer to his sovereign'. Realizing that he had overreached himself, the Cardinal thought it prudent to transfer the property to the King. But Wolsey never recovered Henry's favour after his failure to secure an annulment of the marriage with Catherine of Aragon and he was finally toppled in 1529.

The King moved into Hampton Court and tackled an ambitious building programme. He added a third big courtyard, rebuilt the Cardinal's hall, altered the Chapel and gave the whole place his own stamp. Soon it looked as if the Cardinal had never had anything to do with the palace.

The Great Hall is the outstanding survival from Henry VIII's time here. 40 ft wide, it has a splendid timber roof with Renaissance decoration. There is another remarkable ceiling in the Chapel Royal, a slightly simpler ceiling in the 'watching chamber' next to the Great Hall and two other

Top left: The Great Gatehouse erected by Thomas Wolsey
Top right: The Astronomical Clock and Bell Turret on top of Anne Boleyn's Gateway
Left: Wren's east front from the Fountain Garden

53

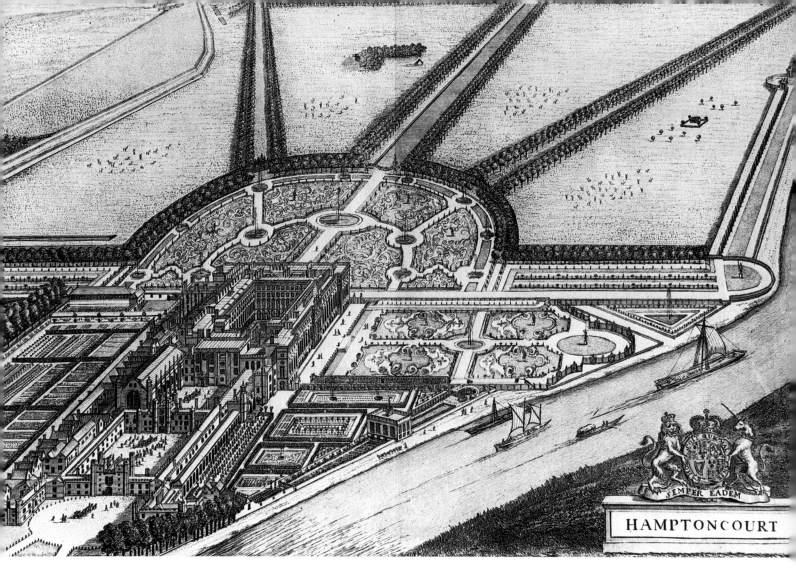

Tudor ceilings of interest in Wolsey's Closet and Wolsey's Chamber – the latter two being the only interiors to survive from the time of the Cardinal. The new kitchens built by Henry VIII are another fascinating survival in more or less their original state. The athletic Henry also added a tilt-yard, bowling alleys, archery butts and the tennis court. He was particularly fond of tennis and apparently 'it was the prettiest thing in the world to see him play, his fair skin glowing through a shirt of the finest texture'. The Royal Tennis court, the oldest in England, is still very much in use and wily old men can be seen outwitting younger opponents at this indoor game which involves such arcane cries as 'Hazard chase the door'.

Hampton Court was the scene of many of Henry's marital ups and downs. Sometime before his divorce from Catherine of Aragon, 'Anne Bouillayne's lodgynges at Hamptone Courte' were being built here. Jane Seymour delivered a frail heir in the palace, dying within a fortnight, and Catherine Howard was cross-examined by Cranmer about her love life in a distressing manner. The gallery outside the Chapel is said to have been haunted by her ever since she ran down in it in terror away from the soldiers who came to take her away. Finally, though, Henry enjoyed a peaceful conclusion to his marital career at Hampton Court with the homely Catherine Parr.

Mary Tudor spent her honeymoon with Philip II of Spain at the palace and had her pathetic phantom pregnancy here.

Top left: An 18th-century engraving by Kip showing the palace when Wren had completed his work
Bottom left: Wolsey's Closet, one of the Cardinal's surviving apartments, with its early 16th-century paintings
Below left: William III's State Bedchamber
Right: The interior of the Chapel Royal, showing the timber ceiling dating from Henry VIII's time

Her half-sister Elizabeth spent some time as a prisoner in the Water Gallery during Mary's reign, but seemed to bear Hampton Court no ill will for some of her more light-hearted adventures with her various suitors took place here. She took a particular interest in the gardens which have always been an outstanding feature of the great riverside domain. The Chamberlains' Company, which Shakespeare joined as an actor, performed in the Great Hall before Elizabeth and her successor James I.

The 'wisest fool in Christendom' held the Hampton Court Conference in 1604 when the Puritan complaints of abuses in the Church of England were rejected, though the Authorised Version of *The Bible* was put in hand. His son Charles I was imprisoned in the palace during the Civil War (later escaping to the Isle of Wight) when the Parliamentarians sold many of its treasures. Cromwell took up residence here as Lord Protector, only to catch the 'bastard tertian ague' which killed him. After the Restoration, Charles II spent his honeymoon at Hampton Court and redecorated the place, remodelling the park.

William and Mary liked the situation of the old building but had the grand notion of asking Sir Christopher Wren to replace it with a magnificent new palace. Sir Christopher drew up plans along the Versailles model, approached by a mile-long avenue across Bushy Park. The avenue was duly landscaped but the money ran out before the whole palace could be rebuilt. As it turned out, Wren pulled down more than half of the rambling rabbit-warren of Tudor structures, remodelling two sides and a courtyard. Because the King and Queen were joint sovereigns, Wren built two sets of state apartments around the elegant Fountain Court, approached by separate staircases. The King's state apartments were on the south front, the Queen's on the east.

A fine fireplace by Grinling Gibbons in the King's Private Dressing Room

Views have differed as to Wren's rebuilding. James Pope-Hennessy has observed that from 'an interesting monument of the English Renaissance, Hampton Court was transformed into a Dutch copy of Versailles'. However, the result can be seen as a pleasing compromise between Tudor and Stuart. There is an enjoyable contrast between the gateways, courtyards, gallery and Great Hall dating from Tudor times and the partially-built Wren palace that lies beyond them, with its grand front facing along the canal and its enfilades of state rooms. It is all a delightful mixture of the romantic and the classical.

Work on the interior was slow, and in some cases unfinished, but there are many objects to see in the way of state beds, state portraits, Italian paintings and all sorts of other treasures. The King's Guard Room has a display of some 3000 arms, arranged in patterns by William III's gunsmith. The state rooms and the Chapel Royal have fine woodcarvings by Grinling Gibbons; whereas the King's and Queen's staircases, the Queen's Drawing Room and their respective bedchambers have wall or ceiling frescoes painted by Antonio Verrio, Sir James Thornhill and William Kent. The themes of these frescoes were often symbolic, expressed in allegorical terms – thus the Roman Emperors on the King's Staircase being given a wigging for their misdeeds are supposed to represent the later Stuarts whom William had replaced.

Many of the craftsmen who worked inside also had a hand in the wide-ranging alterations in the gardens which were virtually laid out afresh. Mary II, like her husband, was a devoted gardener and she was responsible for many of the ornamental iron grilles and gates designed by Tijou. Other features in the garden include William III's Banqueting House, the great vine (with a main branch of over 100 ft) and the famous, if now somewhat undernourished, maze which dates from the beginning of the eighteenth century.

Mary's death in 1694 rather knocked the stuffing out of the rebuilding plans, but 'Dutch William' came back from time to time to keep things moving. Then in 1702, the 'gentleman in black velvet' intervened; the King's horse stumbled on a mole-hill in the park throwing him on to his right shoulder – an accident that was to cause his death. Queen Anne spent little time here but George I found the place an agreeable retreat for himself and his teutonic entourage, notably his mistresses the 'Maypole' and the 'Elephant'. He used the Great Hall as a theatre, having plays brought down from London by Colley Cibber; but there was little else in the way of enjoyment to be had during his stays here.

George II was the last sovereign to live in the palace. As Prince of Wales he had kept a lively Court in the absence of his father in Hanover, but unfortunately he carried on the bad family tradition of quarrelling with his eldest son when he became King. There was the notorious occasion when the Prince of Wales removed his wretched wife from the palace when she was in an advanced stage of labour so as to prevent his mother from being present at the birth. The favourite room of George II and his wife at Hampton Court was the Queen's Gallery; here they would take breakfast together overlooking the gardens.

Following Queen Caroline's death in 1737, George II seldom returned to the palace. His grandson and successor George III fell foul of his grandfather in one of the state apartments and received a sound box on the ears. According to George III's son, the Duke of Sussex, this painful experience so coloured his feelings for the palace that he decided never to darken its doors again.

When he came to the throne George III removed much of the furniture from Hampton Court and began the practice of granting 'grace and favour' residences in the palace. William IV once described it as the 'quality poor house'. As Duke of Clarence, William had been Ranger of Bushy Park and lived at Bushy House nearby.

Queen Victoria opened the state apartments and gardens to the public shortly after her accession. Despite the physical absence of monarchy the rooms were maintained in good order. Today there are almost 1000 rooms given over to the 'grease and fervours', as someone once unkindly called them; they tend to be widows of peers and other distinguished public servants who refer to the palace as 'Hampers'.

It is a pity that this superb setting is not used for more ceremonial occasions, though its continuance as a royal residence would probably have meant the giving up of Windsor Castle. The proximity of Windsor has presumably accounted for the fact that it has rather taken a back seat. In any event, it remains a marvellous place to behold: nothing conjures up the world of the Tudors so colourfully as Hampton Court and, as an elegant bonus, there is the majesty of Wren and the glorious gardens. **HMM**

KEW PALACE (THE DUTCH HOUSE)

Above: Mercier's painting of A Music Party, 1733, showing Frederick, Prince of Wales, and his sisters with the Dutch House in the background

The mellow red brick Dutch House, which in turn became known as the Prince's House and Kew Palace, is the oldest of the royal buildings in Kew Gardens, and the only one there to survive. An earlier house on the same site which had belonged to Sir Henry Gates during Mary Tudor's reign, was known as the Dairy House. It later came into the hands of a Somerset family, the Portmans of Orchard Portman, who sold it to a Dutch merchant, Samuel Fortrey, from whom it acquired the name of the Dutch House.

Samuel Fortrey built the present house of Flemish bond brick in 1631 with three gables on the main fronts. This date, with his and his wife's initials S F C, united by a knot, appear over the entrance. Though known as a palace, the word seems almost a misnomer for what is an extremely unprententious house. Still, the technical meaning of palace is a house belonging to a king, queen, prince, princess or bishop, and a palace it did become.

The builder's son, William Fortrey, sold the house in 1697 to Sir Richard Levett who, in 1701, became Lord Mayor of London. After his death, Queen Caroline took out a lease, and in 1728 her daughters were recorded as living there. In 1734 Anne, the eldest, was at the Dutch House the year she married the Prince of Orange. The house forms the background to Philip Mercier's picture of Frederick, Prince of Wales playing the 'cello to his sisters

57

in the gardens of the White House opposite, and his cypher appears on some of the heavy brass locks. During the time that the Prince leased both the White House and the Dutch House, George III's son, as a boy, spent much of his time at Kew, and after his marriage to Princess Charlotte of Mecklenburg-Strelitz, it was used as an annexe for their many royal children. In 1781 the King purchased the Dutch House.

In 1771 when George's son the Prince of Wales reached the age of nine he was allotted the Dutch House, where he lived with his younger brother Frederick, Duke of York under the governance of a tutor, with language, dancing and music masters in attendance. The younger brothers, according to Mrs Papendieck, went to a house at the top of Kew Green, later called King's Cottage.

Discipline was lax, despite the rigid views of the King and Queen on their children's upbringing. When the Prince of Wales was sixteen he became smitten with the charms of the actress Mary Robinson, after seeing her as Perdita in *The Winter's Tale* at Drury Lane, and he sent her ardent love letters signed 'Florizel.' His household arranged to smuggle her through a private door in the wall on her many midnight assignations with the Prince in the secluded parts of Kew Gardens. Perdita Robinson, as she was subsequently known, was accompanied by Lord Malden on these visits. She wrote that she 'always wore a dark coloured habit: the rest of our party generally wrapped themselves in great coats to disguise them, excepting the Duke of York, who almost universally alarmed us by the display of a buff coat, the most conspicuous colour he could have selected for an adventure of this nature'. Perdita, who became the Prince's mistress, received a bond for £20,000 to be redeemed when the Prince came of age, but by then he was tired of her. Soon after this intrigue the Prince was given apartments at Windsor.

When the White House was demolished in 1802, all the royal possessions were moved to the Dutch House, which then became the sole royal residence in Kew Gardens. The last happy month that George III and Queen Charlotte spent there was in October 1805. During this time Princess Elizabeth planned a surprise dinner at the Queen's Cottage. The only subsequent time the King came back to Kew was a fleeting visit in the following year, *en route* from Windsor to London.

Queen Charlotte returned to Kew in August 1813, after an absence of eight years, a sad lonely woman. King George was then blind and senile, and the Prince of Wales had been Regent for over two years. The King was never to recover his sanity, but the old man, his beard now quite white, survived his Queen by just over a year, dying on 29 January 1820.

The last great day at Kew happened on 11 July 1818, when (following the death of Princess Charlotte, only daughter of the Prince Regent,) the two middle-aged sons of the King and Queen discarded their mistresses to marry for the sake of succession. The two were the Duke of Clarence, later William IV, and the Duke of Kent, Queen Victoria's father, choosing respectively Princess Adelaide of Saxe-Meiningen and Princess Victoire of Saxe-Coburg-Saalfeld, widow of the Prince of Leiningen. This was the second ceremony for the Kents, the first being held at Coburg.

The Dutch House, as it is today and (above) as it was at the end of the 18th century – hardly altered since Samuel Fortrey built it in 1631

Queen Charlotte, then in her last illness, was wheeled into the Drawing Room to watch the ceremony by her eldest son, the Prince Regent. Immediately afterwards she went back to her rooms, and the banquet took place in the King's Dining Room, followed by an *al fresco* party, presided over by the Regent, at the Queen's Cottage.

Just four months later, on 17 November 1818, Queen Charlotte died in her bedroom in the Dutch House, propped up in her chair.

For 80 years Kew Palace (or the Dutch House) was shut up. The new King, George IV, who succeeded in 1820, gave orders for its demolition, but fortunately countermanded them. John Henry Jesse, in his *Memoirs*, tells on a subsequent visit there that 'the housekeeper sometimes goes to dust and air the house.' At length, in 1897, to celebrate Queen Victoria's Diamond Jubilee, Kew Palace was renovated and opened to the public. There are many mementoes of George III, Queen Charlotte and their children: King George's walking stick and favourite chair, the backgammon board on which he used to play with his equerries, and his private prayer book, in which he obliterated with his own hand 'our most religious and gracious king' and substituted 'a most miserable sinner'. There are the tapestry chairs which Queen Charlotte worked, placed near the harpsichord Shudi made in 1740 for Frederick, Prince of Wales, her sketch of a cottage which she threw away but which was retrieved, her privately printed poems, her letters, and the children's toys.

The rooms are labelled as they were when George III and Queen Charlotte lived at Kew. The main entrance opens on to a long passage north to south, with a staircase at the north end. To the left of the passage is the Library Ante-Room, which has good sixteenth-century linenfold panelling, perhaps a relic of the old Dairy House. The Library, a larger room, has seventeenth-century panelling and ornamental woodwork over the chimney piece. To the right of the passage is the King's Dining Room, facing south, measuring 31 ft by 21 ft, with five windows. In the centre of the ceiling is a large Tudor rose of plaster dating from the time of the Fortreys. The next room to its north is the much smaller King's Breakfast Room with wooden panelling and intervening pilasters.

On the first floor there is a similar passage north to south, communicating with the stairs at the north end. The little room on the left is the Queen's Ante-Chamber leading to the Queen's Bedroom, facing north. Queen Victoria placed a brass plate over the chimney piece to commemorate the death of her grandmother Queen Charlotte. Two closed doors once opened on to a passage to the King's apartments.

Across the landing at the head of the stairs on the right is the low-ceilinged Queen's Boudoir, with the motif of *The Five Senses*, illustrated by women in different poses. An example is the centre medallion which shows *Hearing* represented by a woman with a guitar. Then comes the principal room in the house, the Queen's Drawing Room, immediately above the Dining Room, with two dark grey marble pillars with alabaster capitals. Across the passage is the King's Ante-Room, leading to the King's Bedroom. The Princesses' bedrooms were on the second floor, and above is the attic storey.

Though most of the thousands of visitors that flock to Kew come to see the Botanical Gardens, a visit to the Dutch House gives us a glimpse of George III and Queen Charlotte in the role in which they were happiest – that of 'Farmer George and his wife'. **PMS**

THE TOWER OF LONDON

There was a twelfth-century tradition that the mortar used in the building of the White Tower was mixed with blood. In view of the Tower of London's grisly history of imprisonment, torture, execution and worse, this would have been singularly appropriate. An even less reliable tradition is that the Tower was founded by Julius Caesar; in fact, William the Conqueror began building the Great Tower or Keep, called the White Tower, in 1078.

The White Tower, with its four turrets, is the only Norman building in the old royal fortress. It is 90 ft high and the walls are 15 ft thick at the bottom; the keep is the biggest in the country but for Colchester. The Conqueror's son William Rufus completed the building operations, having to attend to repairs following a great storm in 1091. The interior is no-nonsense Norman, a style dictated by the paramount requirements of strength and security. The spiral staircase obliged an attacker to fight southpaw because of its right-handed twist. Down below are the noisome dungeons, including 'Little Ease' – so called as it was impossible to lie down. But there is a stark beauty in the Old Banqueting Hall, the Sword Room and the pristine Chapel of St John the Evangelist (dating from about 1080), as well as the state apartments and the Council Chamber, now used as an impressive museum of armoury.

King Stephen kept Court at the Tower during the civil wars of his reign and the Chancellor of Richard the Lionheart enlarged the moat. At the beginning of the thirteenth century, though, the Tower was still a fairly modest castle. It was Henry III who set about converting the Conqueror's hall-keep into a fortress ringed with a curtain wall and thirteen bastion towers.

In 1241 he had the royal apartments whitewashed, as well as the exterior of the truly White Tower, finding it convenient to take shelter here at the time of the Barons' Wars. He also decorated the Chapel of St John with paintings and stained glass, and added more agreable accommodation to the south of the White Tower (most of which was destroyed by Cromwell). Henry did his best to make the place more like a home: the walls of Queen Eleanor's rooms were decorated with roses, whereas a painting of winter in his own bedroom may have reassured him that it was even colder outside.

Henry also started a menagerie at the Tower which remained there until transferring to Regent's Park in the nineteenth century. In 1235 the Emperor Frederick sent Henry, who was his brother-in-law, three leopards. The keeper of the King's leopard, incidentally, was paid three halfpence a day for his own food but 'sixpence a day for the sustenance of the leopard'. Soon other beasts followed: a camel, a white bear from Norway and a short-lived elephant from Louis IX of France. The Lion Tower (where the bookshop and refreshment rooms are now) took its name from this menagerie, leonine arrivals in the den taking their names from the reigning monarch.

Henry III's powerful son Edward I built the remainder of the outer wall, which his father had started, and also the western section of the inner wall, together with what came to be known as the Beauchamp Tower. Including the moat, the whole area covers some eighteen acres and it was Edward I who was broadly responsible for the fortress we see today.

His grandson Edward III's main use of the Tower was to lock people up in it. Among the notable political prisoners of his reign were David Bruce, King of the Scots, John, King of France, and several French noblemen in the wake of the Battle of Poitiers. The list was to stretch to Rudolf Hess in the Second World War. Edward was a careful steward of the Tower, having a survey done, and wanted the gates, walls and bulwarks to 'be kept with all diligence'. He installed his son, the Black Prince, there to keep an eye on things.

The Black Prince's son, Richard II, kept elegant Court at the Tower, carrying out various elaborate decoration work. He made additions to the Byward Tower, the gatehouse of the outer ward, where parts of a wall painting, showing the figures of St John the Baptist and St Michael depicted against a background decorated with the Leopards of England and *fleurs-de-lis* of France, have recently been uncovered. On the eve of his coronation in July 1377, Richard II attended divine service in the Chapel of St John and created a number of Knights of the Bath who then fulfilled their duties of watching the young King at his ceremonial ablutions, waiting on him at dinner, keeping vigil over their arms through the night in the Chapel and then escorting their sovereign to Westminster. This tradition of the King setting out from the Tower for his coronation, which had grown up from the need to show that the new sovereign commanded the capital from its ancient fortress, was to continue until 1661.

During the Peasants' Revolt of 1381 the fourteen year-old Richard II courageously left the sanctuary of the Tower to reason with the rebels at Mile End. However, while he was out, some 700 of Wat Tyler's revolting peasantry broke in. The damage they did to the actual property was small – only amounting to £3 6s 8d – but the personal insults and injuries suffered by the occupants of the Tower were considerable. The knights of the garrison had their beards tweaked, the King's mother fainted when one of the invaders proposed osculation with her, and the Archbishop of Canterbury, the Treasurer, the Serjeant-at-Arms (the man behind the Poll Tax) and an unfortunate Franciscan friar were all decapitated. In 1399 Richard II was defeated by Bolingbroke's rebellion and obliged to abdicate in the Council Room of the White Tower, resigning the Crown in favour of his cousin Henry IV.

The south face of the White Tower, the great Norman fortress which has protected London for a thousand years

The Tower of London, Commanded in Chief by the Rt. Honble. Robert Ld. Lucas.
la Tour *de LONDRES.*

Above: The Tower in about 1708, showing the 17th-century additions now demolished and replaced by the present Waterloo Barracks
Opposite left: The King's House, sometimes referred to as the Queen's House, built in 1530, and the Gaoler's House where Lady Jane Grey was imprisoned
Right: St John's Chapel, within the walls of the White Tower, is today a Chapel Royal

Henry IV's grandson, Henry VI, was a monarch who spent more time than most in the Tower – though by no means all of it was by his own choosing. During the Wars of the Roses he was imprisoned for five years in the White Tower by his victor Edward IV who allowed him five marks a week and an occasional cask of wine. Thanks to the machinations of Warwick the Kingmaker, the pathetic Henry VI was briefly restored to the throne in 1470 before the collapse of the Lancastrian cause and the death of his son led to his return to the Tower where he died 'of pure displeasure and melancholy'. That, at least, was the official version; others include him among those to have been murdered in the Tower, and his memory is honoured on 21 May every year by representatives from his foundations at Eton and King's College Cambridge.

The bloody roll-call also numbers Edward IV's brother the Duke of Clarence (according to Holinshed, 'privately drowned in a butt of malmesie') and, of course, the King's own sons and heirs, Edward V and the Duke of York – 'the Princes in the Tower'. The Tudors managed to attach the blame for this dastardly deed firmly to the 'wicked uncle', Richard III; but recent research has done much to rehabilitate the character of that greatly maligned monarch

and the responsibility for the deaths of the young princes still remains unproven.

The Tower of London is essentially a medieval place and the Middle Ages are generally regarded as having ended in 1485. The Tower was far from inviting as a palace and its use as a residence became increasingly restricted to ceremonial occasions after Henry VII's Queen died in childbirth in 1503. Its other more ghastly uses speak eloquently down the ages.

Here, in the Bell Tower (possibly dating from early in the thirteenth century) was confined Thomas More who, together with such figures as Anne Boleyn, Catherine Howard and the Duke of Monmouth, passed through the Traitors' Gate under St Thomas's Tower (built by Edward I) on their way to the scaffold. The Bloody Tower (with a gateway built by Henry III and the tower added over it in the reign of Richard II) may have acquired its name from the suicide here of the eighth Earl of Northumberland in 1585; later it was the home of Sir Walter Raleigh for several years, off and on – before the 'off' applied to his head. On the east of the Bloody Tower is the Wakefield Tower where Henry VI was found dead in the Oratory. The Chapel Royal of St Peter ad Vincula (rebuilt after a fire in 1512) is the burial place of various personages who were executed at the Tower, including Lady Jane Grey, her husband Lord Guildford Dudley and the last man to lose his head there – the mountainous septuagenarian Jacobite, Lord Lovat. On his way to the block, in 1747, a woman in the crowd screamed at the 'Old Fox', "You'll get that nasty head of yours chopped off, you ugly old Scotch dog" and he replied "I believe I shall, you ugly old English bitch".

The semicircular Beauchamp Tower has some of the most interesting mural inscriptions on account of it having been much used for famous prisoners. Sir Philip Howard inscribed: 'The more suffering for Christ in this world the more glory with Christ in the next' in 1587. In what is now known as the Queen's House (a good timber-framed building of about 1530, lived in by the resident Governor), the Gunpowder conspirators were interrogated; and it was from here that the Jacobite, Lord Nithsdale escaped in female attire in 1716, on the eve of his intended execution. The Salt Tower has numerous prisoners' inscriptions, not a few by Jesuits.

The young Elizabeth I herself had been a prisoner in the Tower, had indeed even walked through the Traitors' Gate, so it is hardly surprising that she did not regard it as a desirable residence. Her involuntary spell here is commemorated by Elizabeth's Walk (the ramparts between the Beauchamp and Bell Towers). In her reign the chronicler John Stow defined the Tower's contemporary function:

> This tower is a Citadell, to defend or command the Citie: a royall place for assemblies, and treaties. A Prison of estate, for the most dangerous offenders: the onely place of coynage for all England at this time: the armourie for warlike provision: the Treasurie of the ornaments and jewels of the crowne, and generall conserver of the most Recordes of the King's Courts of justice at Westminster.

The Royal Mint was moved to Wales in 1968 but the collection of armoury in the Tower is quite magnificent, ranging from such esoteric items as a suit of elephant's armour probably worn at the Battle of Plassey to the beautiful Flemish silvered armour worn by Henry VIII. The Crown Jewels on show in the west wing of the Waterloo Barracks (built in 1845) include St Edward's Crown which was made for the coronation of Charles II.

It was for this coronation that the sovereign set out for the last time from the Tower, as the next monarch, James II, thought such a tradition was too expensive to maintain. His father and namesake was the last sovereign to keep a proper Court at the Tower, entertaining himself and his guests with the pleasures of bear-baiting in the royal menagerie. In William and Mary's time the surviving domestic apartments, apart from the White Tower, were pulled down.

However, even now the Tower remains a royal 'liberty' and the Chapel of St John remains a royal chapel, the fortress is still the backdrop to some of the pageantry surrounding the sovereign. On Tower Wharf, the Honourable Artillery Company fire off their salutes. And every night at 9.40 pm, as he has for the last 700 years, the Chief Warder of the Yeoman Warders ('Beefeaters'), with his escort, locks the West Gate, Middle and Byward Towers, then returns to the Bloody Tower archway. It is an awe-inspiring experience to see them jangling along in the darkness, overcoming the challenge with the historic password – 'The Queen's Keys!'. After arms have been presented the Chief Warder cries out: "God preserve Queen Elizabeth" and the bugler sounds the Last Post.

There is an old legend that when the famous ravens go, the White Tower and the British Empire will collapse. The Empire may have collapsed, but as the ravens strut around the brass plate on Tower Green marking the site of the scaffold, the Tower still stands, a vivid reminder of a rather disagreeable segment of English history. **HMM**

63

THE PALACE OF WESTMINSTER

Ever since Edward the Confessor built the great Abbey of Westminster from about 1045 to 1065, there has been a palace adjacent between the eastern apse and the River Thames. Our sovereigns ceased to live there from the reign of Henry VIII, but today Parliament still meets in the Queen's Palace.

King Edward's main palace was at Winchester, then capital of England, while he had a royal residence in the City of London at Aldermanbury. In his latter years however, the King's main interest was in the foundation of his new Abbey of Westminster. We know little about his palace, except that here, on 5 January 1066, he died, only eight days after the consecration of the abbey, a ceremony which he was too ill to attend. According to the Bayeux Tapestry, the hall and the royal apartments were grouped together instead of being detached like others before the Conquest, and the King's bedchamber appears over the hall.

After William the Conqueror had been crowned at Westminster Abbey on Christmas Day 1066, he intended to rebuild the Great Hall. Goscelin, a monk at St Augustine's Abbey, Canterbury, tells of a fleet of fifteen ships laden with Caen stone from Normandy being shipwrecked in a storm. Only one ship arrived in port and this was with materials for Canterbury.

It was the Conqueror's son, William Rufus who built the Great Hall of the 'New Palace of Westminster', the largest in England, and some said in Europe, at the time. This fine hall, which still stands, though remodelled by Richard II, measures 235 ft 6 ins long, and 67 ft 6 ins wide, with a gallery round the inside, 20 ft from the ground. A double row of columns separated the hall into three aisles and supported the roof. Even so, when William II returned from Normandy, at Easter 1099, to find it completed, he was reported to have said that this was a mere bedchamber compared with what he had intended to build. He did not destroy the Confessor's old palace which stood alongside his new hall. The name 'Old Palace Yard' to its south still survives.

The following Whitsun the King held his Court for the first time in his new building at Westminster. He had little opportunity for further work there, for in August 1100 he met his death in the New Forest under mysterious circumstances.

The amount of time future kings spent at Westminster varied, but as London had become the capital of the kingdom, this, the chief palace, was thronged with the Court and household, whenever the King was in residence. The restless Henry II was only at Westminster on seventeen occasions during his reign. Walter Map noted: 'He never

The Throne in the present House of Lords is the symbol of sovereignty in the Palace of Westminster. With its elaborate canopy it is considered the greatest creation of A W Pugin

sat down; he is always on his legs from morning to night.' Nevertheless Henry found the palace half ruined after its neglect by his predecessor King Stephen, and he built a new hall, later known as the White Hall, to accommodate his household. This was on the south side, and in line with the Great Hall. For his personal use he also added a new Great Chamber at right angles to the new hall.

The palace grew in splendour. William FitzStephen wrote: 'On the west, higher up on the bank of the river, the royal palace rears its head, an incomparable structure, furnished with a breastwork and bastions, situated in a populous suburb.' The Chapel of St Stephen, later to be rebuilt, adjoined the Great Hall at right angles at the south east corner. Its eastern end stood by the wall on the river bank, and here, in 1177, Ailnoth, 'the builder of the King's houses', built a new quay.

Of all the Plantagenets, Henry III loved Westminster most. Though as a king he was a failure, his religious zeal prompted him to rebuild the abbey as we know it today. Another great achievement was his Painted Chamber within the palace, so called as early as 1307. Though unremarkable from the outside, this chamber had impressive dimensions, being 80 ft 6 ins long, 26 ft wide, and 31 ft 9 ins high. The lavish decorations here included mural paintings of the wars of the Maccabees and the life of Edward the Confessor, hence its name. Here was the King's bed, with posts painted green, and powdered with gold stars. In the 'little chapel at the corner of the King's chamber', Henry's sister, Eleanor, in 1238 married Simon de Montfort, who became his mortal enemy.

In 1322 two Irish friars came to see the Painted Chamber which much impressed them. 'Near the Abbey', they wrote, 'stands the celebrated palace of the kings of England, in which is that famous chamber on whose walls all the warlike scenes in the Bible are painted with wonderful skill, and explained by a series of texts beautifully written in French, to the great admiration of the beholder.'

Fortunately, the paintings, which in the course of time were buried under layers of whitewash and blue paper, were rediscovered in 1819, and were recorded by Edward Crocker, Clerk of Works at the time of alterations, in his unpublished work, in the Ashmolean Museum at Oxford, and by the artist C A Stothard, and were reproduced in colour in *Vetusta Monumenta*, 1842 (Volume vi).

Edward I was born in 1339 in Westminster Palace. (He was known as Edward of Westminster for, to the end of the fifteenth century, members of the Royal Family, like churchmen, were surnamed from their birthplace.) In 1292, in order to outshine St Louis' La Chapelle in Paris, he rebuilt, with great magnificence, the Chapel of St Stephen in similar proportions, except that where La Chapelle had two storeys, St Stephen's had three. The lower chapel which still exists and is misnamed 'the Crypt'

Ciuitatis Westmonasteriensis pars

Parlament House   the Hall   the Abby

The Great Hall has dominated views of Westminster for many centuries. Below, a 16th-century view shows the Hall, the Abbey and St James's Palace. Above, a 17th-century print shows the addition of the Parliament House and opposite, we see the interior in the 18th century when the Hall was the domain of the lawyers

An Ancient View of St James's, Westminster-Abby, & Hall, &c. from the Village of Charing now Charing Cross.

1. St James's Palace.
2. A Public House at the Village of Charing now Charing Cross.
3. Westminster Abbey.

Engraved By Permission from the Antiquarian Repertory.

4. Westminster Hall.
5. A Wall belonging to the Palace now Pall-Mall.
6. Fields now St James's Park.
7. A Conduit supposed standing where St James's Square now

(meaning below ground level) was dedicated to St Mary the Virgin, and the upper to St Stephen. The third, the clerestory, built only to impress, meant that the tiny building, 28 ft wide and 90 ft long, was nearly 100 ft high. The upper storey was supported by flying buttresses, Due to shortage of money, the Chapel took a surprisingly long time to construct, 56 years, by which time Edward III was on the throne.

For great occasions when the King summoned his parliament, the assembly took place in the Great Hall, where more spectators could be accommodated, such as Simon de Montfort's Parliament in 1265; otherwise, lesser chambers were used. Whenever Parliament met at Westminster, the Commons came to hold their sittings in the neighbouring Abbey, either in the refectory, which no longer exists, or the Chapter House. Within the palace, there was only one authority, the King's. Thus the judges who represented him and who were usually assembled in the Great Hall, became the Court.

So many official departments developed at Westminster, that the southern part of the palace became reserved for the personal use of the Royal Family. By the time of Edward III, the Privy Palace as it became known, had its own custodian. It probably extended to the White Hall (or Lesser Hall), the Painted Chamber, and included the Queen's Chamber beyond, as well as the Green Chamber, built by Edward I and the White Chamber of Edward II.

Today there is one survival of the Privy Palace, the Jewel Tower, designed by Henry Yevele and built 1365–66 at the south-west corner, to house the King's personal jewels and other treasures. Surrounded on three sides by a moat, which was connected to the river by a ditch, the tower was originally abbey land. When the Keeper of the Privy Palace, William de Husseborne, died from eating a pike caught in the moat, the Westminster monks recorded their unconcealed pleasure.

Richard II's great contribution to the Palace of Westminster was his remodelling of the Great Hall, which endures to this day. He removed the Norman columns which supported the ceiling, and constructed the beautiful hammerbeam roof which spans the whole width of the hall. The old walls of King William Rufus were retained, but these were heightened and heavily buttressed to take the largest medieval timber roof in Europe. The oak beams, were 23 ft long and 2¼ ft wide, and great angels were carved at both ends.

It is one of the ironies of history that, when the Great Hall was virtually completed in 1399, Richard II was deposed, and the first ceremony to take place there was a meeting of Parliament on 30 September, when the King's abdication was read in Latin and English and accepted by the estates and people. The crown was offered to his rival Henry, Duke of Lancaster, Henry IV.

Henry VII will ever be associated with his Court of the Star Chamber, a name taken from their meeting place in the palace, though the name was only attached to this council in the next reign, when it was given a fixed abode in the Star Chamber. This chamber stood next to the Exchequer building, near where Big Ben now stands, and was rebuilt in 1602 on nearly the same site.

The Palace of Westminster did not suit the flamboyant and athletic young King, Henry VIII. It was draughty and old fashioned, quite unsuitable for a Renaissance prince with grand ideas. A few weeks after Parliament met there in February 1512, a great fire spread through the palace

consuming most of his private apartments, sparing the Great Hall and the Painted Chamber. Stow reported:

> it hath not been re-edified, only the Great Hall with the offices near adjoining are kept in good repair, and it serveth, as before it did, for feast of coronations, arraignments of great persons charged with treasons, keeping of courts of justice. But the princes have been lodged in other places, as at Whitehall and St. James's.

An Act of Parliament of 1536 declared that the limits of the Palace of Westminster were Charing Cross, the Sanctuary Gate, the Thames and the wall of St James's Park. The buildings 'in utter ruin and decay' were a small part of this vast area, which included the whole of Whitehall and St James's Palace. Before long, this Act was ignored and their residences went by their actual names. Westminster was later succeeded as the principal London seat of the court by Whitehall, and then by St James's and finally Buckingham Palace, all within the bounds of the City of Westminster.

The Great Hall of Westminster was the scene of all coronation banquets, of which the last and most splendid was George IV's, and royal lyings-in-state. It housed the state trials including those of Sir William Wallace in 1305, the Duke of Somerset in 1551, his rival the Duke of Northumberland in 1553, the Earl of Essex in 1601, Guy Fawkes in 1606, Strafford in 1640, Charles I in 1649 and the trial of Warren Hastings, which took seven years, from 1788 to 1795. The only time the Coronation Chair left the Abbey was for Cromwell's installation as Lord Protector in Westminster Hall on 26 June 1657.

The Parliament Chamber, previously the Queen's Chamber, was used until 1801 by the House of Lords. This was the building Guy Fawkes attempted to blow up. There were two storeys, and the House of Lords sat in the upper chamber. In the lower, which had been the kitchens, Guy Fawkes stored his gunpowder. In 1801 the Lords moved into the Court of Requests, previously known as the White Hall of the old Norman palace.

The Painted Chamber was used for opening and closing Parliaments. Charles' I's death warrant is supposed to have been signed there. The adjacent Prince's Chamber became the Robing Room.

When St Stephen's Chapel was suppressed in 1547, the House of Commons moved in where they have since remained. The cloisters were rebuilt in 1526–29.

Little of the historic 'New Palace' of Westminster survived the fire which broke out on 16 October 1834. This was the most devastating fire in its long history. It raged all night unchecked, sweeping through the panelled passages and lobbies to the Painted Chamber and the many other mediaeval halls built of timber and plaster. Records were hastily removed to St Margaret's. The Dean and the Keeper of Records waited on the roof of the Chapter House in great anxiety. Lord Melbourne, the Prime Minister, directed that fire engines should be brought to spray the priceless hammerbeam roof of Westminster Hall, and all breathed a sigh of relief that this was not destroyed with the remainder of the palace.

The fire started after two workmen had been told to burn some tallies, notched sticks used until 1826 for keeping exchequer accounts. Usually they were burnt at Tothill Fields when storage space became required from time to time, but on this occasion the men took them to a stove which heated the House of Lords. The stove became overheated, and the panelling caught alight.

It was not that there had been no adequate warning of the danger of fire. Sir John Soane, in his *Designs for Public Buildings*, published only six years earlier, said:

The exterior. . .as well as the interior, is constructed chiefly with timber covered with plaster. In such an extensive assemblage of combustible materials, should a fire happen, what would become of the Painted Chamber, the House of Commons, and Westminster Hall? Where would the progress of the fire be arrested? The want of security from fire. . .calls loudly for revision and speedy amendment.

Among the buildings able to be restored was St Stephen's Hall, formerly Chapel. Sir Christopher Wren had inserted a low ceiling, with panelling and galleries, within the original fabric. The fire destroyed these, revealing Edward I's chapel once more. The Government did not risk a conversion which would have allowed the Church of England to claim it, and thus made the Commons homeless, but as a compromise the lower chapel, which had become the Speaker's Dining Room, was re-dedicated.

The new Palace of Westminster arose from the ashes, but it was not until 1837 that a start was made on rebuilding. The House of Lords moved in during 1847, and the Commons in 1852. That year Queen Victoria made her first public entry and conferred a knighthood on the architect, Sir Charles Barry. In 1857, with the aid of A W Pugin, Barry's elaborate late Gothic palace was completed.

The Crypt Chapel of St Stephen was originally built by Edward I in 1295. In the mid-19th century it was restored after the fire and now provides a chapel for Members of Parliament

On the night of 10 May 1941, during one of London's worst air raids, the House of Commons was destroyed. Across Star Chamber Court incendiaries fell on the roof of Westminster Hall, placing it in great danger. When it became clear that there were not enough pumps and equipment to save both the Commons and the Hall, the decision was taken to give priority to the historic hall which was saved by axing down the locked great doors. The oak to restore the hall came from Lord Courthope's Wadhurst estate, which more than once in the past had supplied timber for that purpose. Once again the House of Commons, designed by Sir Giles Gilbert Scott, was rebuilt in St Stephen's Hall in 1948–50.

Despite great changes during its long history, the Palace of Westminster remains one of the Queen's palaces. Parliament sits within the palace, to which it is summoned to perform its duties by royal proclamation. Every year the Queen comes in state, wearing her crown and robes of state, to open Parliament. Though Westminster has long ceased to be a royal residence the palace is under the overall control of one of the Queen's great officers of state, the Lord Great Chamberlain. **PMS**

and Members of the Royal Family

BALMORAL

As a young married couple Victoria and Albert craved *Gemütlichkeit* ('cosiness' in the Queen's translation) in their domestic surroundings. The royal residences available did not fit the bill and in Albert's view 'monotony of place' was prejudicial to the nervous system. There was nothing new in the idea of a monarch leading a simple country life as a change from pomp and circumstance; but whereas George III's rural retreats had been near London, Balmoral (and for that matter, Osborne) was not in a part of the world that had traditional connections with the sovereign.

Victoria and Albert had fallen in love with Scotland on their first holiday with the Breadalbanes at Taymouth Castle in 1842. Two years later they stayed at Blair Atholl and the Queen considered the scenery of the Highlands 'lovely, grand, romantic, and a great peace and wildness pervades all, which is sublime'. Furthermore, the Queen found the Highlanders 'never make difficulties, but are cheerful, and happy, and merry, and ready to walk, and run, and do anything'; Albert approved of their good breeding, simplicity and intelligence. Even a spell of rough weather on the west coast in 1847 did not dampen their enthusiasm. While they were being drenched by Loch Laggan, the Queen and Prince Albert learnt of the charms of the eastern Balmoral estate from her physician Sir James Clark, whose son was convalescing there at the time.

The following year Victoria and Albert duly took over the lease of Balmoral Castle on the upper Dee in Aberdeenshire. Originally the site of a hunting lodge of King Robert II, the estate had been owned by the Gordons of Huntly, then by the Farquharsons of Inverey and latterly by the Duffs, Earls of Fife, whose trustees had been letting the place to Sir Robert Gordon, the eminent diplomatist. Gordon, a brother of the fourth Earl of Aberdeen, had a lease of some 40 years and decided to improve the estate. In 1833 he set to work on the deer forest and the following year engaged 'Tudor Johnny' Smith to remodel the house. The finished building had mullioned windows with flamboyant tracery, stepped and fancy gable-ends, projecting turrets at angles with lancet windows and round towers topped by cone-shaped roofs. Before his lease was up, however, Sir Robert suddenly died, not inconveniently, at the breakfast table one morning in the autumn of 1847 and the stage was set for Victoria and Albert's arrival in the Highlands.

'It is a pretty little castle in the old Scotch style', wrote Queen Victoria, . . . 'one enters a nice little hall, and a billiard room and dining-room. A good broad staircase takes one upstairs and above the dining-room is our sitting-room . . . a fine large room opening into our bedroom, etc.' Albert asked 'Tudor Johnny' back to plan various alterations. Smith, City Architect of Aberdeen, had been trained in London at the instigation of his colourful father, 'Sink 'em' Smith, a master builder, who was worried that his son would 'gae doon wi' all his plannies' when he returned from

his sojourn in the south by sea in a storm. As they settled into their new home in the Highlands, Victoria and Albert set their hearts on buying Balmoral outright, as well as the neighbouring estates of Abergeldie and Birkhall and the forest of Ballochbuie.

They had to be content with a lease of Abergeldie from the Gordons, but Birkhall was bought outright with 6,500 acres in the name of the Prince of Wales. After protracted negotiations, Balmoral itself was finally bought in 1852 with 17,400 acres for 30,000 guineas from the Fife trustees. Whereas previous royal residences had all been Crown property, this was a private sale; the purchase price came out of a bequest from an idiosyncratic old character, John Camden Neild, who died that year leaving his considerable fortune to the Queen. For Albert, with his passion for architectural projects, this buckshee cash was like an answer to a prayer.

As 'Tudor Johnny' had died, Albert promptly sent for the third member of the redoubtable Smith dynasty, William. Together they chose a new site only 100 yards from the old house for a new castle to be built in the now highly popular Scotch Baronial style. The vogue for the Highlands had really come in; it could be traced back to the Romantic

Movement and the novels of Sir Walter Scott and was furthered later in the nineteenth century by the British aristocracy's love of sport and also by the coming of the railways. Albert and Smith's idea was to create a piece of scenic architecture so that the new castle and the new gardens should conform with the ranges of foothills rising to the summit of Loch-na-Gar. The landscaping was deputed to James Giles, while William Smith tackled the building work.

He wasted no time and the new castle was ready for occupation by September 1855, the old being demolished. Multi-turreted with castellated gables, a *porte-cochère* and a 100 ft tower, the new castle was built of grey Invergelder granite, had 180 windows, 67 fireplaces as well as a central heating system, four bathrooms and fourteen water-closets. 'The new house looks beautiful', wrote Queen Victoria in her journal, '. . . charming; the rooms delightful; the furniture, papers, everything perfection'. Although the interior has been much altered since the reign of Queen Victoria, the arrangement of the rooms then is worth recording. The building was designed so that only where particularly lofty rooms were required did it have two floors. On the west front were the State Drawing-Room, Library and Billiard

The porte-cochère and main entrance to the new castle which was ready for Queen Victoria and Prince Albert by September 1855

Room. Above the drawing-room was Victoria's private sitting-room; above the Library, her bedroom; above the Billiard Room, Albert's bathroom and dressing room. The Queen's 'little room' in the turret gave her an excellent view of Loch-na-Gar. Her bathroom and dressing-room were above the hall which led to the Grand Corridor and an ante-room with encaustic tiled floors and statuary in niches. Halfway along the Grand Corridor on the west side was the Grand Staircase leading to a corridor that stretched along the west side where Victoria and Albert had their private apartments. The princes and their tutor lived on the north side; the princesses on the south.

The south of the Grand Floor provided accommodation for visitors and a suite for the Minister in Attendance, with its own entrance hall. Above the ministerial suite was the second smaller tower capped with a cupola that has been likened to a sugar-castor. On the east side was accommodation for the Queen's ladies; on the north, the dining room and butler's pantry. There were spare rooms on the east side and above the less lofty south and east sides was a second floor for servants. The largest apartment at Balmoral is the Ballroom, measuring 68 ft by 25 ft which has witnessed many a Gillies' Ball.

At the end of each summer, Victoria and Albert returned to their beloved Balmoral. Every year, as the Queen wrote in her journal:

> My heart becomes more fixed in this dear Paradise and so much more so now that all has become my dearest Albert's own creation, own work, own building, own laying-out, as at Osborne: and his great taste and the impress of his dear hand, have been stamped everywhere.

Inside the castle the main effect of this impress was in the ubiquitous tartan and the motif of the thistle.

Tartan, which had been somewhat in abeyance since the beautiful Duchess of Gordon introduced reel-dancing into the late eighteenth-century drawing-rooms of London, was revived in no uncertain manner by the Prince Consort. He designed a special Balmoral tartan of black, red and lavender on a grey background. 'Tartanitis' took over; soon the stuff was literally all over the place. A chorus of chameleons would have died of over-exertion. One of the Queen's granddaughters described the decor as 'more patriotic than artistic and had a way of flickering before your eyes and confusing your brain'. Lord Rosebery unkindly remarked that he had considered the drawing room at Osborne to be the ugliest in the world until he saw the one at Balmoral.

It would be quite wrong, though, to underrate Albert's remarkable achievements at Balmoral, not only in terms of building and landscaping but in the way he took such an active interest in the welfare of the local people. He and the Queen established a notable rapport with the Highlanders, relishing the chance to lead an outdoor life. They would repair to 'The Hut' up Glen Muick, travel incognito on excursions to the Cairngorms, enjoying sport which was then run along far more simple lines before the big business it later became, as fashionable figures migrated to Highland lodges in pursuit of the grouse and the stag. At the end of the 1861 Scots sojourn, Albert recorded in his journal: 'Go out shooting for the last time and shoot nothing'. It was indeed the last time at Balmoral for he died a few months later.

Queen Victoria, who described herself as 'his broken-hearted widow' in the granite pyramid she erected in memory of 'Albert the Great and Good' on the spot where he had shot his last stag, now came slightly less frequently to Balmoral. The Queen's love of the Highlands endured, however, and her devoted servant John Brown personified what she liked most in upper Deeside. A lot of rot has been written about the Queen's relationship with Brown; it is worth remembering that he was Albert's particular gillie long before the Prince Consort's death and that, apart from anything else, Brown's primary appetite was for whisky. Towards the end of the Queen's life in 1901, the atmosphere at Balmoral became rather stodgy, giving rise to the expression 'Balmorality'.

Below: 'A pretty little castle in the old Scotch style':
Balmoral painted by W Wyld before the new castle was built
Opposite top: The Ballroom, Balmoral's largest apartment
Bottom: The garden front of Birkhall

The entrance front at Birkhall with its sturdy rustic porch glimpsed through the wooded hillside

Edward VII and Queen Alexandra had previously spent holidays at Abergeldie and now came to Balmoral no more than about a month every year. The castle is essentially Victorian, and George V, who was more of a Victorian than his father, had a greater affection for it. He and his son George VI used to come for at least two months in the autumn, a practice followed by the present Royal Family.

Balmoral remains a special private holiday home for the Royal Family, a world apart. Their hereditary love of the Highlands has, of course, been amplified by the Scots blood of the Queen Mother. The place has also inspired some notable artistic expressions from the jottings and sketchings of Queen Victoria to the present Prince of Wales best-selling book for children *The Old Man of Loch-na-Gar*.

Birkhall The Queen Mother's retreat on the Balmoral estate remains the delightfully secluded Birkhall, a small white house well sheltered behind a steep wooded hillside. 'You have to imagine a house halfway down the slope of a teacup', was the way the present Prince of Wales once described this Deeside shooting-box to a friend. As we have seen, Birkhall had originally been purchased for a previous Prince of Wales, the future Edward VIII, in 1852. Never notably keen on life north of the Border, Albert Edward sold it back to his mother Queen Victoria in 1885. The house had been built in 1715 by Charles Gordon, a Captain in Lauder's Foot and a Commissioner of Supply, who married a distant kinswoman Rachel Gordon, the tenth Laird (or, in her case, Lady) of Abergeldie. The year of Birkhall's building was a significant one for the Gordons were staunch Jacobites.

After the fiasco of the '45 and the butchery of Culloden, Joseph Gordon of Birkhall and his wife Elizabeth gave sanctuary to Laurence Oliphant of Gask and his brother. While they were in hiding at Birkhall the brothers were known as 'Mr Brown' and 'Mr White'. The Oliphants did not forget Elizabeth Gordon's kindness and kept in touch with her from Sweden to which country she had arranged their escape.

White-harled with a blue-slated sloping roof and a sturdy rustic porch, Birkhall is an early example of the type of non-fortified Scottish 'ha-house'. The bow-fronted wing was added in the 1950s by the Queen Mother to a clever design, which affords a fine vista from the French windows to the spire of Ballater Church seven miles away. Birkhall has been a cherished home for the Queen Mother and the Royal Family since it was given to her husband after their marriage.

The Queen and Princess Margaret enjoyed some idyllic childhood moments here in the beautiful terraced gardens dipping away sharply from the whitewashed house down to the River Muick. The summerhouses are a beloved feature; in one wooded corner of the garden is the 'Wendy House' which was presented to the little princesses by the *Aberdeen Press* in 1935. Twelve years later Princess Elizabeth and the Duke of Edinburgh spent part of their honeymoon at Birkhall; their fond feelings for the place were happily not marred in spite of the Duke catching a cold. Honeymoons have also been spent in this secret hideaway by the Duke and Duchess of Kent and by Princess Alexandra and her husband. Birkhall has continued to be a place of enchantment for the Queen Mother's grandchildren who have delighted in the gardens, crossing the river by the swaying, if steel, bridge. Inside, the Queen Mother has applied her special gifts, creating an elegant and comfortable atmosphere with colour schemes of pale gold, oyster, pink and blue.   **HMM**

BARNWELL MANOR

Barnwell Manor, showing the ruins of the old castle, which has survived since the reign of Henry III

At the present time England's royal residences are located, with one exception, in three distinct areas, London and the Home Counties, the West Country and East Anglia. The one exception is the gabled grey stone Elizabethan house of Their Royal Highnesses the Duke and Duchess of Gloucester and his mother, Her Royal Highness Princess Alice, Duchess of Gloucester. The house, of course, is Barnwell Manor, Northamptonshire.

The manor was purchased in 1938 by the Duke's father Prince Henry, Duke of Gloucester, just over two years after his marriage on 6 November 1935 to Lady Alice Montagu Douglas Scott, daughter of the seventh Duke of Buccleuch, who, sadly, had died shortly before the wedding.

Barnwell Manor had been part of the ancestral estates of the Buccleuchs and their ancestors, the Montagus since the reign of Henry VIII, so there was only a slight break in continuity, a mere 26 years, between the sale in 1912 by Princess Alice's father and the purchase by her husband. Princess Alice is twelfth in direct descent from Sir Edward Montagu, who was granted the manor in 1540.

Barnwell lies on the brook of the same name in a rural part of the East Midlands. Close by is Oundle, home of one of England's public schools. There were originally two parishes, each with its own manor, Barnwell St Andrew's (the present manor) and, half a mile away, Barnwell All Saints. All Saints Church was demolished in 1825, except for the chancel which contains the memorials of the Montagus, Earls of Sandwich, and the parishes were united.

Across the lawn from Barnwell Manor to the south-west stands the old ruined castle of Barnwell, whose sturdy 700 ft curtain walls, 12 ft thick, have survived from the reign of Henry III. Today they rise to a height of 30 ft. At each corner there is a round tower, with two more at either side of the great gateway. The latter has two pointed archways, and the slit from where the portcullis descended is still visible. The castle, which is hidden from the road by trees, is important as a prototype of the Edwardian castles like Harlech, which were built soon afterwards in Wales.

This ancient castle, however, was not the first to be built at Barnwell. Its predecessor, a motte and bailey fortification, has left earthworks flanking the lower road. Here lived six generations of the powerful le Moyne family, a name derived from *monachus*, a monk. The land was granted by the Abbot of Ramsey between 1114 and 1130 to Reginald le Moyne, who had lived at Barnwell as the Abbey's tenant as early as 1091.

The last of the le Moynes was Berengar who, in 1266, built the castle whose ruins we see today. Four years later, having been granted a twice weekly market at Barnwell and an annual fair there for a week, following the vigil of St Michael, he set off to fight in the crusades, bearing as his coat of arms, Argent a cross paty gules. He returned home safely, but either because he had fallen on hard times or because he had no son to follow him, he sold Barnwell and other manors back to the Abbot of Ramsey in 1276 for £1,666 13s 4d, with prayers for himself and for the souls of his parents, Reginald and Rose.

This much is history, but according to ancient Northamptonshire legends, Black Berengarius, so called from his dark complexion, seized with jealousy, built his younger brother into the walls of Barnwell Castle. His cousin Beatrice, who preferred his brother, is said to have drowned herself in the Nene. Charles Henry Montagu Douglas Scott tells the story in verse in his *Tales of Northamptonshire*.

Barnwell Castle became the occasional residence of the Abbot, but was used principally by successive stewards to control their surrounding estates. The castle was neglected and part fell into ruin. Remains of the inhabited part can still be seen in those chambers with later fireplaces and windows, which were used 'for meane houses for farmers'. When Henry VIII dissolved Ramsey Abbey in 1540, the castle and manor of Barnwell were granted to the immensely rich Sir Edward Montagu, Chief Justice of the King's Bench and Speaker of the House of Commons. For the last twenty years he had been Steward of Barnwell on behalf of the abbey. He also purchased Boughton near Kettering in 1536 and added extra buildings to make it his chief seat.

There is a story, not always accepted as true, that when one of Henry VIII's bills of subsidy did not pass, Sir Edward was sent for by the King who said – "Ho! Will they not let my bill pass?" and laying his hand on the head of Montagu, who was kneeling before him, said, "Get my bill to pass by such a time tomorrow, or else by such a time this head of yours shall be off!" The bill passed.

In 1568 the Chief Justice's son, also Sir Edward Montagu, built the present manor in the castle grounds and added the stables. The antiquary Camden described it as 'a little castle, repaired and adorned with new buildings by the worthy Sir Edward Montacute Knight'. Sir Edward left to his wife Elizabeth Harington of Exton, Rutland, a cousin of Sir Philip Sidney, 'all householde stuff in my castell of Barnewelle'.

Two of his sons lived extensively at Barnwell, his heir, a third Sir Edward who, in 1621, was created Lord Montagu of Boughton, and the youngest, Sir Sidney. After the Civil War broke out, Lord Montagu used the old castle as an arsenal in the royal cause. He died in 1644 in custody at the Savoy, London, but his third wife Anne lived at Barnwell Manor during her four years of widowhood. During this time, in August 1645, Charles I came here on his way to Bedford.

Lord Montagu's brother, Sir Sidney Montagu, James I's Groom of the Bedchamber, lived at Barnwell, probably in the Manor of All Saints, now demolished, before he brought Hinchingbrooke near Huntingdon from another brother, the Earl of Manchester, who had acquired it from the Protector's uncle Sir Oliver Cromwell. At the end of his life, Sir Sidney returned to Barnwell after he was released from the Tower.

Sir Sidney had three children, Henry, Edward and Elizabeth, whose history is bound up with Barnwell. In April 1625, shortly before his third birthday, little Henry fell into the brook there and was drowned. There is a memorial to him in All Saints Church, which portrays him standing under a curiously tapering alabaster canopy, dressed in a red and gold gown, holding in one hand a white square cap, the work of the sculptor Gerrard Christmas. The inscription reads – 'A wittie and hopefull child, tender and deere in the sight of his parents, and much lamented by his friends.'

His younger brother, Edward, born at Barnwell two months after the drowning tragedy, became the famous Earl of Sandwich. Like Henry, he too was drowned. In 1672, while commanding the Blue Squadron in the battle against the Dutch of Sole Bay, or Southwold, his flagship, the *Royal James*, was set alight by fireships; three-quarters of the ship's company also lost their lives.

Their sister Elizabeth Montagu, dearly loved Barnwell. She married a Northamptonshire baronet, Sir Gilbert Pickering of Titchmarsh, and when her daughter, Elizabeth Creed, was widowed she made her home at All Saints Manor, Barnwell. Her cousin, the poet John Dryden, often stayed with her, and she became celebrated for writing epitaphs and painting altar pieces in churches near Oundle. She died at Barnwell in 1728.

It was the third Lord Montagu, subsequently created Duke of Montagu by Queen Anne, who demolished much of Barnwell Castle. Stukeley related in 1748 that John, second Duke, lamented that his father pulled down the castle. That the ruins have been preserved is due to this second Duke (known as 'The Planter' from his passion for planting avenues of trees), who prevented its further use as a quarry for building stone.

In 1845 Barnwell, along with other Montagu estates passed into the family of the fifth Duke of Buccleuch. But Barnwell was not always the home of members of the family. In the early years of this century it became the home of Lady Ethelreda Wickham, youngest daughter of the tenth Marquess of Huntly, who was a link between Marie Antoinette and the reign of Queen Elizabeth II. Her grandfather, the ninth Lord Huntly used to recount that he danced as a young man with the Queen of France and in his old age with Queen Victoria. Lady Ethelreda survived until 1961.

Additions were made to Barnwell in 1890 by the sixth Duke of Buccleuch, and later, in 1913, by the new owner Mr Horace Czarnikow, after the estate was sold by the Duke's son, the seventh Duke, when Earl of Dalkeith.

Today Barnwell is run as a highly mechanised farming unit, considered one of the most efficient of its size in the Midlands. The late Duke of Gloucester took an active part in the running of the estate when his duties permitted. He virtually designed the farm buildings himself, and was proud of his pedigree herd of Guernsey cattle with a high milk yield.

There are six farms on this 2,500 acre estate, two of which were owned by Prince William of Gloucester, the Duke's elder son. The Prince played a large part in the running of the estate. His death in a flying accident in August 1972 resulted in his younger brother Prince Richard becoming his father's heir.

A month before Prince William was tragically killed, he was best man at his brother's wedding at Barnwell Church to Birgitte van Deurs, daughter of a Danish lawyer. They had met at Cambridge where Prince Richard was an undergraduate, and she was studying at a language school. Prince Richard became a full time partner in a firm of architects, but increasing royal duties and his share of running the Barnwell estates after his brother's death took up more and more time. On the death, in June 1974, of his father, Prince Henry Duke of Gloucester, who had been an invalid for some years, Prince Richard became the second Duke.

Both the present Duke's mother, Princess Alice, and his wife play a large part in local affairs and, twice a year, in the spring, the Barnwell gardens are opened to the public in aid of charity. The Duke and Duchess have three children: a son and heir, Alexander Earl of Ulster, born in October 1974, Lady Davina born in November 1977 and Lady Rose, born in March 1980. All the children were christened at Barnwell Church.

The Duke of Gloucester is a keen photographer and has written several books on architecture, illustrated with his own photographs under his professional name of Richard Gloucester. He once said "one part of me is an architect, one is now a farmer, and one is a prince, really in that order. Being all three does pose certain strains, but I hope to be able to fit all three together." **PMS**

GATCOMBE PARK

The Gatcombe estate in Gloucestershire was bought for Princess Anne and Captain Mark Phillips in 1976 from the Conservative elder statesman Lord Butler of Saffron Walden. Here Captain Phillips farms a total of 1,263 acres (some of which is rented from one of the Queen's properties nearby) where an eighteenth-century owner, Edward Shephard, successfully crossed his Ryeland sheep with the newly introduced Spanish Merinos.

Shephard was a rich clothier who built the present house in about 1770. His son sold it in 1814 to David Ricardo, the son of a Dutch Jew who made a fortune on the London Stock Exchange. Ricardo Junior had retired from business and now concentrated on the classical theory of political economy – a school of which he is recognized to be the founder – publishing *The Principles of Political Economy and Taxation* in 1817 and entering the House of Commons two years later. Soon after this he commissioned one of Sir John Soane's most brilliant pupils George Basevi, a connection of Disraeli's, to remodel the house.

Gatcombe's central block of two storeys and a basement is faced in ashlar. There is a finely-moulded cornice with a balustraded parapet; the centre of the building breaks forward with an open pediment above a Venetian window

Gatcombe Park: the house remodelled by Basevi for David Ricardo, with its bowed wings and conservatory. David Hicks and other hands have redecorated the interior for Princess Anne and Captain Mark Phillips

arrangement. Above the porch of four Doric columns is a balustraded balcony. The bowed wings are one-storeyed. The decoration inside the house is recorded to be of high quality. There are tall Doric columns in the hall and the principal rooms have marble chimneypieces; one in a bedroom is made of onyx with ormolu decoration. The library on the east wing has bookcases by Basevi. Little has changed since his time; even the conservatory on the west side was here by 1829.

The grounds are splendidly landscaped, with some fine stone vases. The Ricardo family remained here until the estate was sold in 1940 by Lieutenant-Colonel Henry Ricardo, the political economist's great-grandson. It should, of course, be mentioned that the estate is situated in the Beaufort country where the modern Royal Family are now congregating so densely. The stables at Gatcombe, built round a polygonal yard, are of a suitably high architectural standard for two Olympic equestrians. **HMM**

HAREWOOD HOUSE

When the present Earl of Harewood was born in 1923 he became the first grandson of George V and was sixth in line to the throne. A photograph was taken of him with his mother the Princess Royal, her father George V and Queen Alexandra, Lord Harewood's great-grandmother. Today, Lord Harewood hovers just outside the top twenty in the order of succession but he is still a member of the Royal Family. Keenly interested in classical music since he was a boy, he now divides his time between running the English National Opera from the Coliseum in London and managing the family estate at Harewood in Yorkshire.

The estate was bought in 1739 by Henry Lascelles, a politician and director of the East India Company. His son Edwin, later created Lord Harewood, built Harewood House of local yellow stone to the design of Carr of York twenty years later with a portico overlooking the valley. Shortly afterwards, Robert Adam, recently returned from Italy, was given the whole interior to decorate and all was finished in 1772 when Capability Brown set to work landscaping the park.

Lord Harewood's cousin Edward succeeded to the property in 1795 and was created an Earl in 1812. His eldest son, a noted patron of the arts who made the collection of Sèvres and Chinese porcelain in the house and commissioned watercolours of the place from Girtin and Turner, never succeeded to the Earldom, dying unmarried two years later. His brother, the second Earl, was known as 'Beau Lascelles' because he 'used to dress at and after George IV'. Queen Charlotte referred to him as the 'gay Lothario'.

The third Earl of Harewood employed Sir Charles Barry

The garden front of Harewood, as it is today, with the alterations by Sir Charles Barry. The park was landscaped by Capability Brown

to build additional floors for the extra bedrooms which his wife (a daughter of the second Marquess of Bath) wanted. Barry also remodelled the exterior, erecting a massive Italian balustrade and removing Carr's portico. The sixth Earl, who was a personal ADC to George V, married the King's only daughter Princess Mary, the Princess Royal, in 1922 and the bedroom wing was altered for her. The Princess had trained as a nurse and, having done much useful work in the First World War, ran Harewood as a hospital in the Second.

Her Royal Highness and the sixth Earl collected the superb Italian paintings that fill two of the main rooms at Harewood. They include works by Bellini, Titian, Veronese and Tintoretto. The portrait of the Princess Royal, who died in 1965, above the fireplace in the dining room is by Sir Oswald Birley; among the other artists responsible for family portraits were Reynolds, Gainsborough, Romney, Hopper, Lawrence, Richmond and Winterhalter. The collection of furniture is outstanding and features some of the very best of Chippendale's work. Two of the state rooms still have carpets designed by Adam; the one in the Music Room reflects the ceiling with its roundels painted by Angelica Kauffman. The Gallery, which is almost a triple cube with a painted ceiling by Rebecca, is the finest room at Harewood. The park was devastated by storms in 1962, but Lord Harewood has been working hard to rescue the delectable landscape. **HMM**

HIGHGROVE

Highgrove, the new home of the Prince and Princess of Wales, lies in one of the most picturesque parts of England, the South Cotswold country of Gloucestershire close to the Wiltshire border, at the little hamlet of Doughton. A mile to the north is the small town of Tetbury, and Gatcombe Park, home of his sister Princess Anne and her husband Captain Mark Phillips, is only eight miles away.

Despites its lack of grandeur – it has 30 rooms and is about the same size as Gatcombe – this pleasant late eighteenth-century grey house of Cotswold stone should prove ideal for the Prince, for he has always preferred compact and comfortable houses which can be easily run to those which are larger and more pretentious.

Highgrove, built between 1796 and 1798 by John Paul Paul, is a three storey rectangular building in classical style of five by three bays, with the principal fronts facing north and south. The house is built of brick with an exterior facing of stone and there are four shallow pilasters running through the upper floors. The four principal reception rooms include the drawing room which has a marble fireplace with a dolphin motif, and a large library. Views from

the house stretch towards the parish church on high ground, which dominates the market town of Tetbury.

The grounds contain a formal garden, dominated by a large Lebanese cedar, and there is a well appointed stable block. Prince Charles takes a great interest in farming, a trait which he no doubt derives from his favourite ancestor, George III, popularly known as 'Farmer George'. Perhaps the 347 acre estate will become a farming enterprise, echoing Captain Mark Phillips' Gatcombe Park, and the larger Barnwell, belonging to the Duke of Gloucester.

The builder of Highgrove, John Paul Paul, was born in 1772, of a family who had been well known at Tetbury for over 100 years. His curious double name arose because at his birth he had the surname of Tippetts. In 1789 his father, Josiah, changed his name to Paul on inheriting from his maternal uncle, John Paul of Tetbury. He did not, however, own the land on which Highgrove was built, for this was inherited by John Paul Paul from his maternal grandfather, Robert Clark.

John Paul Paul was a notable figure in the Tetbury neighbourhood, holding such offices as a trustee of the Tetbury

Savings Bank, Vice-President of the Tetbury Dispensary, and High Sheriff of Wiltshire. In 1819 he purchased for £25,000 the old manor of Doughton which once included Highgrove within its boundaries. Doughton was formerly spelt 'Dofton', as appears in the Tetbury parish registers in the eighteenth century, and it is still so pronounced today.

On John Paul Paul's death in 1828 he was succeeded by his son Walter Matthews Paul, and in 1838 his combined estates consisted of 650 acres. In 1860 he sold the two estates to Colonel Edward Stracey who, through his mother, was connected by marriage with the Paul baronets. Four years later the Colonel inherited Boston House near Brentford, Middlesex, from the Clitherows, his mother's family, and added their surname after his own. He thereupon sold Highgrove and Doughton to William Hamilton Yatman, a Warwickshire barrister. Mr Yatman rebuilt the loftly pinnacled church tower and spire at Tetbury, which was completed in 1893 as a memorial to his only son, a captain in the 3rd Dragoon Guards, a fact which is commemorated by a plaque in Tetbury Church. Highgrove was seriously damaged by fire during that year, which occasioned him to sell the two estates.

The purchaser was Captain Arthur Charles Mitchell of the Gloucestershire Regiment, seventh and youngest son of a rich London merchant with Jamaican connections, who lived in Upper Wimpole Street. On completion of the purchase, Captain Mitchell in 1894 restored the burnt parts of Highgrove at the cost of £6,000 by rebuilding the south front and east side. At the same time he added a block containing kitchens and offices. After his death in 1917, Highgrove continued to be the home of his widow, Constance Lucy, who was an Elwes of Colesbourne Park near Cheltenham, until her own death in 1945. In the meantime her stepson, Lieutenant-Colonel Francis Arthur Mitchell, on retiring from the Royal Gloucestershire Hussars, in 1935 carefully restored the manor of Doughton and made it his home. The two estates then parted company, for Highgrove was sold to Lieutenant-Colonel Gwyn William Morgan-Jones of the Life Guards, who farmed the estate and extended its acreage.

After Colonel Morgan-Jones died in 1964, the estate was purchased by Maurice Macmillan, son of the former Prime Minister, Harold Macmillan. Mr Macmillan is a Conservative Member of Parliament, who served during Edward Heath's administration as Secretary of State for Employment and as Paymaster General. In 1966, soon after purchase, he demolished the nineteenth-century additions of the kitchen block, and inserted some fireplaces from other houses, which date from the eighteenth century. He sold Highgrove in 1980, to join his father at Birch Grove, Sussex.

Prince Charles, who represents the seventh family to possess Highgrove, has returned to the district of some of his ancestors. Edward III's son, Edmund Duke of York and his son held the manor of Doughton, and later Henry VII gave to his wife, Elizabeth of York, in dower, the manors of Doughton and Charlton, both in the parish of Tetbury.

In addition to this, the Prince of Wales' grandmother, Queen Elizabeth the Queen Mother, is a descendant, through her mother, the Countess of Strathmore, of the Breuse and Berkeley families who for generations were lords of the manor of Tetbury. In 1632 when Lord Berkeley sold the lordship to the Feoffees of the town. The Feoffees still administer Tetbury. **PMS**

THE CASTLE OF MEY

The Castle of Mey, in the most northerly parish of mainland Great Britain, Canisbay, (which also contains John o'Groats six miles to the east) is the home of Queen Elizabeth the Queen Mother. This is her very own possession, which she bought and converted herself. Views from the windows look out northwards upon Dunnet Head, across Pentland Firth to the Orkney island of Hoy. But Mey is no barren outpost. Surrounded by little trees, which hide the castle from the road a mile down the drive, the estate contains high-walled gardens and hothouses. The 25 acres of grounds also include a deer park and trout ponds.

Shortly after King George VI died in 1952, the Queen Mother went to stay with her great friends, Lady Doris and Commander Vyner, who lived nearby at Dunnet Head. One afternoon they visited the ancient Barrogill Castle, then up for sale. Storms had damaged the roof, the ceilings leaked and the walls were damp. The Queen Mother came twice in June, and after five more visits in August, she decided to buy the castle to save it from being demolished. She had fallen in love with the Castle of Mey, which she had decided to call by its original name.

The castle took three years to renovate before the Queen Mother could move in. In 1955 her daughter the Queen and Prince Philip came to the housewarming in HMS Britannia. The Queen Mother also bought the adjoining 120 acre Longgoe Farm, where she has a herd of pedigree Angus cattle. She is patron of the Aberdeen Angus Cattle Society.

Mey is not a large castle. It is one of the few sixteenth-century houses in the locality and is built on the traditional 'Z' plan with a tall battlemented tower with turrets whose conical roofs were removed in the nineteenth century, and replaced by sham battlements. A double staircase leads from the entrance to the charming drawing and dining room on the first floor. In the drawing room, which has windows to the north, overlooking the sea, is a large seventeenth-century tapestry covering one wall. The dining room, which is decorated simply and looks out on to the walled garden, has in contrast a richly embroidered tapestry 9 ft by 7 ft, of the Queen Mother's coat of arms, showing in its border flowers from her garden. Further up the spiral staircase is her writing room, and her bedroom with panelled walls painted in aquamarine.

The Queen Mother herself sought out many of the contents and furniture from local antique shops, and managed to trace the missing Caithness Sword of State resting in a Glasgow museum, which was presented to her. It was placed in a niche on the entrance landing, close to the blackamoor figure which once stood at her home at 145 Piccadilly.

For centuries the Castle of Mey was the seat of the Earls of Caithness. Originally a Norman family, 'the lordly line of high St Clair', as Sir Walter Scott termed them, became

An exterior view of the exterior of the castle, the ancient seat of the Sinclairs of Mey

in time the rulers and then Earls of Orkney, a dependency of Norway, until James II of Scotland compelled them to exchange their islands for the Earldom of Caithness. Thus they were introduced to that county, and the Earl became Chief of the Sinclairs.

It was George Sinclair, fourth Earl of Caithness, who acquired the Barony and Castle of Mey, which he purchased in the 1560s from the Bishop of Caithness. The Bishop had already built a fortified stone house, which was to form the nucleus on which the Earl rebuilt the castle. The gunloops can still be seen on two levels. There still exists Lord Caithness's coat of arms impaling those of his wife, a Graham of Montrose, with the date 1566.

This Lord Caithness was a friend of the notorious Lord Bothwell who was to become Mary Queen of Scots' third husband, and was said to have been at supper with him at Holyrood Palace the night that Riccio, the Queen's secretary, was murdered. He was foreman of the jury who tried and acquitted Bothwell of murdering Mary's husband, Lord Darnley.

Nevertheless, Lord Caithness was not a lover of justice. As Justiciar of Caithness and Sutherland, he had authority to banish or kill as should be most expedient, and certainly used his great power to the fullest extent. Even his relations were not safe, for both his brother and his eldest son, the Master of Caithness, were thrown into the dungeons of Girnigoe Castle, and the latter was slowly starved to death. Lord Caithness was assisted in this barbaric act by his second son, William Sinclair, to whom the Castle of Mey was granted, and who, like many of his family, came to a violent death. For while the lord was visiting his brother's cell the prisoner was able to muster enough energy to exact his revenge by crushing the unwelcome visitor to death with an iron embrace.

Thus perished Mey's first laird, from whose natural son was sprung the Sinclairs of Ulbster. Their descendant to-day, Viscount Thurso is a not too distant neighbour at his Castle of Thurso. Mey, however, was given by Lord Caithness to his third son, George Sinclair, from whom it passed directly from father to son until 1890.

Lord Caithness's princely mode of living brought him into financial difficulties, and despite frantic efforts to regain his lost affluence, he left an impoverished estate to his son and heir. In the meantime his younger son, George Sinclair, the laird of Mey steadily improved his position. 'A man of ability who lost no opportunity of promoting his family interests, and considerable additions to the estate were made by him', said a family chronicler. Nevertheless, he had his worries, one of which must have been the unruly behaviour of his schoolboy son.

When young William of Mey was a scholar of Edinburgh High School during the year 1595 the authorities decided to curtail the usual period of vacation. Taking advantage of the headmaster's absence, the scholars mutinied and managed to obtain possession of the school. They laid in a stock of provisions and firearms, and successfully barred the entrance to authority for a whole day. The following day the town council resolved to take strong measures to crush the rebellion, and a posse of officers tried to prise open the schoolroom door. The boys refused to unlock it to any but the headmaster, and threatened to 'put a pair of bullets through the cheeks' of the good bailies of Edinburgh.

At length young Sinclair of Mey, evidently one of the ringleaders, aimed a gun at John MacMoran, one of the bailies, through the window, and fired, shouting that they were all "naught but 'buttery carles'". The bailie fell backwards to the ground dead, and Sinclair, with seven of his

The elegant drawing room of the Castle of Mey. On the right hand wall, facing the window, is the 17th-century tapestry

accomplices, was marched off to prison. He was later pardoned by the King.

He grew from a wild youth into a respected laird who received a knighthood. In 1628 he was visited by the noted Scottish traveller William Lithgow, who penned a tribute to the Castle of Mey, dedicated to the Earl of Caithness, and 'his honorable cousin and first cadet of his house, the right worshipful Sir William Sinclair of Catboll, knight, Laird of Maji (Mey),' in which he spoke of the two square courts, and its

Halls, high chambers, galleries, office bowers,
Cell rooms and turrets, platforms, stately towers.

Mey's lairds continued to increase in power, and in 1631 Sir James Sinclair was created a baronet by Charles I. With the second baronet, the line nearly came to an end at the castle, for he fell into debt, and Mey had to be made over to his creditors at his death. Fortunately his uncle, Viscount Tarbat, purchased it and conveyed it to the next laird a few years later.

Soon the baronets were to aspire to a higher title, for in 1789 died the eleventh Earl of Caithness, a colonel who had fought the Americans in the War of Independence. Sinclair of Mey thus became the Chief of the clan, and although inheriting no estates from his impoverished kinsman, he petitioned the House of Lords for recognition as the twelfth Earl of Caithness.

The next Earl 'vastly improved and moderned the castle' in the nineteenth century, and inserted the double staircase and added a dining room wing to the west.

His son, John Sinclair, the fourteenth Earl of Caithness and seventeenth successive laird of Mey, became a Lord-in-Waiting to Queen Victoria, who created him a peer of the United Kingdom as Lord Barrogill, by which name the castle was then known. King Edward VII and Queen Alexandra, when Prince and Princess of Wales, came to the castle and planted two chestnut trees in the forecourt to commemorate their visit. A diarist then noted its 'grey, quaint picturesque look in keeping with the scenery amid which it is placed and the grey sea over which it looks.' He went on to say, however, that 'inside it is a most comfortable house. . . . The windows are little rooms in themselves, for the walls are of immense thickness.' They are in fact 9 ft thick.

Known to his tenants as their most genial laird, he died during a visit in 1881 to New York. Much to their regret, the castle became severed from the Sinclair family nine years later, when his son bequeathed the property to a school friend, Frederick Granville Heathcote, who thereupon took the name of Sinclair, a very remote kinsman having succeeded to the Earldom.

The Queen Mother is herself descended from the Sinclairs through the marriage of her ancestor, John Lyon, Earl of Kinghorne, with Lady Anna Murray, great-great-granddaughter of Lady Eleanor Sinclair, whose nephew built the castle, and whose father the second Earl of Caithness fell at Flodden. **PMS**

NETHER LYPIATT MANOR

The recent private purchase of Nether Lypiatt Manor near Stroud in Gloucestershire by Prince and Princess Michael of Kent has added a small country house of considerable architectural merit to the properties owned by the Royal Family.

In 1944, when the house was occupied by the tenth Viscount Barrington, Mr and Mrs Gordon Woodhouse and Miss Walker, the architectural historian James Lees-Milne, then working for the National Trust, went to lunch. He describes 'this wonderful little house' in his diary:

> The house is perched high on a hill, overlooking a built-up village. It is compact and tall, with two flanking wings, one new so as to balance the other old one. It is unspoilt . . . and perfect in every way. In fact an ideal, if not *the* ideal small country house. It retains all its wainscoting, doors with high brass handles and locks, one lovely chimneypiece in the hall, of white stone against a ground of blue slate. The rich staircase has three twisted balusters to each tread . . . The forecourt enclosure with stone piers and balls, the contemporary wrought-iron gates . . . the garden . . . is enchanting with modern yew walks and a flourishing lime avenue.

A few details can be added to this characteristically fine description by Mr Lees-Milne. The house was built from 1702 to 1705. The main block is only 46 ft square but comprises a full cellar storey, a basement above ground, a principal floor (or moderate English version of the *piano nobile*), a bedroom floor and an attic storey with dormers. The attic was reconstructed by P Morley Horder, who also built the modern wing in 1923. The buildings are faced in Cotswold ashlar of admirable quality and roofed with Cotswold stone slates. The rainwater heads of 1717 have Judge Coxe's crest upon them. The wrought-iron grilles linking the screen of stone piers have been attributed to Warren. A porch of two detached fluted Ionic columns supports a segmental pediment. The elevation of the main building owes something to Sir Roger Pratt's lovely house at Coleshill (demolished in 1952 after a fire).

Coleshill would have been familiar to Judge Coxe, the builder of the present house at Nether Lypiatt, as it was on the road to London from Gloucestershire. Coxe was Clerk of the Patent Office in London and sat for Cirencester and then Gloucester in the House of Commons, as well as being a Justice of the Brecon, Radnor and Glamorgan circuit. This busy lawyer had married the heiress of the Nether Lypiatt estate, Mary Chamberlain, in 1693; his wife inherited the property through the long-established Freme family. The Judge was succeeded here in 1728 by his son John, also MP for Cirencester and Clerk of the Patent Office. John's great-granddaughter married another MP, Robert Gordon of Auchendolly; but their daughter, Miss Gordon, gave the place away to some cousins called Sheppard. Nether Lypiatt rather came down in the world, eventually being mortgaged and sold off to A W Stanton of Stroud in

the early years of this century. Stanton carried out some urgent repairs and promptly sold the house again to Corbett Woodall who rehabilitated Nether Lypiatt with the help of Morley Horder, the architect. Further improvements were made by Mr and Mrs Gordon Woodhouse after they had become the owners in 1923. Mrs Woodhouse was a noted performer on the early keyboard instruments she kept in the house.

Inside, all the principal rooms survive and most of them, apart from the hall, have stone-moulded bolection chimneypieces. Princess Michael, herself a professional interior decorator, is taking personal charge of the current restoration work. Her Royal Highness will be riding to hounds with the Beaufort and no doubt she will be hoping to find a mount as reliable as the builder of the house who erected an obelisk, in the woods below the formal gardens, in memory of his horse. The inscription records that this animal 'served his master good and true, and died at the age of forty-two'. **HMM**

Above: The south front of Nether Lypiatt Manor, showing the sheltered garden court
Below: The main staircase and the hall

SANDRINGHAM

'This house was built by Albert Edward and Alexandra his wife in the year of Our Lord 1870': the east or entrance front with its great porte-cochère

'Very flat, Norfolk,' goes the famous line in Noel Coward's *Private Lives*; the charms of the Sandringham part of the world cannot be said to be everyone's taste. When Albert Edward, Prince of Wales (later Edward VII), became Sandringham's first royal occupant, his wife's Lady of the Bedchamber, Lady Macclesfield, reported that it would be difficult to find 'a more ugly or desolate looking place'; the icy north-east winds blowing over the Wash were 'unendurable'. It seemed inexplicable to her that, with the whole of England to choose from, this spot had to be chosen. Norfolk, however, has an individual, separate character that has been largely unaffected by industrialization; this vast agricultural county abounds in fine churches, solid country houses and pleasant villages. To those who know the place there is nowhere quite like it. 'I have always been so happy here,' wrote George VI to his mother, 'and I love the place.' His father, George V, loved 'dear old Sandringham' better than anywhere else in the world.

For Edward VII himself Sandringham was 'the house I like best'. Initially the two principal attractions of Sandringham, when he first saw it in February 1862, were the shooting and the distance from his mother at Windsor. It was his father's idea that the wayward Prince should have somewhere to put down rural roots away from the fleshpots on his coming of age, but nothing had been settled by the time Albert died at the end of 1861. In keeping with her husband's wishes Queen Victoria went ahead with the scheme and duly purchased the house and 8,000 acres at Sandringham for £220,000 shortly after her son's tour of inspection.

Sandringham Hall (as it was then called) had been built in 1771 by Cornish Henley, whose wife's family the Hostes had acquired the estate in 1686 from the Cobbes. The Hostes were of Dutch origin and connected to Sir Robert Walpole by marriage; a notable member of the family was Sir William Hoste, one of Nelson's commanders at the Battle of the Nile. Henley was a pioneer of fox-hunting in Norfolk and a far-sighted squire typical of the eighteenth century. In 1770 the agriculturist Arthur Young noted that at Sandringham:

. . . are very considerable tracts of sandy land, which are applied at present only to the feeding of rabbits. It is a very barren soil but not, I apprehend, incapable of cultivation: it lets from 1s 6d to 2s 6d an acre in warrens. Mr Henley has tried some experiments on it lately, with a view to discover how far it will answer cultivating. The value of it is prodigiously advanced by planting. That gentleman has formed several plantations, which thrive extremely; all the firs do well, and will pay a better rent for the land than any husbandry.

Cornish Henley's new house at Sandringham replaced what is reputed to have been a rambling Elizabethan structure with a plain Georgian building of stucco exterior, slate roof and small gables on either front. It had two and a half storeys with a west front of seven bays with a two-storey central bow and straight gables over the centre and end bays; the east front was of five bays with a central one-bay straight gable and two-bay two-storey wings. Henley did not live to see the house finished and his son sold the place to a neighbour, John Motteux of Bechamwell, in 1836.

Although Motteux never actually lived at Sandringham he extended the acreage and planted some pear trees before he died in 1843 leaving the estate to his *protégé* Charles Spencer Cowper. This fortunate young man was the youngest son of the fifth Earl Cowper, whose widow married Lord Palmerston, the great politician seated at Broadlands, and was herself the sister of Queen Victoria's benevolent Prime Minister Lord Melbourne. Cowper decided to cheer up Sandringham's rather dull appearance, commissioning Samuel Teulon to add a somewhat bizarre three-storey east porch in the Elizabethan style and also a conservatory of brick and various kinds of stone, notably the local dark brown carstone.

These romantic additions to what was basically a hunting lodge were to please Cowper's wife Lady Harriett, whom he married in 1852. Her previous marriage to Count d'Orsay had never been consummated because her mother the Countess of Blessington was availing herself of the Count's favours in a notorious *menage à trois*. The Cowpers' daughter died as a baby and Lady Harriett busied herself in setting up an orphanage at Sandringham. Cowper was happier in Paris than in East Anglia; he was therefore quite content when his wily stepfather Lord Palmerston engineered the sale of Sandringham to the Prince of Wales.

In 1863 the Prince brought his bride Princess Alexandra of Denmark to their new home. If her Lady of the Bedchamber, Lady Macclesfield, found Sandringham unsympathetic the Princess was in her element. Chill winds and gaunt landscape recalled her Danish childhood; at Sandringham she was reminded of the simple life she had enjoyed as a child, walking across the park to the church and picnicking at the seaside nearby. For her husband, though, the house was simply not big enough; more room was needed for family, household and guests. He was one of nature's hosts, never happier than when entertaining. To alleviate the space problem several lodges were built for the staff, a new kitchen and domestic offices were added to the house and two other buildings were put up in the grounds: Park House beyond the church and the Bachelor's Cottage to the south. The Prince planned a new wing for the hall itself which became known as the 'Big House' to distinguish it from the other buildings. However, the design for this wing did not prove satisfactory so the Prince came to the conclusion in 1865 that the best course was to knock the whole place down and start again.

Everything was accordingly razed to the ground save for the conservatory which became a billiard room. To this the Prince was to add a bowling alley (later a library) – an innovation he had been impressed by at the Duke of Sutherland's seat at Trentham. The Prince's faithful architect A J Humbert, a fairly indifferent performer who had been responsible for some earlier work on the Sandringham and Osborne estates and had also worked on the mausoleums at Frogmore, was given the go-ahead in 1867.

The present Sandringham House is of red brick with yellowish Ketton stone dressings in a sort of 'Jacobethan' style. The east front has a five-bay central block of three and a half storeys with a central porch and *porte-cochère*, and three straight gables above the parapet; and, then, on either side, two bays with a straight gable, and a bay with a two-storey bow crowned with a segmental pediment, plus another straight gable – making a front of eleven bays in all. The west front has a similar central block of three and a half storeys – this time of seven bays, balustraded and with dormers, with a central three-bay canted and balustraded bow to full height, flanked on each side by two bays and then a third with a shallower bow to full height, again crowned with a segmental pediment and with additional projecting bow on the ground floor and similar gables. To right and left are three bays with, again, similar central bows, and at the right-hand end of the front, a polygonal domed turret. Beyond this is Teulon's conservatory and Humbert's bowling alley. The north front is of three bays and three storeys, with three bows to full height and three shaped gables. That is the bald description of Sandringham's architecture; with the best will in the world it cannot be said to have much merit.

Over the porch were inscribed the words 'This house was built by Albert Edward and Alexandra his wife in the year of Our Lord 1870', but in April of that year, while they were renting Lord Suffield's place at Gunton nearby, the Prince and Princess found the new house far from ready. When the Prince returned in September to see heaps of rubble and unfinished ceilings he threatened to cancel the labourers' dinner to be held on his birthday (9 November) unless the building work was complete by then. Happily Goggs Brothers of Swaffham, the builders, ensured that it was.

Sandringham House (as it was now called) was warmed by a series of parties, such as the birthday ball for Princess

Alexandra on 2 December at which 300 guests arrived by brougham and coach in a brilliant light. This was provided by the gas illuminations from a plant installed in a new farm on the estate built by the Prince. 'I now have gas everywhere,' wrote the Prince to his mother Queen Victoria, 'which is a great improvement (of course, not in the living rooms!)' Eleven years after the completion of the house a one-storey ballroom of four bays was added to the designs of Colonel R W Edis, a professional architect who succeeded the artist Lord Leighton as commanding officer of the Artists' Rifles.

The Prince was due to celebrate his 50th birthday at Sandringham in 1891 and, in preparation for the arrival of the guests, fires were lit in the bedrooms. The brickwork in one chimney, however, was defective and timber caught fire. The conflagration was at its worst on the third floor, where the bedrooms for the ladies of the household were situated, as it was built in the open-timbered style and the spaces between floor and ceiling had been filled with sawdust to soften the sound of footsteps. Consequently the blaze caused the roof to collapse; if the second floor had not been constructed in iron girders and concrete the whole house would have been burnt to the ground. The fire was discovered in the early hours of Sunday, 1 November but

it was noon before the staff manning the Sandringham fire engine, with assistance from the King's Lynn brigade, had matters under control. On the upper floors, fourteen rooms were totally destroyed; the overall damage was estimated at £15,000. The party took place, though, under a roof of wood, tarpaulins and corrugated iron.

Unfortunately Prince George (later George V) promptly went down with typhoid and had to be removed to London away from the damp. His erratic elder brother the Duke of Clarence died of pneumonia the following year, shortly after his engagement to Princess May of Teck. This was the second of Albert Edward and Alexandra's sons to die at

Opposite: An aerial view of the west or garden front, showing the lake and church. A good show of some of the 200 different varities of rhododendrons growing at Sandringham can be seen
Below: Crocquet outside the billiard room (formerly the conservatory) in 1864. Albert Edward, Prince of Wales, is on the right
Bottom: Princes Edward (later Edward VIII), Henry (later Duke of Gloucester), George (Duke of Kent) and John with Princess Mary (Princess Royal) skating at Sandringham in January 1908. Their tutor, Mr Hansell, is on the left. It was said of Prince Edward that he suffered from an excess of Hansell and not enough Gretel

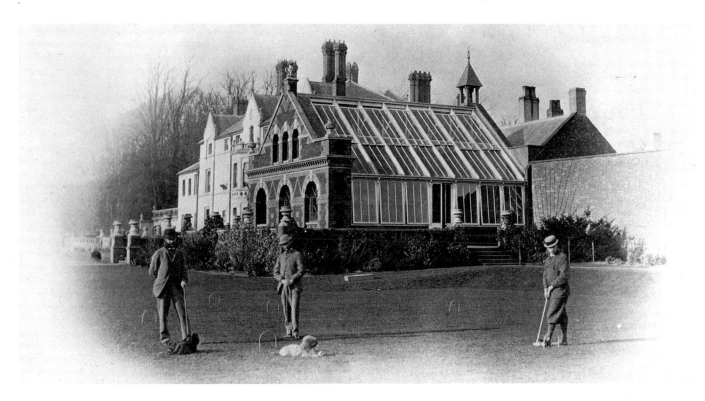

Sandringham as Prince John had died there aged only one day in 1871.

The fire was a blessing in disguise as far as the architectural appearance of the house was concerned. Edis, a considerably more talented designer than Humbert, added the long wing to the east which joins on to the billiard room (originally the conservatory and the only part of the old house to survive the rebuilding of 1870). This wing is in a more attractive combination of red brick and the local orange-brown carstone.

The grounds had seen fundamental changes brought about by the landscape gardener W B Thomas. The ornamental lake was thought to be too close to the east front of the house so two new lakes of more elegant shape were excavated further to the south. The spoil from these was used to fill in the original lake but while working at this task Thomas broke a leg, much to the consternation of Princess Alexandra who kindly nursed the gardener; in return he sent her white roses on his birthday for the rest of her life.

One of the two new lakes was called the Upper Lake, the other came to be known as York Cottage Lake after the old Bachelor's Cottage was given to Prince George, Duke of York, and renamed York Cottage. Prince George married his late brother's fiancée Princess May and they spent their honeymoon at York Cottage; as their family grew – all the children, save for the future Edward VIII, were in fact born there – this 'most undesirable residence' had to be enlarged twice by different architects, who should perhaps remain anonymous. Sir Harold Nicolson described York Cottage in his official biography of King George V:

It was, and remains, a glum little villa, encompassed by thickets of laurel and rhododendron, shadowed by huge Wellingtonias and separated by an abrupt rim of lawn from a pond, at the edge of which a leaden pelican gazes in dejection upon the water lilies and bamboos. The local brown stone in which the house was constructed is concealed by rough-cast which in its turn is enlivened by very imitation Tudor beams. The rooms inside, with their fumed oak surrounds, their white overmantels framing oval mirrors, their Doulton tiles and stained glass fanlights, are indistinguishable from those of any Surbiton or Upper Norwood home.

Even after he became King on the death of his father in 1910, George V continued to live at York Cottage; it was his favourite home for 33 years. He respected his father's wish that Queen Alexandra should continue to live in the 'Big House' until her death in 1925. "It is my mother's house", he said. "My father built it for her." The new Queen was less understanding, according to Edward VIII: she pointed out that "as a practical matter, it was rather ridiculous for one old lady to reside in grandeur in that vast mansion, while the King and Queen lacked room in their congested cottage for a single guest".

Inside the 'Big House', the Great Saloon is reminiscent of a Jacobean hall, with a wooden gallery on round arches and fluted columns, and the Great Drawing Room has an elaborate ceiling with *putti* and a painted centrepiece of blue sky and pheasants, as well as painted overdoors. The Dining Room is hung with tapestries (two of which are woven after cartoons by Goya) given in 1876 by King Alfonso XII of Spain, punctuated by fluted Ionic pilasters. Although some of the woodwork has been whitened and the palm trees and some of the knick-knacks have disappeared, the

Opposite: The Main Drawing Room where the Royal Family and their guests assemble for dinner. The cases contain Chinese ornaments carved in jade and other precious stones

Alexandra, Princess of Wales, outside the old Sandringham in 1863, the year she first visited the house

atmosphere of Sandringham's interior remains splendidly Edwardian. There are fine royal portraits in the Saloon, notably Edward Hughes's full length study of Queen Alexandra when Princess of Wales in 1896. The Sandringham collections include carved semi-precious stones, Worcester porcelain and marble statues. A bronze inkwell in the form of a harpy is a self-portrait of the great actress Sarah Bernhardt. As might be expected, though, it is the sporting pictures and cases of game that make the strongest impression. Shooting has always dominated life at Sandringham and the clocks used to be kept half an hour fast ('Sandringham time') in order to fit in an extra half-hour's shooting on the dark winter days.

Edward VII made Sandringham into an outstanding game reserve under the guidance of the Earl of Leicester; the careful treatment of pheasants and partridges resulted in a remarkable density of game. The King was perhaps more interested in the size of the bag than the sport itself: 30,000 head a season was a standard figure. In Edwardian times the army of beaters wore a uniform of blue blouses, black chimneypot hats with a red ribbon, and a red badge and individual badge for each beater. They chivvied the birds under the watchful eye of the mounted head keeper who, as Edward VIII recalled, wore 'one of those half-top hats, a 'cheerer', and silver horn – on a cord of red braid with tassels hung over his green brass-buttoned coat of Melton cloth'. These picturesque outfits persisted until the time of George V who died at his beloved Sandringham in 1936. "I'll fix those bloody clocks," Edward VIII is reported to have said on the night of his father's death, but little else at Sandringham was affected by his brief reign and George VI, another dedicated shooting man, was very much at home here. If anything he loved it even more than his father had; it was appropriate that he should die in his sleep at Sandringham in 1952 after a good day's hare shooting.

Above: The Dining Room with its tapestries presented by King Alfonso XII of Spain in 1876. The subjects of the tapestries are taken from cartoons by various Spanish artists, including Goya
Below:York Cottage, George V's favourite home for 33 years

Opposite: The Small Drawing Room with its cabinet of 18th-century porcelain and portrait of Queen Alexandra's mother, Queen Louise of Denmark. The tapestry on the wooden armchair on the right was worked by Queen Mary. This room is used by the Lady in Waiting in attendance

It was said of Edward VII that the interests of everything in the Sandringham estate were subordinated to the shooting but George VI was a model landlord; under his stewardship a substantial amount of land was reclaimed from the Wash. The estate now consists of about 20,100 acres (8,100 hectares) and includes the villages of Wolferton, West Newton, Appleton, Flitcham, Anmer and Sherbourne. The activities on the estate range from arable, stock and fruit farms and forestry to recreational parks and nature trails, pigeon lofts (which saw active service with the RAF in the last war) and, of course, part of the Queen's thoroughbred stud. There are over 100 employees on this thriving property.

The nineteenth-century gardens at Sandringham itself have been sympathetically adapted to the modern age, the lakes now being bordered by carstone rocks and flowering shrubs. Many of the trees that have now grown to maturity to the west and south of the house were planted up to the turn of the century and the tradition of planting trees has been carried on by generations of the Royal Family up to the present day. There are more than 200 different varieties of rhododendrons growing at Sandringham; they make summer walks along the glades especially memorable together with the azaleas and primulas, following the daffodils and the camellias in spring. The formal North Garden was laid out by G A Jellicoe for George VI; the eighteenth-

century statue of 'Time' close by was bought by Queen Mary in 1950 whereas the gilded Kuvera (a Buddhist divinity) was presented by Admiral Sir Henry Keppel (a great-uncle of Edward VII's friend Alice Keppel) in 1869. The Norwich Gates on the main road were designed by Thomas Jeckyll, wrought in iron by Barnard's of Norwich, exhibited at the Great Exhibition of 1862 and presented to the Prince of Wales on his wedding in 1863. His bride's dairy where she took tea, rather in the manner of Marie Antoinette, is another special feature of Sandringham, as is the lovely church with its memorials.

Anmer Hall The Queen's cousin, the Duke of Kent lives on the estate at Anmer Hall, a late-Georgian house that replaced an earlier building once known as Castle Hall or Bersford. Anmer was acquired in Charles II's reign by a local family called Coldham who continued to own the place until 1896. The present house has a long eleven-bay front, with a three-bay central pediment. It is of two storeys and dormers. The windows on the ground floor and the central windows on the upper floor are set in blank arches; there is a semicircular porch on two Tuscan columns. Standing in ten acres of park, Anmer, with its four bedrooms and nursery wing, has served as an agreeable country house for the Kents since 1973, following their departure from Coppins near Iver in Buckinghamshire.

The finances of Sandringham have always been of some concern. When Sandringham was auctioned in 1836 it only fetched £76,000 but the Prince of Wales had to pay £220,000 for the place 26 years later. However, his father's shrewd eye for an agricultural investment had not blinked; the development of the estate and its acres has more than proved him right. With regard to the house itself, Albert allowed a sum of £60,000 in his reckonings for improvements; in the event Edward VII spent over £300,000 and his grandson, Edward VIII, called the place a 'voracious white elephant'. By the mid-1970s the house badly needed modernization and plans to demolish 91 of the 274 rooms, as well as rebuild kitchens and staff quarters, were drawn up. These improvements were reported as being likely to cost anything between £250,000 and £400,000 and the figure was virtually doubling every year. After Christmas 1975 the Queen and the Royal Family spent five weeks in the six-bedroomed Wood Farm at Wolferton (where her epileptic uncle Prince John had lived out his thirteen years) in order that work could begin; but at a time of national economic crisis the Queen had a change of heart, feeling 'it would be insensitive and inappropriate' to carry out the improvements to the 'Big House'. At the same time it was announced that the Queen would open Sandringham House to visitors during the summer months (the country park and gardens were already open).

Opposite: The late Georgian Anmer Hall, the country home of the Duke and Duchess of Kent
Above: Wood Farm, Wolferton where the Royal Family often stay on their visits to the Sandringham estate. Here lived Prince John, the epileptic son of George V and Queen Mary

A further announcement explained that 'the house is to be made weather-proof as it now stands and the Queen will decide whether or not it might be practicable to adapt it so that she and her family may stay there in the future easily and economically.' The Royal Family still come to Sandringham after spending Christmas at Windsor and the shooting continues to exert its own pull at other times of the season.

So now the public can see inside this fascinating private residence of the Royal Family. Sandringham is far from a palace; it is easy to sneer at its lack of architectural distinction, but it is full of interesting artefacts collected by Queen Alexandra and her successors, and expresses the role of monarch as country squire better than anywhere else. Above all, it is on a personal scale; it is a home and has always been a special place for the modern Royal Family. When the present Prince of Wales was born, his grandfather, George VI, wrote excitedly to his mother Queen Mary that now there was the prospect of five generations at Sandringham.   **HMM**

The only house within the boundaries of the royal park of Richmond still in private hands is the early eighteenth-century Thatched House Lodge, home of H R H Princess Alexandra and her husband the Hon Angus Ogilvy. The name is taken from the thatched gazebo, or summer house, lying between the lodge and the road, in three acres of grounds which are surrounded by a high fence to keep out the deer. In late spring the grounds, studded with rhododendron bushes, are a blaze of colour.

The earliest record of the lodge occurs in 1673, during the reign of Charles II. In that year John Somervile and Thomas Burford, Keepers of the New Park, as Richmond Park was then known, were provided with 'a convenient abiding place in the Park, a brick built building lately erected on a hill in the said Park near to the village of Ham.' The Ranger was then the Duke of Lauderdale, the King's Great Minister, who dwelt at Ham House in the vicinity.

By 1716 the house was known as Aldridge's (or Aldrich's) Lodge, a name taken from the keeper Charles Aldridge, as appears from an item of £40, spent on its repair. There are traces of the original house in blackened oak which became exposed in the ceiling of a room in one of the wings. Aldridge lived in the days when the Hydes were Rangers. Lauderdale had died in 1682, and was followed by Lawrence, Earl of Rochester, son of Chancellor Hyde and an uncle of the future Queen Anne. In turn, he was succeeded in 1711 by his son Henry, who later also inherited the senior Earldom of Clarendon. He was accused of neglecting the park, which became 'a bog and a harbour for deer-stealers and vagabonds'. This may have been an exaggeration, but his rule certainly had become very lax.

In 1725 George II bought the Rangership of the park for £5,000 and bestowed it upon Robert Lord Walpole, son and heir of his Prime Minister, Sir Robert Walpole, who later built for his own use Stone or the New Lodge, eventually becoming known as White Lodge.

Though the younger Walpole was nominally the Ranger, his father, keenly addicted to hunting, spent £14,000 of his own money in improving the park and rebuilding many of its lodges. Consequently he considered himself quite justified in shutting up the gates and taking away step ladders on the walls, only admitting those 'respectable persons in the daytime and such carriages as had tickets'.

Having found that 'there was not any mansion better than the common lodges of the keepers', Sir Robert set to work to enlarge two of them, to make them suitable for the Ranger. One of these was the Old Lodge, demolished about 1837. The other house, the smaller of the two, was Aldridge's Lodge near Ham. Walpole built the present Thatched House Lodge in about 1727, at the same time as White Lodge. Facing south with a grey slate roof, the house has a cove of white brick three windows wide, with a canted bay in the middle. The house, minus the west wing which was added later, was basically what we see now, though the dining and drawing rooms in the middle of the garden front were remodelled in the nineteenth century.

Horace Walpole, the Prime Minister's youngest son, noted in his copy of Robertson's *Topographical Survey of the Great Road to Bath and Bristol*, 1792, which is now in the British Library, that his father in about 1727, built 'the thatched room at the smaller lodge'. This thatched gazebo, justly celebrated as one of the earliest of its type in existence, consists of two octagonal rooms, the smaller forming the entrance hall to the larger. From the balcony under the high peaked roof of thatch, there is an entrancing view of the Thames Valley to the south-west. Here, traditionally, Walpole entertained his monarch, George II, after a hunting expedition. The gazebo is built over deep cellars, which were originally used as an ice well.

In 1762, during the Rangership of George III's Prime Minister, the Earl of Bute, the house appears on a map as Burchett's Lodge, though officially, as we shall see, it was one of the two Ranger's lodges. Even so, it must already have been popularly called Thatched House Lodge, for the flat ground lying below is shown as 'Thatched House Plain',

in a map of 1771. The house itself was first so termed in 1813. Both the two Keepers, Charles Aldridge, who died in 1736, and John Burchett, whose death was 60 years later, are buried in Petersham churchyard. Whether these two Keepers lived in Walpole's lodge or in a less grand cottage nearby has not been ascertained.

The lodge was then granted to the 31 year-old Colonel William Medows (as he spelt his name), whose father Philip Meadows of Thoresby, Nottinghamshire, was Deputy Ranger to Lord Bute. The Colonel, who became General Sir William Medows, gained renown in 1776 fighting at the Battle of Brandywine against the American colonists. He must have been continually away from home in distant lands, leaving his wife, Frances Hamerton from County Tipperary, to superintend the celebrated paintings in the gazebo, which date from the Adam period.

The late Mr Edward Croft-Murray suggested that the decoration is more likely to be the work of the Venetian, Antonio Zucchi, Robert Adam's chief decorator, than of his wife Angelica Kauffman, to whom it has generally been attributed. The ceiling of the smaller room showed Apollo and one of the Muses, with her other eight sisters each occupying a medallion in the surrounding cove. In the larger room, painted on the superb blue-grey walls, appeared representations of the birth or *Sea Triumph of Venus*, and the story of Cupid and Psyche. These are currently being renovated, and in due course will be hung at Cornwall Terrace, Regents Park.

In earlier days, William Medows had ardently desired to marry his young cousin Lady Louisa Stuart, youngest daughter of the Ranger and Prime Minister Lord Bute, who would not hear of the match. Nevertheless the two remained attached to the end. Louisa, who never married, became her father's devoted companion, and apparently bore him no resentment for dismissing her suitor. She had considerable literary gifts, and was a close friend of Sir Walter Scott, who called her his best critic. She was the first to read his *Marmion* and *The Lady of the Lake*, and it was from her notes that Scott included the scene in Richmond Park in *The Heart of Midlothian*, described in the chapter on White Lodge. Her MSS were never published and were destroyed at her death, but some of her letters have been carefully preserved.

Lady Louisa's mother, Lady Bute, was a daughter of

Opposite: The garden front which faces south over the Thames Valley
Above: The north front facing the drive approached through Richmond Park

that redoubtable leader of fashion the eccentric Lady Mary Wortley-Montagu, who was also Sir William Medows' great-aunt. In 1785 Sir William resigned his tenancy in favour of Lady Louisa's brother, the Hon Sir Charles Stuart who, like him, achieved military fame, particularly in 1798 when he captured Minorca. In that year the architect, Sir John Soane, then Deputy Surveyor of Woods and Forests, carried out some alterations to the dining room of the lodge, plans of which are to be seen in Sir John Soane's Museum. Sir Charles Stuart died in 1801 at the lodge. There is a white marble monument to him by Nollekens in Westminster Abbey, and tablets to him and his wife – she survived him by 40 years – in Petersham Church.

In 1957 the lease was sold by the Crown Estates to the Earl of Westmorland who, two years later, sold it to the Duke of Sutherland on moving from Sutton Place near Guildford. The Duke had served King Edward VIII as Lord Steward of the Household; and it was on his land in Scotland that the Duke of Kent met his death in 1942 while serving with the RAF. The plane in which he was travelling, crashed into a hill.

On 24 April 1963 the Duke of Kent's only daughter, Princess Alexandra, married the Hon Angus Ogilvy, son of the Earl of Airlie, and Thatched House Lodge became their home. The Duke of Sutherland having died two months prior to their wedding, the Princess and Mr Ogilvy initially rented the house from the Duke's executors, and subsequently purchased the lease from his estate.

Here were born the two children of Princess Alexandra and Mr Ogilvy, James in February 1964 and Marina in July 1966, the only births to a member of the Royal Family in Richmond Park after that of the Duke of Windsor at White Lodge.

Secluded from the road near Ham Gate and hidden by a small hill, Thatched House Lodge has retained the atmosphere of a house in the depths of the country, despite being so close to London. It has been a happy home for the Ogilvys ever since their wedding, and here their two children have grown up. **PMS**

Bridewell
As it appeared

This View shews the PALACE of BRIDEWELL, with the
as they appeared a short time previously to their
BRIDEWELL in its original state, was a building of
from the banks of the Thames southwards as far
noble castellated Front towards the River: the
with cloisters, gardens, &c. as represented in the
entertainment of the Emperor Charles V.th but it
the reign of the former, being converted into an
the maintenance and employment of Vagrants and
corporation with Bethlem Hospital. A very small part

The Thames Front of Brid...

Published for the Proprietors, by

Palace,
about the year 1660.

ENTRANCE to the FLEET RIVER, part of BLACK FRIARS, &c.
destruction by the GREAT FIRE of LONDON, in the year 1666.
considerable magnitude, as well as grandeur, extending
north as to the present Bride Lane, and having a
interior was divided into different squares, or courts,
Vignette. KING HENRY VIIIth built this Palace for the
retained the dignity of a Royal Residence only during
HOSPITAL by EDWARD VIth who gave it to the City for
idle Persons, and of Poor Boys, uniting it in one
of the original structure now remains.

lace when perfect An.1540

W. Herbert, Penlington Place, Lambeth, 1817.

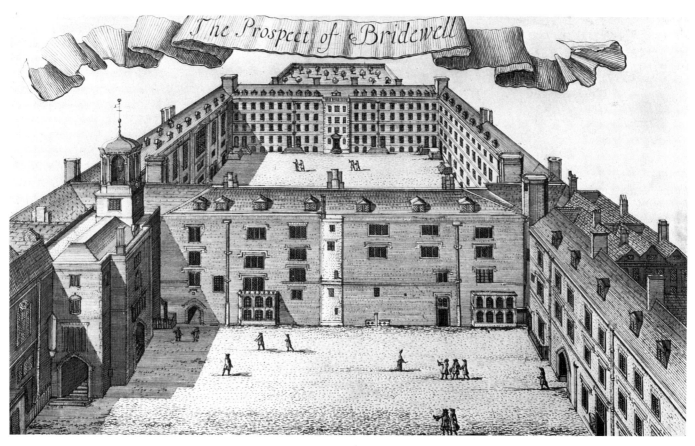

The Prospect of Bridewell

BRIDEWELL PALACE

Henry VIII's Palace of Bridewell stood on the west bank of the River Fleet where this small tributary flowed into the Thames. It thus lay outside the walls of the City of London, but within the Liberties. Today, the Fleet has been demoted to a sewer which flows southwards under New Bridge Street. Bride Lane, a turning off the street and leading to St Bride's Church, formed the northern boundary. This church, 'the cathedral' of London's press, is dedicated to St Bride (or St Bridget), the fifth-century Abbess of Kildare.

King Henry urgently needed an imposing palace in London after the two great fires in 1512 had destroyed both the old Palace of Westminster – where only the Great Hall and the Painted Chamber escaped – and the royal apartments of the Tower of London. Apart from the smaller and more insignificant Baynard's Castle, a little further downstream on the Thames, he had only Richmond or Greenwich palaces which were outside London.

Nearly all the land he required had originally belonged to the Knights Templars up to their suppression in 1312, and subsequently to the Knights Hospitallers of St John of

Above: An 18th-century engraving of the palace, then being used as a house of correction

Jerusalem. In 1509 Wolsey, who leased the Vicarage of St Bride from Westminster Abbey, also acquired Bridewell from the Knights Hospitallers. It then consisted of 'an orchard and twelve gardens.' (It was also the Knights Hospitallers who, six years later, leased him Hampton Court).

Wolsey obsequiously ceded this land to the King, who also required another small piece of land in Bride Lane occupied by the inn (or town residence) belonging to Faversham Abbey. He purchased this in 1521 for £100 and demolished the inn.

Bridewell Palace was begun in March 1513 by Thomas Larke, Surveyor of the King's Work, and cost in all £39,000. The palace was ranged round three courtyards, two on the north side and one on the south. The main entrance was approached from Bride Lane through a gateway leading south into Chapel Court. This was the north east quadrangle. On the south side of this court was the Great Staircase, one of the first in England to be specially designed for state occasions, and leading up to the principal rooms on the first floor. On the left of Chapel Court, a gatehouse led to a quay on the River Fleet.

A larger gateway led from Chapel Court westwards to the Great Court. At its southern end was the Great Hall, 80 ft long, with deep bay windows, dividing off the Southern Court. The Great Hall extended westwards across the present Bridewell Place. From the western range of the Great Court, the Long Gallery extended past the Southern Court to the Thames, marking the western boundary. Here, on the river bank were two hexagonal towers. At the northern end of the Long Gallery were the King's apartments, mentioned in the repair accounts of 1534. To the south of the palace was a broad terrace extending to the Thames. What we know of the layout comes from early maps, such as those of Ralph Agas and Joris Hoefnagel, a plan of 1791, plus the findings of recent excavations. Unfortunately, there is no detailed plan, so the sites of the Chapel, the Queen's apartments and the domestic offices are unknown.

Bridewell Palace was nearly completed in 1522 when the Emperor Charles V came on his first visit in full state to Henry VIII, bringing with him a retinue of over 1000 men. Bridewell was lent to the Emperor, who decided to stay at the Priory of the Black Friars on the opposite bank of the Fleet, leaving his entourage quartered in the palace. A half-timbered bridge was hastily built across the Fleet, and a gallery, cut through the wall, gave access from his apartments. During his visit the Emperor obtained the blessing of his aunt, Catherine of Aragon, Henry's Queen.

The King and Queen were often at Bridewell in the next few years. Henry, with no son to follow him on the throne, attempted to obtain a papal annulment on the plea that his marriage to the widow of his elder brother Arthur was 'not good'. The eventual outcome was to have a far-reaching effect on the future of Bridewell. In the meantime, when Cardinal Lorenzo Campeggio came from Rome as Papal Legate to investigate the matter concerning the marriage, he was lodged at Bridewell. Here, in the Great Hall, during October 1528, the Cardinal first appeared in public with the King and Cardinal Wolsey.

In the following month, also in Bridewell's Great Hall, Henry called a great meeting, to which he summoned the nobility, the Lord Mayor, Aldermen, principal merchants and lawyers, whom he addressed on his conscience and motives, but added that if the Queen was adjudged his lawful wife, 'nothing will be more pleasant or more acceptable to me.'

The whole of Shakespeare's third act of *King Henry VIII* is set in Bridewell Palace, and the Queen who lodged there during the sitting of the Legatine Court at Blackfriars was commonly called 'the Martyr of Bridewell'. On 18 June 1529 the Legatine Court, charged with the task of passing sentence on the King's marriage, opened and dragged on to July. Cardinal Campeggio, to extricate himself from these proceedings, announced that an adjournment was now necessary as, according to Roman Law, no cases could be tried during the summer vacation, and he took great care that the court was not re-convened. During the vacation Cardinal Wolsey went to Bridewell to see the Queen, promising her on Henry's behalf that if she would agree to the divorce, she would receive great riches and honours. Of course all this was of no avail.

As Henry did not obtain his divorce from Rome, Cardinal Wolsey fell from power. The King cast his eyes on the magnificent York Place, Wolsey's riverside palace at Westminster, which had grown in splendour year by year. Then in November 1529, four days after the Cardinal was sentenced in the King's Bench, Henry VIII moved in, obtaining official confirmation from the new Archbishop in the following year. The King renamed York Place, Whitehall Palace, and then lost interest in his own palace of Bridewell.

In 1552 Nicholas Ridley, Bishop of London, wrote to Cecil with the request that the young Edward VI would give him Bridewell for charitable purposes. 'There is a wide large empty house of the King's Majesty called Bridewell which would wonderfully well serve to lodge Christ in, if He might find friends at court to procure in His cause'. Edward VI made the grant and founded the Royal Bridewell Hospital as 'a House of Correction for vagrants of both sexes'. A few years later, a part of Bridewell was used for training purposes, as Ridley had intended.

During the Great Fire of London in 1666, the southern quadrangle was completely destroyed, and the site used for dwelling houses and warehouses. The roof of the Great Hall fell in, but was later restored, as was the Court Room. The Chapel Court fared better. In 1818, William Boydell, later the Guildhall Librarian, wrote:

This (Chapel Court) received but little injury in the Fire . . . Much of the north side backwards still remains in its original state, built of the red – or, as it is called by antiquaries, Tudor – brick with small, heavy stone-framed windows. Some of the hexagonal towers also (of which there are several at various angles of the structure) may yet be seen. They are brick with stone dressings and in the prevailing style of buildings of Henry VIII's day.

An engraving of a drawing by John Wichelo in 1803 shows the corner of the east range and the southern (Great Hall) range of the principal courtyard. Shortly afterwards, despite what Boydell wrote, the whole of Chapel Court was rebuilt, when the present court room and entrance, at 14 New Bridge Street, was constructed. This retains the sculptured head of Edward VI on the keystone of the arch.

In 1830 the school removed to Lambeth and in 1855 the House of Correction at Bridewell was abolished. The foundations thus became entirely educational. In 1860 the name was changed to 'King Edward's School' and seven years later the boys removed to Witley, Surrey, the girls remaining in London. Today, this ancient school stands in 400 acres of Surrey countryside at Witley.

Excavation of Bridewell Palace took place in two areas during 1978 prior to redevelopment. At 9–11 Bridewell Place, evidence was found that much survived of the palace's massive foundations. The foundation of a polygonal stair turret for a spiral staircase was discovered where the eastern range of the principal court joined the southern range. Another stair turret was discovered at the south east corner of this range. At the other site, 1–3 Tudor Street, at the southern end of the palace, the remains of 'the two towers upon Thames' were located. **PMS**

The reconstructed gateway of the palace, now 14 New Bridge Street

BAYNARD'S CASTLE

William the Conqueror established 'two very strong castles', Baynard's and Montfichet's, on the western walls of the City of London, and a stronghold which evolved into the Tower of London on the eastern side, in order to overawe its 'vast and fierce populace', who had been able to hold out for two months after the Battle of Hastings in 1066. The public house, The Baynard Castle at the corner of St Andrew's Hill and Queen Victoria Street, is on the original site of the castle. The castle owed its name to its first custodian, Ralph Baignard. The site then lay on the west side of St Andrew's Hill which climbs up from Thames Street to Carter Lane to the south west of St Paul's Cathedral. The Baynard family remained in possession until 1111 when it was forfeited by William Baynard.

Later custodians were the FitzWalters, lords of Dunmow in Essex, of whom the most famous was Robert, leader of the 25 barons who forced King John to grant his Magna Carta. Stow suggested that King John destroyed the castle in 1212 when Robert FitzWalter joined the barons against him. In 1278, Robert's grandson, another Sir Robert Fitz-Walter, received a licence to sell Baynard's Castle to the

Archbishop of Canterbury who returned it to the King. The land was then granted to the Convent of Dominican or Black Friars. Later, in 1361, the King's Wardrobe was established on the opposite side of St Andrew's Hill, next to the church of that name.

Baynard's Castle was rebuilt on the other side of Thames Street on a site stretching down to the river. The new building first appeared in records in 1338. Henry VI granted the castle to his uncle and one time Regent, the Duke of Gloucester, whose popularity with merchants resulted in his being called 'good Duke Humphrey'. After a serious fire the Duke in 1428 built the castle anew. The Duke of Gloucester was arrested and attainted, and Baynard's was then granted to the King's powerful kinsman and rival, Richard Duke of York, who with 400 of his men, was there in 1438. On 30 October 1460, the weak King Henry VI of the House of Lancaster acquiesced in recognising the Duke of York as his ultimate successor in place of his own son, but his more spirited Queen did not do so and brought the issue to combat at the Battle of Wakefield two months later, when the Duke of York was killed.

By a series of successes, the Duke of York's son, Edward Earl of March, at the age of nineteen and regarded as 'the handsomest man in England', suddenly and unexpectedly found himself regarded as the King of England. About 4000 people who assembled at St John's Fields, Clerkenwell, were asked if they would have young Edward as King, and shouted "Yea, yea!" His captains came to Baynard's Castle to give him this news, and two days later the hastily constituted Council also came there to offer him the Crown, including in their number, the King's uncle, Richard the Kingmaker, Earl of Warwick and the Archbishop of Canterbury. Edward IV then went to St Paul's in procession

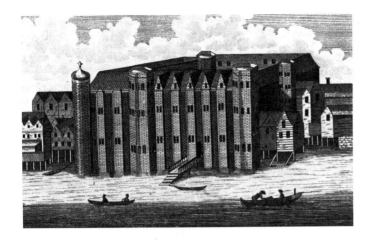

Opposite: A model of Baynard's Castle which is today in the Museum of London. It shows old St Paul's and the buildings in Ludgate Hill before the Great Fire of London
Left: An engraving of 1784 shows what then remained of the palace. Today there is nothing, although a public house (below) stands on the site and preserves the name

The King and Queen were often here, and their son Prince Arthur and Catherine of Aragon spent a few days in the castle in 1502. At Baynard's Castle Philip of Austria, King of Castile, came with his wife on their visit in 1505, having been shipwrecked on the Dorset coast.

The castle later became the jointure of Catherine of Aragon, who stored her contents here. The inventory taken at Baynard's Castle after her death included some of the property of the House of York, such as some 'very worn' hangings carrying the badges of falcon and fetterlock, rose and sun.

Baynard's Castle passed to Anne Boleyn, but after her execution was granted to Henry VIII's illegitimate son, the Duke of Richmond, who died in the same year, 1536. Anne of Cleves was living there in 1540.

In the middle of the sixteenth century three new wings were built round a court on the site of the former garden. Five earlier buildings were replaced by a new north wing. By this time a series of distinctive towers had been erected on the waterfront, including a private watergate and landing stage. During the excavations carried out in 1974 and 1975, the north wall of the castle which had a window to the street was uncovered together with a gateway and a cellar.

Later keepers of Baynard's Castle were Sir William Sidney, Henry VIII's favourite and Lord Chamberlain, who was also grandfather of Sir Philip Sidney, and Sir William Herbert, later Earl of Pembroke, who married Anne Parr, sister of Henry VIII's last Queen, Catherine Parr.

Queen Elizabeth I held the Pembrokes in high regard. On the Queen's first Garter Day of her reign, St George's Day of 1559, she came to Baynard's Castle for supper, and later left in procession up the Thames. This was to prove the first of many visits.

When the profligate Philip, fourth Earl of Pembroke, married his learned second wife, Lady Anne Clifford, in June 1630, it was to presage for her much sorrow. She was a redoubtable lady, with six great castles in the north of England. Dr Donne said 'she could discourse of all things from predestination to slea-silk'. After being together for four years, they parted, he living in lodgings at the Cockpit, Whitehall, and she at Baynard's Castle when not superintending her own estates. In her memoirs she described Baynard's Castle as 'a house full of riches and more secured by my lying there'.

The last custodian of Baynard's Castle was the Earl of Shrewsbury. A few days after Charles II had supped there, on the second day of the Great Fire of London, Monday 3 September 1666, the flames consumed it, and the castle was still burning at 7 o'clock on the following morning. The walls collapsed into the courtyards, as is shown in Hollar's engraving of the ruined city. All that remained was 'a little tower next the water side', which survived until 1720. Buildings and wharfs were built on the site. Fragments of the lower part of the castle were built into the houses, but the whole site was demolished early in the nineteenth century.

Castle Baynard remains one of the wards of the City of London. There is a model of the castle in the Museum of London. **PMS**

where a *Te Deum* was sung and to Westminster Hall where he donned the royal regalia and sat in the marble chair.

A later king was also offered the throne at Baynard's Castle. Edward IV was now dead, and the throne had come to his thirteen year-old son Edward V, the elder of the Princes in the Tower. On 26 January 1483 the boy's uncle, Richard Duke of Gloucester, received a deputation there, led by the Duke of Buckingham who entered the courtyard. Richard, from a balcony, after a show of reluctance, accepted the Crown and following shouts for 'King Richard' he descended to his nobles, who attended him on his ride to Westminster Hall. Shakespeare set the scene at Baynard's Castle in his *Richard III*.

The next King, Henry VII, decided to rebuild Baynard's Castle. According to John Stow, in his *Survey of London*, 'about 1501, the sixteenth year of his reign, repaired, or rather new built this house, not embattled, or so strongly fortified castle like, but far more beautiful and commodious for the entertainment of any prince or great estate'. The dock on the west side was filled in, and a walled garden put in its place. The castle soared high above its neighbours, and was luxuriously furnished. From the riverside the mansion seemed to be set in, rather than upon the river, like a veritable Venetian palace. Stow's date of 1501 is probably too late, for accounts show that the re-roofing occurred in 1498.

The main gateway from the north opened on to Thames Street. The square building surrounded a court, with an octagonal tower in the centre and two in front, between which, according to Holinshed, there were several square projections from top to bottom, with the windows in pairs, one above the other. Beneath was a bridge, and stairs led down to the river.

CAERNARVON CASTLE

Edward I's majestic castle of Caernarvon was one of a series he built in order to maintain his conquest of Wales. With Harlech, Conway and Beaumaris, Caernarvon is one of the 'big four', which became the envy of all Europe as masterpieces of military architecture. Caernarvon was singled out for special honour as Edward's capital under the terms of the Statute of Rhuddlan proclaimed in 1284, under whose terms Wales was to be governed for the succeeding three and a half centuries. Not only that, but he arranged for his son, Edward, the first 'Imperial' Prince of Wales to be born there.

The castle is on a strongly defensive position on a peninsular where the River Seiont flows into the Menai Strait. The third side to the north, beyond the walled town of Caernarvon, is formed by the little River Cadnant, which now flows underground. Nearby was once the Roman fort of Segontium, named after the river, and on the same site as the present fortress was a motte and bailey castle built by William the Conqueror's second Earl of Chester, Hugh Lupus (the wolf), whose motte resulted in the 'hour glass' design. The castle reverted into Welsh hands with Llewelyn the Great, but on the death of the last Welsh Prince of Wales, Llewelyn ap Gruffydd, in December 1282, the English regained Caernarvon.

Edward I's architect was the Savoyard, James of St George, Master of the King's Works in Wales, and construction started in the summer of 1383. At the beginning of these operations, on 13 July, Edward I brought his Queen Eleanor to Caernarvon for a month's stay. They lived in substantial timber framed apartments, which 42 carpenters had hastily erected within the castle site.

The following Easter, the King and Queen returned, when eight royal chambers were ready to receive them, with windows newly glazed. The Queen had a special lawn. A fortnight later, on 25 April 1384, their son Edward was born. At that time he was not heir apparent, for an older son, Alfonso, then ten years old, was alive, but he died four months later.

Whether there is any truth in the oft-told legend that King Edward presented his son Edward of Caernarvon, who could not speak a word of English, to the Welsh people as their Prince, cannot be proved, but it is possible. In 1301 the Prince was formally created Prince of Wales. The other story, dating from the reign of Elizabeth, that the Prince was born in the little room in the Eagle Tower must be wrong, because the walls are known not to have reached that height at the time of his birth.

The castle walls are 6 to 7 ft thick, fortified by thirteen towers, of which the strongest and largest is the Eagle Tower at the extreme western boundary. The fortress is long and narrow, running from east to west, and occupies the summit of an extensive rock. There is now only one entrance, the King's Gate, in the centre of the northern wall. Two massive towers flank the entrance, above which is a statue of the first Prince of Wales, erected when he was reigning as Edward II.

Originally the main gate was the Queen's Gate at the western end. From the north, the castle was protected first by a moat and then by the great ditch, hewn out at the beginning of the castle's construction, beyond which was the town of Caernarvon, walled by Edward I. It was therefore not considered to be exposed from this direction. The early work was all concentrated on the southern flank, which was mainly built before 1292.

Then, when Edward of Caernarvon was aged ten, there was consternation. In 1294, Madoc ap Llewelyn, a cousin of the last Welsh Prince, managed to raise a revolt. The Sheriff of Caernarvon was murdered, and the town wall

Opposite: Caernarvon Castle today, reflected in the quiet waters of the River Seiont
Above: An 18th-century view showing the castle and keep still virtually intact
Left: A drawing by Forestier showing how the castle looked in medieval times

badly damaged. Madoc and his men were able to penetrate the castle and burn the timberwork before being repulsed. Immediately the town walls were repaired, the northern walls of the castle prepared, and the main entrance became the King's Gate.

The Eagle Tower is built so strongly that it resembles a keep. It has three fine turrets, and after completion a hexagonal turret was added in 1316. The tower had received its name by 1317, when three eagles decorated the battlements, one on each turret, of which that on the western turret is still fairly complete.

The final building period ended in 1327, the last year of Edward II's reign.

Among the later kings who came to Caernarvon was Richard II, by which time the castle could only offer him a straw bed. In the Civil Wars, it was twice garrisoned by Royalist forces, and three times besieged, but very little damage was done owing to its strength and the perfection of its fortifications. After the Restoration, Charles II ordered its demolition, but this does not seem to have even been started.

On 8 August 1832, the Duchess of Kent brought her young daughter, the future Queen Victoria, to Caernarvon, and as the Princess climbed up the spiral stairs of the Eagle Tower to see her ancestor's alleged birthplace, the Duchess stayed in the courtyard below. Queen Victoria's son, the Prince of Wales (later Edward VII) came here in April 1868 on the anniversary of the birth of the first Prince of Wales.

On 13 July 1911, Edward, Prince of Wales (later Edward VIII) became the first Prince of Wales to have been invested on Welsh territory, at Caernarvon Castle, an event masterminded by David Lloyd George, Member of Parliament for Caernarvon. This was followed by the investiture of the present Prince of Wales on 1 July 1969. **PMS**

CARLTON HOUSE

Carlton House in London's Pall Mall, like Brighton Pavilion, will always be associated with that cultivated spendthrift, the Prince Regent. It occupied the site between the lower end of Regent Street and the Duke of York's Steps, a red brick house with wings and a stone entrance, which was built in 1709 for the Secretary of State, Henry Boyle, later Lord Carlton (then often spelt Carleton) of Carlton, Yorkshire. Though the house was unremarkable, the gardens were both extensive and beautiful. They were laid out by William Kent, and extended along the south side of Pall Mall to the fine house Wren built for the Duchess of Marlborough, Marlborough House.

When Lord Carlton died at Carlton House in 1725, his heir was his nephew, Richard Boyle, Earl of Burlington, famous as an architect and collector, and the builder of Chiswick House. Two years later he parted with Carlton House to Frederick, Prince of Wales, son of George II. After the Prince's death, his widow continued to make it her London home, and increased its size by buying the house next door from George Bubb Dodington.

When her grandson (and George III's son), the 21 year old Prince of Wales was given his own establishment in 1783, he took up residence at Carlton House on the understanding that he would not part with any land and be responsible for all repairs to the house and garden. The house had become neglected in the last eleven years, and was not grand enough for the Prince's tastes. Accordingly he called in Henry Holland to alter, enlarge and improve it: to turn it, in fact, into a splendid palace.

In the autumn of that year, Holland started work. It was decided to build an elaborate sequence of rooms, filling the shell of the existing building. In the centre of the Pall Mall facade, Holland erected a Corinthian portico; and inside, a splendid oblong hall, decorated with two Ionic columns of brown Siena marble on all four sides. This led to an octagon and to the right was the fine double staircase. Beyond the Music Room was the Chinese-decorated Drawing Room, later to be dismantled, and its contents sent to Brighton. Holland also erected a colonnade of Ionic columns to screen the palace from the street.

Horace Walpole described the scene enthusiastically on 17 September 1785 to the Countess of Ossory:

We went to see the Prince's new palace in Pall Mall and were charmed. It will be the most perfect in Europe. There is an august simplicity that astonished me. You cannot call it magnificent; it is the taste and propriety that strike. Every ornament is at a proper distance, and not one too large, but all is delicate and new . . . and there are three most spacious apartments, all looking on the lovely garden, a terreno, a state apartment and an attic.

The portico, vestibule, hall and staircase will be superb, and to my taste, full of perspectives; the jewel of all is a small music room that opens into a green recess, and winding walk of the gardens. . . .

I forgot to tell you how admirably all the carving, stucco and ornaments are executed; but whence the money is come I conceive not, all the tin mines in Cornwall could not pay a quarter. How sick one shall be, after this chaste palace, of Mr Adam's gingerbread and sippets of embroidery!

Opposite top: The north front and its portico from a painting by W Westall
Bottom: The same artist's view of the south front
Above: Wild's painting of Nash's splendid Gothic Dining Room

To celebrate the completion of the first stages, the Prince gave a great ball in March 1784; but it was not until 1791 that Carlton House was completed. Long after that the Prince continued to lavish money on the palace. In fact, these were the most expensive operations undertaken at a royal residence until his work at Windsor after he became King. In six years his unpaid bills reached £133,505, and a further sum was owed to tradesmen for personal items of £90,804. His father asked Parliament to vote this money in return for the Prince's promise 'to confine his future expenses'. This did not happen, and a Committee of Inquiry was instituted, which eventually resulted in his vast debts being paid upon his agreeing to the disastrous marriage to his cousin, Princess Caroline of Brunswick.

Here, at Carlton House, he spent his wedding night in 1795, and here in the following year was born their only child Princess Charlotte, who in May 1816 was to marry, in the Grand Crimson Drawing Room, Prince Leopold of Saxe-Coburg, who later became King of the Belgians and Queen Victoria's favourite uncle.

Holland had died in 1806, and in the following year his successor, Thomas Hopper, added the large Gothic Conservatory, designed in the style of Henry VII's Chapel in Westminster Abbey. Further alterations by James Wyatt in

Above: The Gothic Conservatory, built en suite with the Dining Room, by Thomas Hopper
Opposite: From Pyne's Royal Residences (above) the Entrance Hall and (below) the Rose Satin Drawing Room on the upper floor

1804 and 1805 included redecoration of rooms on the basement floor of the garden front. Then, in 1813, John Nash entirely remodelled and replenished this floor, overcoming the difficulty that, owing to the slope of the ground, it looked out only onto the garden and had rather low rooms. These apartments linked Hopper's Gothic Conservatory to Nash's own Gothic Dining Room. The magnificence of Carlton House was illustrated in Pyne's *Royal Residences* in 1819 – the Golden Drawing Room and Gothic Library, the Throne Room, the Circular Drawing Room and the Rose Satin Drawing Room on the upper floor.

A succession of great ceremonies took place at Carlton House, including the Regency ceremony of swearing in. At noon on 5 February 1811, the Grenadier Guards marched into the courtyard and struck up the National Anthem, as Privy Counsellors were arriving. That afternoon, the Prince, now grown 'enormously large', made his way through the Circular Drawing Room to the Grand Saloon where he sat at the head of a long table. One by one, in strict order of precedence, came the Archbishops, the Lord Chancellor, the Privy Counsellors, and many others, to hear the Regent's oath of loyalty. They then, in turn, approached the Regent to kneel before him and kiss his hand. During the ceremony, Princess Charlotte, outside on her horse, peered through the windows.

The Prince Regent had a grandiose scheme for Nash to build a 'royal mile' leading from Regent's Park to Carlton House, to be named Regent Street, but before this was completed, he had in 1820 become King.

King George IV now had to deal with the question of his London home. Despite the thousands which had been lavished on Carlton House, he now complained of its low ceilings and unpalatial air. He told Lord Farnborough, in front of Nash, "I tell Nash before you, at his peril, never ever to advise me to build a palace. I am too old to build a palace. If the public *wish* to have a palace, I have no objection to build one, but I must have a *pied à terre*. I do not like Carlton House standing in a street, and moreover I tell him that I will have it at Buckingham House; and if he pulls it down he shall rebuild it in the same place; there are early associations which endear me to the spot."

To offset the vast expenditure needed for the Buckingham Palace project, he was determined to demolish Carlton House and embark on a building scheme in its place. In 1825 Nash was summoned to undertake the rebuilding of Buckingham Palace, and in 1827 Carlton House was demolished. 23 chimney pieces went to Windsor, and also the floors of the Ballroom, Great Drawing Room, the Circular Drawing Room and the Gothic Dining Room. Other fittings and materials went to public auction, when columns of the portico were used at the National Gallery. The whole Regent Street scheme which had led to Carlton House, now had to have a *raison d'être*. Thus came about the idea of St James's Park as a southern counterpart to Regent's Park. Carlton House Terrace arose in the gardens of the former house. It was not so very long before, in 1789, that the *New Town and Country Magazine* had called Carlton House 'a national ornament and the only habitable palace Great Britain can boast'. **PMS**

ELTHAM PALACE

Eltham Palace, Kent, two miles to the south of Woolwich and now surrounded by a dormitory suburb of south-east London, was one of the favourite homes of our kings, from the reigns of Edward II to Henry VIII. The later Plantagenets liked to escape as much as possible from the ceremonial which surrounded them at Westminster, and they found peace and tranquility at Eltham. The palace is justly famed for its existing Great Hall, with its magnificent hammerbeam roof. This is one of the three important halls still to survive, the others, which are slightly larger, being at Westminster and Hampton Court.

Even before Eltham became a royal palace, kings used to come here to stay. Henry III spent Christmas there in 1270, and his son, Edward I, dated several charters at Eltham. Anthony Bek, Bishop of Durham, who was one of Edward's chief advisers, acquired the manor in 1295 from William de Vesci. About 1300 he rebuilt the moated and turretted manor, which formed the basis of the palace. This is roughly a square shape, approached by a bridge across the moat from the north side.

Bek quarrelled with the King and was dismissed, but he remained a close friend of Edward of Caernarvon, Prince of Wales, and gave him the reversion of the manor. By the time the Bishop died in 1311, the Prince had become Edward II, and he immediately made Eltham Palace over to his Queen, Isabella of Valois. In August 1316, their second son, John of Eltham, later Earl of Cornwall, was born there.

Edward III, who had taken over Eltham from his mother about 1343, entertained several sovereigns there, including his brother-in-law David II, King of Scots, John II of France, Waldemar IV of Denmark and the crusading King Peter of Cyprus. He did considerable work at Eltham, including the erection of new apartments on the eastern side of the palace.

Richard II, Edward's grandson, made further additions, and we first hear of the Outer Court, beyond the moat, in his reign. Richard II gave audience to Froissart, who arrived from the continent with a gift for the King, 'a fair book, well illuminated' of his own poems. . . 'I shewed him how it treated matters of love.' Froissart called Eltham 'very pleasant and shady, for those galleries were then covered with vines'.

Henry IV embarked on new royal apartments on the west side of the Chapel, consisting of a chamber with a study, a parlour kitchen, buttery and laundry, which were constructed of timber with stone chimney stacks, the chamber and the study standing over a cloister 60 ft long, which led to the Chapel. The roof of the King's chamber had 68 wooden bosses carved with angels bearing escutcheons and scrolls. The Queen's chambers were also rebuilt in two storeys.

Henry V, in his short reign, did little rebuilding at Eltham, but his son Henry VI, in 1445, ordered new buildings to be erected 'in all haste possible', to receive his bride, Margaret of Anjou. Eleven years later, reference is made to the 'new hall'. Although no plan of the palace is known, this and the 'old hall', were evidently demolished when Edward IV built the magnificent Great Hall, begun soon

after November 1475, which now exists. This measures 100 ft by 36 ft of six bays, with massive carved pendants from the roof and fine oriel windows.

As well as the hall, King Edward may have constructed the existing stone bridge over the moat. The editor of *The King's Works* states that owing to the lack of documentary evidence, it is impossible to state with certainty that this is so, but architectural evidence would suggest that it dates from his reign.

The two youngest of Edward IV's children were born at Eltham: Catherine in 1479, who married William Courtenay, Earl of Devon, and Bridget in the following year. Bridget was taken as a child to Dartford Abbey, and she remained there as a nun for the rest of her life.

Lambard, writing in 1576, referred to Henry VII's building new apartments in brick along the west side of the Great Court. 'It is not yet out of memory that the King set up a fair front over the moat there.' In 1499, when the King and his elder son were away, the eight year-old Prince Henry, later Henry VIII, acted as host when Erasmus came to Eltham, accompanied by Sir Thomas More. The great man was much impressed with the boy's 'right royal bearing', and added that 'during dinner the stripling sent me a short epistle, as a kind of challenge, to write something for him'. Three days later he composed a Latin verse in praise of the Prince's father, Henry VII.

Henry VIII, at the beginning of his reign, built a new chapel, whose foundations are still traceable on the north east side of the Great Court. A tunnel under the moat from the Kitchen Court was probably made at the same time.

*Opposite: The celebrated 1835 engraving by Samuel and Nathaniel Buck showing the Great Hall and gatehouse
Below: A 19th-century romantic view of how the hall would have looked in about 1365*

Henry much preferred his birthplace of Greenwich not far off, and rarely came to Eltham, but his household ordinances, prepared by Cardinal Wolsey, were issued from Eltham. Among the many rules to be observed, it was forbidden for the scullions to go about 'naked or in such vileness as they now do, nor lie in the nights and days in the kitchens or stand by the fireside'. Waiters must not wipe their hands on the tapestries, and the royal barber must be ready every morning in the Privy Chamber with water, cloths, knives, combs and scissors to trim the King's beard and hair. The barber was also warned not to go near 'vile persons' at any time.

Queen Elizabeth appointed her favourite, Sir Christopher Hatton, as Keeper of Eltham, and James I, occasionally came to hunt. In 1606 he brought with him his brother-in-law, King Christian of Denmark, 'and killed three buck, with much pleasure, on horseback'. When Charles I came in 1629, the palace was in a sorry state of disrepair.

The Parliamentary Surveyors in 1649 considered Eltham to be untenantable, and Evelyn, in 1654, found 'both the palace and chapel in miserable ruins, the noble wood and park destroyed by Rich the Rebel'. (This was Colonel Nathaniel Rich, who bought the lands in 1651). Eltham reverted to the Crown on the Restoration, but then only a little of the Inner Court within the moat and the bridge which linked it with the Outer Court, still stood. The surviving Inner Court buildings, became a farmhouse, and the Great Hall a barn, then strangely called 'King John's Barn'. The windows were blocked up and a door inserted into the southern oriel for carts to enter.

By the early eighteenth century the Great Hall had lost its louvre turret, and the lead roofing had been replaced with tiles. Wainscoting had disappeared round the walls, and of the woodwork only the main roof and a little of the screen survived. In 1735 a view from the north-east, showing the Great Hall, gatehouse and the bridge over the moat, was engraved by Samuel and Nathaniel Buck, and in 1790 Turner painted a water colour showing the interior of the Great Hall used as a barn.

Robert Smirke, Surveyor of Woods and Forests, reported that the hall was unsafe in 1823, although a few temporary repairs were then made. Four years later, Sir Jeffry Wyatville, then rebuilding Windsor Castle, was reported to be considering the removal of the roof to Windsor, but the expense prevented this plan from materialising. The farmer became scared that his grain would be exposed, and an outcry developed, when the matter was taken to the House of Lords.

As a result of this campaign, several artists came to Eltham, and between 1828 and 1830 three books appeared on the hall with detailed drawings, the last by Pugin, with prints based on those now in the Royal Institute of British Architects' library, made in 1827 by John Nash. Repairs were begun in 1828 including beams put in to hold up the roof, which remained until the end of the century. The Great Hall had been used as a coach-house, drill hall, and for parish fêtes and flower shows. In the three years before the first World War, the roof was strengthened and the windows re-glazed.

In 1931 Eltham Palace was leased to Stephen Courtauld, and a few years later, Seeley and Paget erected a new house for him next to the hall which was carefully restored. Bomb damage occured in the second World War and was repaired in the 1950's. The Institute of Education now leases Eltham Palace, and the Great Hall is open to the public. **PMS**

FALKLAND PALACE

In 'the Kingdom of Fife', beneath the Lomond Hills, lies the old royal burgh of Falkland. Here sits the historic hunting palace of the kings and queens of Scotland, including the celebrated courtyard facade of the sixteenth century, which has been called the finest monument to 'the auld alliance'.

The palace fell into near ruin in the eighteenth century, until it was lovingly restored, at his own expense, by the Hereditary Keeper of Falkland Palace, the third Marquess of Bute. This careful work of restoration and maintenance, not only of the palace but its gardens and precinct, has been carried out by Lord Bute's descendants as Keepers, together with the National Trust of Scotland in co-operation with the local authority. Like Edinburgh Castle and the Palace of Holyroodhouse, Falkland Palace is still owned by the Queen. Her present Keeper is Ninian Crichton Stuart, who succeeded his father in 1981.

Falkland Palace is formed of three ranges, the north, east and south, round a square courtyard. The fourth side was a wall, higher than the present one, and was 5½ ft nearer the courtyard. The first range to be built was the north, an extension of the old castle, but nothing now remains but

its foundations. The east and south ranges were built by James IV and embellished by James V. The east block, which contained the royal apartments, is now roofless. The south range, with the Chapel Royal, is the best preserved.

To the south, facing High Street, the facade is a fine example of Scottish Gothic architecture, with its five massive buttresses and projecting battlement linking up with the two towered gatehouse. The two fronts on the courtyard side, however, which were completed by French masons for James V, became what Mark Girouard, writing in *Country Life*, terms 'a display of early Renaissance architecture without parallel in the British Isles'. Nevertheless, there were few successors to Falkland or James V's other masterpiece in the classical style, Stirling Castle, and for the rest of that century architecture continued to be Scottish.

The long vanished old castle of Falkland was probably built in the twelfth century by the Earls of Fife, whose seat it was. This was one of the seven ancient earldoms of the Kingdom of Albany. In the tenth century they were styled mormaers, and by the early twelfth century, Earls. The Macduffs, Earls of Fife, occupied the first place among the seven, and had special privileges, such as seating the King on the coronation stone.

The last of the warlike line of Macduffs was Isabel, Countess of Fife in her own right. She married four times, but since she had no issue by any of these ventures, in 1371 she ceded the earldom to Robert Stewart, Earl of Menteith, brother of her second husband, and second son of Robert II, King of Scots. In 1398 Robert became Duke of Albany and was the most powerful man in Scotland. Henceforward Albany became the usual title of the King's second son down to the union of the two kingdoms.

By this time his eldest brother was King, for their father

Robert II had died in 1390. He was baptised as John, but as this name was considered unlucky (John Balliol had surrendered Scotland to Edward I), he too, reigned as Robert. As Robert III, he became one of Scotland's most ineffectual kings, and the Duke of Albany took over the reins of government as Regent. When the King's eldest son and heir, David, Duke of Rothesay, reached the age of twenty, he was appointed Regent for a period of three years, but when his term of office ended this capable but arrogant young man did not step down.

Albany arrested his nephew and brought him back to Falkland under strong guard and held him prisoner in 'a befitting chamber'. Then, at Easter 1402, when the Duke of Rothesay was 24, it was given out that he had died of dysentery at Falkland, but it was commonly believed that his uncle had starved him to death.

Sir Walter Scott, in his *Fair Maid of Perth*, accepted the latter view, but transferred the scene to a cellar in the east range which had not then been built.

Robert III sent his second son James, now his heir, for safety to France, but on the passage he was captured by an English vessel and taken to the Tower. After his eventual return to Scotland as King James I, neither he nor his son, James II, ever forgave the Albany family. James II came into possession of Falkland in 1425, after beheading, in Stirling, Murdoch, second Duke of Albany, together with his two sons and father-in-law. He found Falkland Castle consisted of a great round well-house tower, 'a hall, and a chapel, divers chambers, a gallery, a kitchen, a brewery, a bakery, and a kind of office or count-house. There was also very extensive stabling and a large fleshery establishment'.

The last of the old castle to survive was the Chapel, which formed part of the Great Tower, to the north of the

Opposite: The Chapel Royal with its fine ceiling is the only surviving original interior
Above: The gatehouse with its turrets facing High Street

palace's east range. A few years after the new Chapel Royal was built, this was allowed to crumble, being last repaired in 1540. The tower, long used as a prison, had completely disappeared by the seventeenth century. In recent years, an ornamental string-course was discovered round the remains of the circular tower.

James II, known as 'the fiery face', from his birthmark, made Falkland Palace over to his wife, Mary of Gueldres, whom he married in 1449. He started to build the north range of what became known as 'the Palace' after 1458, when the royal burgh was created. This range included the Great Hall which, as at Linlithgow, was termed the Lyon Chamber from decoration of the royal arms. How much was erected by him and how much by his son James III, is not known, but as there is a resemblance between this Great Hall and that at Stirling Castle, of which the architect was James III's favourite, Thomas Cochrane, one supposes he may have been responsible for both.

James II was killed at the age of 30 in 1460, when a gun which he was watching exploded. His widow, Mary of Gueldres, became Regent to her nine year-old son, James III. She gave sanctuary at Falkland to the exiled English Queen, Margaret of Anjou. A year after her husband's death, Mary built a new chamber at Falkland, with a special door which led to her private garden. Her memory still survives with the Gilderland Walk through the Falkland woods.

Their grandson, James IV, was much given to architecture. As well as building the east and south ranges at Falkland, he did much work at Stirling, Linlithgow and Holyrood. His royal apartments at Falkland were on the first floor of his new east range, with the Queen's above. She was Margaret Tudor, Henry VII's daughter.

The King's Bedchamber was in the projecting cross-house in the centre of the east range. Galleries stretched on either side to the north and south, with views over the Forest of Falkland beyond. Much of the cross-house, with the King's Bedchamber, had to be rebuilt last century by the Marquess of Bute, due to bad condition. Behind were the King's Guard Hall, a long room, leading to the Presence Chamber, and beyond was the Privy Dining Room. Here, a stairway in the Dovecote Tower at the north-west corner of the palace, led to the kitchen. This tower is at the angle where the east and north ranges join. Some of the surviving masonry of the Great Hall in the vanished north range projects into the east range.

James IV built the Chapel Royal, reached by the Turnpike Tower at the east end of the south range. This was already under construction in 1501, and completed eleven years later, shortly before James IV fell at Flodden. The Chapel was not consecrated until his son, James V, came of age. This contains the only original interior still to survive, and was rescued from ruin by Lord Bute, along with the beautiful carved entrance screen of oak. He restored with great care the fragments of the royal pew and pulpit.

From a stair in the cross-house in 1528, James V, as a sixteen year-old boy, escaped the clutches of his hated step-father, Archibald Douglas, Earl of Angus. He borrowed clothes from one of his yeomen of the stable, and rode to freedom at the Castle of Stirling, where he began his personal rule. One of the repercussions for the Douglases was the burning as a witch of Angus' sister, Lady Glamis.

In the reign of his son James V, the east wing was roofed, and in 1537, when he had reached the age of 25, the royal apartments were handsomely redecorated, ready to receive his royal bride from France.

That year he went to France in order to marry Francis I's daughter Madeleine, but she died seven months later, shortly after her arrival in Scotland. In the following year he married Mary of Lorraine, daughter of the Duke of Guise. Consequently Falkland Palace was prepared for one bride and completed for another.

The French master mason, Nicholas Roy, came to Scotland to beautify the south range by carving the round medallions which, in pairs, flank the five great windows of the upper storey. Though they represent classical figures of mythology, by tradition they are in the likenesses of James V and his two Queens, his parents, and several others at Court.

James V's architect for the south range was his cousin Sir James Hamilton of Finnart, who had also reconstructed Linlithgow and Stirling. He was later executed for treason, and within two years, in 1542, James V's own death put an end to work at Falkland.

In 1541 James V completed the gatehouse, flanked by twin towers with conical roofs. Above the gate, is the central gargoyle of the royal lion of Scotland. He also built the Royal Tennis court in 1539, the only one in Scotland to survive from such an early period, and comparable with Henry VIII's court at Hampton Court.

When James V lay dying at Falkland Palace in December 1542, the Lord Lyon rode from Linlithgow to tell him that the Queen had given birth to Mary, the heiress to the throne (two infant sons had died at Holyrood in a space of a few days the previous year). James commented that the crown 'came with a lass, and will gang with a lass!' Drummond, in his version, added 'King Henry will either take it by his arms or marriage', which proved incorrect. Within a week, the King was dead.

Falkland became the favourite home of his daughter, Mary Queen of Scots, who was here every year bettween 1561 and 1565. In the restoration of the Chapel, the name *Marie Stuart*, was revealed in the easternmost window, perhaps owing its origin to the Queen. Her son, James VI, later also James I of England, made Falkland over to his wife, Anne of Denmark, on their marriage in 1590, and often stayed here to hunt. Here he had to listen to a rebuke from the founder of Scottish Presbyterianism, Andrew Melville, calling him "God's silly vassal," adding "Now again I maun tell ye there is twa Kings in Scotland. Thair is Christ Jesus, the King and his kingdom, the Kirk, whose subject King James the Saxt is, of whose kingdom nocht a king, nor a lord, nor a heid, but a member."

To celebrate Charles I's coronation in 1633 at Holyrood, a painted wooden frieze was placed in the Chapel Royal, running the whole length of the north wall between the painted moulding and the ceiling. This depicts lattice windows above the real ones, and carries the King's, Queen's and their son Charles' monograms, with the date. The Chapel's ceiling was also repainted for the King's stay, with various Tudor and Stuart royal badges, and the King's initials CR (*Carolus Rex*), his Queen's MR (*Maria Regina*) and their son's CP (*Carolus Princeps*).

Charles II came to Falkland in 1560 and 1561. He was the last sovereign there until the present Queen's visit in 1958, marking the 500th anniversary of granting the charter to the royal burgh. In 1650 the King ordered that new colours should be presented to the Scottish troops who had been chosen to guard him, and first constituted them the Scots Guards. (That is why today Scots Guards and members of their association with the badge are admitted to the palace free.)

In 1564, Cromwell's troops came to Falkland to turn the palace into a garden, and they burnt down the whole of the north range. Since the garrison continued afterwards this was presumably their carelessness rather than a deliberate act of violence.

Captains, and later Hereditary Keepers, were appointed to be responsible for Falkland. The first family was that of Beaton (or Bethune) of Creich, to which belonged Mary Beaton, one of Mary Queen of Scots' four Maries. From them the Keepership passed by marriage to the Stuarts, Viscounts of Stormont, who in time turned it over to their kinsmen, the Earls, later Marquesses and Dukes of Atholl. Though they continued until 1787, Falkland became more and more ruinous.

When eventually in 1887, the third Marquess of Bute became Keeper, this office returned to the family of Stuart; for he descended from John, Keeper of Rothesay, a brother of Robert, Duke of Albany, who was the first Stewart (or Stuart) to live at Falkland. He restored the Captain's chambers in the gatehouse, which had become ruined by the early nineteenth century.

The Forest of Falkland ended when Cromwell felled the oaks to provide timber for a fort, but the palace garden, noted ever since the fifteenth century, was laid out at the Keeper's own expense, in a manner similar to that which appeared in a seventeenth-century engraving. The palace precinct too, is a conservation area.   **PMS**

The Great Hall is all that survives of the palace

HATFIELD PALACE

Just as Henry VIII considered that Cardinal Wolsey's palaces of Hampton Court and York Place, Westminster, were too great to be enjoyed by a subject, so he coveted the fine home of the Bishops of Ely at Hatfield, Hertfordshire.

The Bishops of Ely had possession of the manor of Hatfield since early in the twelfth century, hence the name of Bishop's Hatfield. The greatest of these, Henry VII's chief minister John Morton, who successively became Archbishop of Canterbury, Lord Chancellor and a Cardinal of the Church, rebuilt Hatfield Palace in 1496 on a magnificent scale, and died four years later.

All that now remains is the Great Hall, which Sir Nikolaus Pevsner describes as 'the foremost monument of medieval domestic architecture in Hertfordshire', and the gatehouse of a simpler style. This stands on the slope of a hill just to the east of Hatfield Church. We do not know the architectural details of Morton's palace beyond that the buildings were entirely of red brick, ranging round a principal quadrangle. The surviving Great Hall, which measures 230 ft by 40 ft, stood in the centre of the west range. The open timber roof is a fine example of the late medieval period. The north, south and east ranges appear to have been added later. There is a plan among the papers at Hatfield House before the Tudor palace was partly demolished, from which one can get an idea of its appearance early in the reign of James I. Almshouses were adjacent to the gateway, and orchards stretched to the south.

When Nicholas West, Bishop of Ely, died in 1533, Henry VIII offered the see to Thomas Goodrich with the stipulation that Hatfield should be exchanged for less valuable manors elsewhere within his diocese. Thus the King acquired Hatfield, but he seldom came there. Both Princess Elizabeth, then three months old, daughter of Anne Boleyn, the then Queen, and Princess Mary, daughter of the discarded Queen Catherine of Aragon, were sent to Hatfield.

The two princesses received very different treatment. Mary's mother Catherine of Aragon had been discarded by the King, so unlike Elizabeth, she was not treated as a princess.

When Elizabeth was aged ten she was joined by her younger half-brother, Prince Edward, son of Jane Seymour, Henry VIII's third wife, and they had lessons together. When Henry died in 1547, this boy, now Edward VI, was escorted by his uncle Edward Seymour, then Earl of Hertford, to the Tower of London prior to his coronation. King Edward later granted Hatfield to Elizabeth, where she enjoyed life as a young girl, riding in the park and studying under Grindall and Ascham to become one of the best educated princesses in Europe. When Mary became Queen, circumstances changed. Elizabeth was imprisoned at the Tower, and then kept at Woodstock under surveillance, having been accused of complicity in Wyatt's rebellion. When this spell was over, she was allowed to return to Hatfield in October 1555, being placed under the guardianship of Sir Thomas Pope, the founder of Trinity College, Oxford.

During shrovetide of 1556, Sir Thomas provided a masque at his own expense for the Princess's amusement. For this occasion the Great Hall at Hatfield was grandly decorated with cloth of gold and pomegranates. Afterwards came a splendid banquet, followed on the next day with a performance of the tragedy of *Holofernes*. Queen Mary did not approve of these festivities, and instructed him that such follies must cease. However, in the following year, Mary came down to Hatfield herself, and the two sisters watched a bear-baiting after Mass, and in the evening a play performed by the Children of St Paul's, a company of choristers from London. This was the last occasion on which the sisters were to meet.

Less than one year later, on 17 November 1558, Queen Mary was dead. A deputation, headed by the Earls of Pembroke and Arundel, rode to Hatfield to tell Elizabeth that she was now Queen. They are said to have found her sitting under an oak tree in the park, quietly reading a Greek testament. She then fell on her knees on the grass, exclaiming from the Psalms, "*Domino factum est et mirabile in oculis nostris*". (It is the Lord's doing; it is marvellous in our eyes.)

The new Queen was to stay at Hatfield for a few days, taking stock of the situation. On 20 November she held her first Council, when William Cecil was sworn in as Principal Secretary of State. Thus the first act of her reign brought about the partnership between them which was to last for 40 years. Kat Ashley who had served her since Elizabeth was a child, became her Chief Lady of the Bedchamber, and Robert Dudley her Master of the Horse. Then, on the 23 November, the 25 year-old Queen set out for London.

Hatfield was not to see Elizabeth again, apart from a few visits for a day or two of hunting. Her successor, James I, after reigning in England for four years, gave up possession in 1607 to Robert Cecil, Earl of Salisbury, son of Elizabeth's great minister, William Cecil, Lord Burghley; for the King exchanged Hatfield for Salisbury's Theobalds in the same county.

In 1611 the splendid new Hatfield House arose, the home of the Cecils, Lords Salisbury. Much of the Tudor palace was demolished to provide materials for its successor. Only the Great Hall was retained, but part of this was demoted in 1628 to stables. The hall was restored by the fourth Marquess of Salisbury, son of the Prime Minister, in the early years of this century. Hatfield had been a royal palace for a mere 74 years. **PMS**

KEW
(THE WHITE HOUSE)

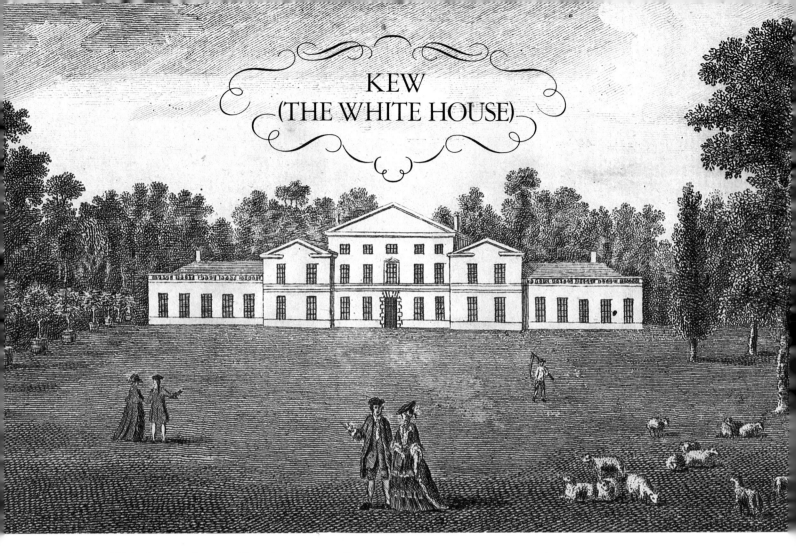

The garden front of the royal palace at Kew engraved in 1776. The royal palace is Kew House, called the White House

George III had two palaces at Kew, both often referred to as such, which has resulted in confusion between them. The older of these, also known as the Dutch House, still survives. The larger house, which was rebuilt by the King's father Frederick, Prince of Wales, also went by the name of the White House or Kew House. To distinguish them I have principally referred to them as the Dutch House and the White House.

In 1731 Frederick, Prince of Wales, son of George II, took the house on a long lease. He found that it was rat infested, and on one occasion the catcher delivered over 500 still alive to the Prince's London home, Leicester House. Almost at once the Prince decided to rebuild, and employed William Kent to undertake the work.

Sir William Chambers, in his folio work of 1763, includes the 'North and South elevations of the Palace, designed and executed by the late Mr Kent'. In his description of the house, the north front was faced by three courts, the Central which was approached from Kew Green, the Kitchen Court on the right, and the Stable Court on the left. The vestibule led to the Central Hall, two storeys high, and lit from windows in the upper storey. This contained two large vases of carved statuary marble, and several portraits of sovereigns and statesmen, including William III and Mary, and Lord Burghley.

From the hall a passage led to the garden, having on its right a suite of apartments for royal use: the Ante-Chamber, Drawing Room, Cabinet, Gallery and waiting rooms. The Drawing Room, hung with tapestry, contained more royal portraits, and in the Cabinet were panels of japan, a gilded ceiling and chimney piece 'designed by the late ingenious Mr Kent'. The Gallery, with other portraits, had wainscot-

ting of blue overlaid with gilded ornament. To the left of the passage were the apartments of the Women of the Bedchamber, with their drawing room, and ascending the Great Staircase to the first floor, there was a further drawing room hung with green silk, with pictures by Domenichino, Paul Veronese and Claude amongst others. The ceiling depicted the story of Leda. This floor contained the Prince's Bedroom and Dressing Room, and a suite of apartments for the royal children and their attendants. Chambers does not mention the second floor, with the housekeeper's and servants' quarters.

By 1735 Kent, with Thomas Ripley as Comptroller of Works, had completed his task. The Prince had spent over £8,000. Of the furniture Kent designed for the house he sadly noted that much was ruined by games of indoor baseball, played by the whole family in the Drawing Room after dinner.

Soon after Prince Frederick moved to Kew, a rift developed with his parents which was to last for the rest of his life. The King called him 'a monster and the greatest villain that ever was born,' and the Queen stated that 'my dear first born is the greatest ass, the greatest liar and the greatest *canaille* and the greatest beast in the whole world, and I most heartily wish he were out of it'. Short tempered, inconsiderate and immoral he undoubtedly was, but he had many points in his favour. He had inherited his mother's intellect and had wide interests which included astronomy, gardening and music. He was accomplished at the 'cello, and sung French and Italian songs 'to his own playing'. He was also a keen cricketer.

At the White House the Prince's Court rivalled his father's. He surrounded himself with gifted people, such as Alexander Pope the poet, who once presented him with a dog, and composed the familiar couplet for its collar:

I am his Highness's dog at Kew
Pray tell me, Sir, whose dog are you?

When in London the Prince used to be rowed up the river to Kew in his stately barge designed by Kent, which is now in the National Maritime Museum.

The Prince had a succession of mistresses from an early age. One of the first was said to have been Madame d'Elitz who had also served his father and grandfather. George Selwyn, when discussing her with a friend who commented that "there is nothing new under the sun", rejoined with "or under the grandson", a *bon mot* which was widely circulated.

In 1736 the Prince of Wales married Princess Augusta of Saxe-Gotha, a no less enthusiastic gardener than he. Both expected their household visitors to assist them in the gardens. Bubb Dodington, the Prince's Treasurer, noted in his diary during February 1750, 'Worked in the new walk at Kew'. On the following day, 'All of us, men, women and children, worked at the same place – a cold supper'.

The Prince encouraged Augusta to take an interest in their friend John, Lord Bute, an ardent botanist. According to Horace Walpole, when Frederick wished to be alone with Lady Middlesex, he would 'bid the Princess to walk with Lord Bute'. When the Princess was widowed in 1751, she threw all her energy into beautifying the gardens under the unofficial direction of Bute. Gossip and lampoons suggested that they had more than a botanical interest in each other, Bute usually being portrayed as a 'Jack Boot'.

In 1757 the Princess appointed William Chambers as her architect. Having been to China he built for her at Kew the pagoda, standing 163 ft high. He also built the Orangery, completed in 1761, which has been compared with Wren's at Kensington though 25 ft less in length, several temples, and a ruined arch and mosque, all placed in Kew Gardens. William Aiton came in 1759 to establish the Physic Garden, and remained at Kew to be inherited by George III and Queen Charlotte.

When the Princess Dowager died in 1772, George III decided to move to the White House, while his increasing family spread to the Dutch House and other houses in the vicinity. According to the plans at Windsor he contemplated extending the house, using Chambers' designs. These included the conversion of the left hand wing into a library and the right hand into a music room, and the addition of a new north front whose facade was extended by 18 ft. It is not known how far these alterations were made. When work on the White House was completed, Richmond Lodge was demolished.

In 1779 the Royal Family moved to Windsor, where the Queen's Lodge was now ready for occupation, but the King and Queen, with the eldest princesses, still returned to Kew every week of the summer to hold the Thursday Drawing Room, sleeping at the White House on Wednesday and Thursday nights.

When Fanny Burney joined the Court in 1786, her diary describes her experiences. A month after her arrival she wrote:

Kew life you will perceive is very different from the Windsor.

As there are no early prayers, the Queen rises later, and as there is no form of ceremony of any sort, her dress is plain, and the hour for the second toilette extremely uncertain. The Royal Family are here always in so very retired a way, that they live as the simplest country gentlefolks. The King has not even an equerry with him, nor the Queen any lady to attend her when she goes her airings.

It was this simple life that 'Farmer George' preferred. He only undertook ceremonial as a duty, disliked London, and seldom visited the houses of the nobility whose expensive habits were repugnant to him. Queen Charlotte was of the same mind.

In October 1788 George III showed signs of what was wrongly assumed to have been insanity and is now known to have been porphyria. On 27th the Royal Family moved to Windsor against the Queen's inclinations. At the end of November the doctors decided to move the King back to Kew so that he could take exercise unobserved. The Queen also thought that this was unwise, but they gave an undertaking that force would not be used. After a great struggle the King left for Kew on the understanding that he would be able to join the Queen there. The Prince of Wales had already ridden to Kew to re-allot the rooms, chalking the occupants' names on the doors. When the King arrived he turned to the left to enter the Queen's apartments only to find that the doors had been bolted. He complained to Greville that he had been deceived.

The Rev Frederick Willis, a clergyman who for 30 years had run a private asylum in Lincolnshire, assisted by his sons, was placed in charge, and treated the King with the utmost severity. Every time the patient refused food because he could not swallow, or threw off his bedclothes during sweating attacks, he was placed in a strait-waistcoat, sometimes from five in the morning till two in the afternoon, or strapped in a restraining chair, which the King sadly called his 'coronation chair', so that he could not move. The senior Willis boasted to an equerry that 'he broke in (patients) as horses in a menage'.

The King was not allowed to see the Queen until 13 December. Fortunately, the attack passed, and by mid-March, the Royal Family could return to Windsor. A thanksgiving service was held on St George's Day at St Paul's Cathedral.

A further attack happened in London during the spring of 1801, with identical symptoms during which he nearly died. The older Willis had by then retired, but his sons took charge. Later, instead of the patient being allowed to rest at Windsor, the Willises tried to kidnap him when he took his daily ride, and, when this failed, entered his room by force. The King exclaimed "Sir, I will never forgive you whilst I live". He was a month at the White House under their supervision, a confinement which only came to an end when the King 'went on strike', the only occasion in history when a monarch has done so. He told Lord Eldon that unless he was allowed to go to the Queen 'no earthly consideration should induce him to sign his name to any paper or to do one act of government whatever'. The Willises were defeated and left, and the King walked across the road to the Dutch House to join the Queen.

These unhappy events could not have endeared the White House to the King, and plans for erecting a new palace had started in earnest. This time James Wyatt was employed to build a huge castellated palace on the river bank, slightly to the west of the White House and Dutch House. In 1802 the White House was demolished and in the meantime the King and Queen moved to the Dutch House. **PMS**

KEW
(THE NEW PALACE)

Sir William Chambers died in 1796. When in 1800 George III decided to embark on a grandiose scheme to build an elaborate Gothic palace at Kew he turned to James Wyatt, Surveyor General of Works. The new Surveyor had just redesigned the state apartments at Windsor Castle, and in the following year embarked on the palace at the original estimate of £40,000. The new site was on the bank of the river opposite Brentford, a little to the west of the Dutch House and the White House, which latter was demolished in 1802 to make way for this project. The King's eldest daughter, the Princess Royal, eagerly noted in 1802 that she thought this would be 'Lulworth Castle improved'.

The large rectangular palace had round towers at each corner, with smaller ones on each face. The building, which has been called 'a sort of late Georgian Nonsuch', had a central keep and spacious courtyard. Within the quadrangle was an inner square building, distinguished by a series of round towers and turrets, while rising still higher in the centre of the pile was a larger square tower crowned by a wind vane. In all, there were three dozen towers and turrets, all crenelated, the walls being pierced with loops and topped with battlements.

As the palace rose it evoked strong criticism. Sir Nathaniel Wraxall, in his *Memoirs*, alluded to its situation opposite 'the smoky and dusty town of Brentford, one of the most detestable places in the vicinity of London', and to its appearance as 'very unkingly, as well as incommodious'.

The river frontage of the castellated palace – the only royal palace never to have been occupied

He added that, 'though still unfinished, unfurnished and uninhabited, as it will probably ever remain, it presents to the eye an assemblege of towers and turrets, forming a structure such as those in which Ariosto or Spencer depicted princesses detained by giants or enchanters'. Sir Richard Phillips, the publisher, likened it to the Bastille. The rooms, he said, consisted of no more than a series of large closets, boudoirs or oratories, which had 'its foundation in a bog close to the Thames'.

By 1806 at least £100,000 had been spent on this white elephant of a palace. Now however, the King, who had entirely lost the sight of his right eye and was nearly blind in the other, lost interest. Queen Charlotte much preferred the old Dutch House, and in that March the workmen were discharged. By that time the exterior was complete and much of the interior also. The imperial staircase was installed and the rooms 'rendered nearly undestructible by fire by means of cast-iron joists and rafters'.

George IV thought the palace was of deplorable taste, and in 1827 gave orders for it to be blown up. The staircase and floors were carried to Buckingham Palace. Only one fragment still exists: a window which was built into a garden shed at Kew. There are plans of the palace in the Royal Library at Windsor Castle.   **PMS**

118

KEW
(RICHMOND LODGE)

Richmond Lodge was once the residence of the Ranger of Old Richmond Park, that is the Old Deer Park, which now also comprises the riverside half of Kew Gardens. The New Park – the present Richmond Park – did not exist before being enclosed by Charles I. The lodge was situated to the east of the present Kew Observatory, just to the south of the present Kew Gardens. The historian Lysons said that the earlier Tudor house built in 1518 by Dean John Colet, founder of St Paul's School, was on the same site, but of this there is no proof. Colet had obtained a lease of land from the Prior of Sheen a year before his death, and later, Cardinal Wolsey came here for a short time after his fall in 1530 when Richmond Palace was forbidden him.

In 1693 William III started to enlarge the lodge and extend the park, on which he spent £3,500. In 1704, James, second Duke of Ormonde, the Ranger of the park, who had succeeded Marlborough as Commander-in-Chief, obtained the lodge on a 99 year lease, and started to build an elegant and extensive house, which he renamed Ormonde Lodge. When George I came to the throne, Ormonde was dismissed from all his offices, and in 1715 fled to the continent. When his tenancy was thus abruptly terminated his house was not quite finished, though the south-west or garden front was complete.

George I granted the lodge in 1722 to his son, the Prince of Wales (later George II), his wife Caroline and their daughter Princess Anne, again on a 99-year lease, and they

Paul Sandby's water colour of Richmond Lodge, showing the south front

made it their summer residence. In that year John Macky wrote that this was:

> a perfect Trianon. . . . It does not appear with the grandeur of a Royal Palace, but is very neat, very pretty. There is a fine avenue with runs from the front of the house to the town of Richmond at half a mile's distance one way, and from the other front to the river-side, both inclosed with balustrades of iron. The gardens are very spacious and well kept. There is a fine terrace towards the river. But above all, the wood cut out into walks, with the plenty of birds singing in it, makes it a most delicious habitation.

The Prince and Princess of Wales grew attached to their 'sweet villa' where she could indulge in her landscaping activities in a rural setting yet so close to London. Nevertheless there were drawbacks which hardly make it seem 'a perfect Trianon', and architecturally its pedimented façade concealed an irregular plan. The walls were damp, and a frequent visitor, Lord Hervey, said that 'what was said in one room might be often overhead in the next'.

One of George II's first acts after his accession was to turn Richmond Lodge over to his Queen, who spent large sums of money in beautifying the gardens and improving the house. She proposed to rebuild the lodge after the Palladian style. Among the drawings preserved of Sir Ed-

119

ward Lovett Pearce, Surveyor General of Ireland, is a set of plans and elevations which shows four facades, each 173 ft in width and terminating in corner pavilions. Pearce, however, died in 1733 before they were put into execution.

William Kent, Pearce's successor, in 1735 also designed a palace, of which there is a pearwood model, now at Kew Palace. Though this was not proceeded with, Kent made some alterations to the lodge by adding the Library wing on the north front, and possibly also the Music Room, which is shown in Sandby's water colour of the lodge to the right of the south front, though the latter may date from the beginning of George III's reign.

Kent, with the aid of the gardener Charles Bridgeman, redesigned the gardens for Queen Caroline, and erected two celebrated follies, the Hermitage grotto in about 1732, and Merlin's Cave, about 300 yards to the south, three years later. Between them now stretches George III's lake.

The Hermitage, 'very gothique', contained an octagonal room full of marble busts of philosophers. Merlin's Cave was a summer house of three rooms, each with a conical thatched roof, looking like the kraal of a Zulu chief, and containing a small library. Round a table sat life-sized wax figures of Merlin, Queen Elizabeth with her nurse, and Elizabeth of York, the first Queen who lived at Richmond Palace in what Horace Walpole termed an 'unintelligible puppet show'. Another likened the cave to 'an old haystack thatched over'. The King refused to look at his wife's plans, announcing that 'he did not care to see how she flung away her own revenue'. In fact, she astutely obtained payment from the Treasury.

At the same time, a mile away at the White House, Kew, was living Frederick, Prince of Wales whom both parents grew to despise. Only a narrow lane to Brentford Ferry separated the King's Richmond Gardens from the Prince's Kew Gardens.

Queen Caroline's death in 1737 put an end to her embellishment of the gardens, though George II continued to come to Richmond from time to time. On his death, in 1760, his grandson, George III became King, (his father the Prince of Wales having died nine years earlier).

As early as October 1760 the new King decided to rebuild the lodge and turned to William Chambers who was doing much work for his mother at Kew. Chambers' drawing of the north front was exhibited at the Society of Artists in 1762. Nothing resulted, and an undated estimate for a palace 'to be erected in the Royal Gardens at Richmond', includes some of the same details as in Chambers' design, of which several drawings exist. They show a palace of

Merlin's Cave, the summer house near Richmond Lodge, built for Queen Caroline

Palladian character with pavilion towers at the corners and a Corinthian portico. Its model at Hampton Court, unfortunately destroyed in 1922, was probably that presented to the King in 1765.

These attempts had to be postponed because of the purchase of Buckingham House in London and the expense which followed.

Capability Brown was commissioned to adapt the Richmond gardens in a style which had become popular, and he swept away Queen Caroline's gardens, walks, wildernesses and follies, not without some verbal opposition. William Mason, in his *Heroic Epistle to Sir William Chambers* (the newly appointed Comptroller of Works), was to write:

. . . To Richmond come, for see untutor'd Brown
Destroys these wonders which were once their own;
Lo! from his melon-ground the peasant slave
Has rudely rush'd and levell'd Merlin's Cave
Knock'd down the waxen wizard, seiz'd his wand
Transform'd to lawn what late was fairy land. . .

On the site of Queen Caroline's gardens, Chambers built the Observatory near the lodge, so that the King could watch the transit of Venus in June 1769, which Captain Cook and Banks also witnessed in Tahiti.

In that year George III started in earnest with plans to rebuild. Mrs Papendieck, daughter of a German page, recalled that 'we remained in the late season at Richmond as His Majesty was greatly occupied in digesting plans with Sir William Chambers for a new palace'. In August 1770, Lady Mary Coke wrote that:

the King had laid foundations for a Lodge (alas not a Palace) in Richmond Gardens, very near where the old house now stands. This was to have a frontage of 140 ft, and was to be built on arches in order, as I suppose, to command a greater prospect.

One of the many plans at Windsor shows a design in which the front measured about 130 ft so Lady Mary was not far out. A further delay was caused by the refusal of the Richmond vestry, who administered the parish, to sell a small piece of ground which did not belong to the royal manor, needed 'for the purposes of elegance and convenience'.

By 1722 the new building had got as far as the ground floor, when the King's mother died. This altered all his plans. George III and Queen Charlotte moved to the White House in her place, and the new building was abandoned.

About this time, certainly before 1774 when it was mentioned in the *Gentleman's Magazine*, George III built for Queen Charlotte the charming little thatched cottage in the Richmond gardens for breakfast, tea and picnics. This was decorated in 1805 by their artistic daughter, Princess Elizabeth. The Queen's Cottage is still standing, in 37 acres of grounds. These are kept in a semi-wild state as requested by Queen Victoria when she handed them to Kew Gardens to mark her Diamond Jubilee in 1897. During the spring the cottage is surrounded by a carpet of bluebells.

The present Kew Gardens evolved from the union of the gardens of Richmond and Kew. The right of way which divided them, Love Lane, was no longer needed after a bridge was built at Kew, and George III obtained an Act of Parliament in 1785 to close the lane, giving the parish some other land in its place on which to build a workhouse. This closure did not take effect until 1802. By this time the King and Queen had moved to the Dutch House, the present Kew Palace. **PMS**

LINLITHGOW PALACE

The roofless palace of Linlithgow between Edinburgh and Stirling is so well preserved that there have been several attempts to restore it to use. The former Prime Minister, Lord Rosebery, wanted to make it a national museum. Linlithgow, which has been termed 'the fairest royal house in Scotland', was one of the most used royal palaces of its kings and queens from the time of James I to James VI.

The palace is in a good defensive position, on a promontory projecting into the southern part of Linlithgow Loch close to Linlithgow, until recently a royal burgh. It is approached from the town up the Kirkgait, leading northwards to St Michael's Parish Church. By the west end of St Michael's is the gateway, the outer entry, called in earlier times 'Foir Entress' which leads into the Outer Close. Beyond, to the left, is the Peel, which takes its name from the peel or palisade built by Edward I to defend the fortress.

Linlithgow Palace is of simple design. Four high ranges surround a square courtyard, the Inner Close, with square towers at each corner. Nevertheless it was unique in Scotland during the Middle Ages. Spiral stairs, known as turnpikes, gave access at the four corners. At the south-west was the King's Turnpike and north-west the Queen's. The north-east was the Kitchen Turnpike, and that on the south-east served the Chapel and the Great Hall, known as the Lyon Chamber.

The ground floor contained guardrooms, while in the basement below, were the wine cellar, the 'laich' kitchen, with its well, and the windowless prison, a vaulted pit of 25 ft by 12 ft, where prisoners were thrust through a hatchway from the guardroom.

The principal apartments were on the first floor. South of the Court kitchen, in the north-east corner, was the Great Hall, situated between the corner towers on the east front, and taking its name from the large tapestry made in Bruges, which had one hung there, of the lyon rampant of the royal house of Scotland. Hooks for tapestries are still to be seen. This hall has a hammerbeam roof, except for the southern end above the fireplace, which was vaulted in stone. The fireplace, of three compartments, is one of the finest of its kind in Scotland. At this south end of the Lyon Chamber was the dais, to take the King's table, and at the northern end was an oak screen which supported the minstrel's gallery. Over the vestry, between the Lyon Chamber and the Chapel at the south-west corner, was the Chamber of Dease (*Chambre d'aise*) or Withdrawing Room, where the King retired from the high table. The Chapel led to a hall, and along the east front were the King's apartments, the King's

Linlithgow Palace seen from the south-east, looking across the loch. St Michael's Parish Church, close to the 'Foir Entress' is to the left of the picture

121

Hall, the Presence Chamber, and the King's Bedchamber with his Oratory; on the north front, until it was rebuilt by James VI, were the Queen's apartments.

In the centre of the Inner Close is an octagonal fountain, originally 19 ft high, of three tiers, the first and finest in Scotland. At its corners, on the buttresses, are all kinds of ornamental work, including remains of figures of a mermaid, a drummer, a whistler and St Michael. A lion supporter survives, sitting on a pedestal. This bears figures of nude boys, one playing a lute, one a whistle and the other bearing a scroll. Another has a winged deer, bearing figures of two gallants in slashed doublets, holding their sides with laughter, on either side of a twisted column.

The first mention of a royal manor at Linlithgow was in 1139, during the reign of David I. It would then have been of a motte and bailey design. During the wars of Scottish independence, Edward I of England established a fort here, spending the winter of 1301–1302. His architect was the experienced Savoyard, James of St George, who had built his Welsh castles, including Caernarvon. His masons were told 'to hasten the King's Chamber'. No doubt he had trouble from his workmen, for later, when they were at Dunfermline, 60 carpenters and 200 ditchers told him they were owed so much money at Linlithgow that they would rather go into exile than work for him again. In 1302, the garrison consisted of 83 men at arms and 100 foot.

Two winters later Linlithgow served as the base for an assault on Stirling Castle, and siege engines were taken there, while others were constructed on the spot. After Stirling surrendered that August, the hay stored in the Peel of Linlithgow was distributed among the army commanders.

In 1313, Linlithgow was still held by the English, though by then the King was the pleasure loving Edward II and not his stern father. Writs from London that year ordered that victuals and stores should be despatched from Berwick. Later the same year there occurred the well known episode, told by Barbour in his epic poem *The Bruce*. William Bunnock, a local farmer, who regularly delivered hay to the garrison, on this occasion hid eight armed men under the hay in his large wain, while a servant drove the oxen. Bunnock, walking at the side, arranged for the drawbridge to be lowered, the gate opened and the portcullis raised. As the wain stood in the middle of the gateway, interposing a complete barrier to its descent, Bunnock gave the prearranged signal. The driver cut the ropes which harnessed the oxen, the men leapt out of the wain and attacked the gate guard and Bunnock killed the porter. A party of armed men who lay hidden, helped to put the few English, most of whom were outside harvesting the hay, to the sword. Robert the Bruce rewarded Bunnock with grants of land, and the present family of Binning trace their descent from him. The heroic deed of their ancestor has resulted in the haywain featuring in their coat of arms. The following year Bruce won his victory over Edward II at Bannockburn, and the English fortifications were demolished.

Robert the Bruce's son, David II, rebuilt his royal manor, only to have it destroyed in 1424 by a fire. James I, back from his long captivity in England, immediately started to rebuild, the work continuing for most of his reign. Bringing his English Queen, Jane Beaufort, he frequently came to see the work in progress, such as in 1434 when they watched Matthew, the King's painter, decorate the royal apartments. Much of the palace which we see today was James I's work.

Though James I's grandson, James III, carried out some repairs in 1470, the next major work took place in his son's reign. However, he gave sanctuary after the Lancastrian defeat at Towton in 1461, to that sad king, Henry VI and his fiery wife, Margaret of Anjou. Margaret soon travelled to the continent to seek assistance, but saintly Henry remained at Linlithgow Palace for over a year.

Two years after James IV came to the throne, in 1488, he began to carry out work at Linlithgow, which was only concluded on his death on the battlefield of Flodden in 1513. Linlithgow was his favourite residence, and when in 1503 he married Princess Margaret, daughter of Henry VII, he made the palace part of her jointure. For her he rebuilt the south facade in the late English Gothic style. His work included the Chapel, which contained the organ made in 1513 by a Frenchman called Gilyem and he laid out gardens and orchards and surrounded the palace with dykes. He participated in many sports, away from the cares of state in Edinburgh, including archery on the Bowbutts, the flat ground by the loch, where he once lost his stakes in a match.

Queen Margaret's favourite retreat was a little vaulted chamber with window seats above the top of the north-western tower. This is still known as Queen Margaret's Bower, reached by 323 steps up the Queen's Turnpike to the top of the tower, and then a further seventeen from which, on a clear day, the peaks of the Grampians can be seen. Above was a watchman's post. In her bower, by tradition, the Queen waited in vain for the return of her husband when he was fighting at Flodden. Sir Walter Scott describes the scene in *Marmion*:

His own Queen Margaret, who, in Lithgow's tower,
All lonely sat, and wept the weary hour.

In the palace in 1512 was born their third son, James V, who became King of the Scots at the age of a year. His work at Linlithgow began when he reached the age of 21, and lasted for the rest of his reign.

James V altered the main entrance from the centre of the east front to the south front. The old entry, approached by steps, has three canopied niches. The central niche had a statue of the Pope, still there in 1689 when it was seen by an English visitor, Thomas Morer, and on each side were figures of a knight and a labourer. Above were angels holding scrolls.

As the result of the new entry, James V in 1535 built the new outer gateway by the west door of the church. On either side of its arched doorway is a semi-octagonal turret with a small gun-looped firing post. On the south side are carved representations, made in 1845, of the insignia of the four orders of chivalry which James IV held, the Garter, the Thistle, the Golden Fleece and St Michael, replacing the originals which were lost. He also erected the King's Fountain, which we know from a lead pipe excavated, was dated 1538.

On 8 December 1542 Mary Queen of Scots was born in Linlithgow Palace, six days before the death of her father, James V, who never saw her. Lisle and Tunstall reported in England that 'the Queen was delivered before her time of a daughter, a very weak child, and not likely to live'. Here she lived for the first seven months before her mother

The Inner Close of Linlithgow Palace, showing its most celebrated feature, the octagonal fountain, which was copied later at the Palace of Holyroodhouse

removed her to Stirling, the strongest castle in Scotland, for more safety.

Mary Queen of Scots' last visit to Linlithgow was on 23 April 1567. The next day, on her way to Edinburgh, she was abducted by Lord Bothwell, who was to become her third husband.

Her son, James VI, was often here before he inherited the English throne, and in 1585 took the unusual step of holding Parliament in the palace instead of in Edinburgh.

On his marriage to Anne of Denmark, Linlithgow Palace was given to her as part of her dowry, and in 1599 he appointed his cousin, Alexander seventh Lord Livingston, a nephew of one of his mother's favourite ladies, Mary Livingston, as his Hereditary Keeper of Linlithgow Castle. The next year at the christening of his son, the future Charles I, Livingston became Earl of Linlithgow, which became his principal residence. The new Earl was made responsible for the education of the King's two daughters, Elizabeth and Margaret. Margaret died at Linlithgow in March 1600, 15 months old, but Elizabeth became the grandmother of George I, and hence is an ancestress of the present Queen.

James embarked on considerable 'new work' at Linlithgow Palace from 1618 to 1620, employing William Wallace, his master mason, in rebuilding the north front in the Scottish Classical Renaissance style. During this work he probably removed the room which was the birthplace of his mother, Mary Queen of Scots.

James's son, Charles I, was the last king to sleep in the palace. When he came here in 1633, there was much bustling activity. All 'middens and bakers whin heaps' had to be cleared from the street, houses near the palace approach with turf roofs had to be replaced by slates, and the inhabitants had to wear suitable clothes for the occasion. After his departure the palace became neglected. It was commented at the time that with the departure of the King, the royal swans left the loch, only to return at the Restoration.

When Cromwell came in the winter of 1650, he was only concerned with military operations, and for the erection of his fortress, he pulled down the hospital, Minister's house, the school and Town House, for their materials. In 1668, Lord Fountainhall said in his diary: 'the Palace which have been werie magnificent is now for the most part ruinous.'

James II came to Linlithgow as Duke of York, as did his grandson, Bonnie Prince Charlie on Sunday 15 September 1745, on his way from Stirling to make his triumphant entry into Edinburgh two days later. Then, in the campaign against the Prince, on 31 January 1746, the palace was burnt due to the carelessness of Butcher Cumberland's soliders. His troops kindled fires, and when they left the palace these were still burning. The straw on which they lay caught fire. The magistrates, who were mostly anti-Cumberland, did nothing, but many of the burgesses of the burgh took some of the contents to their own homes until they were ordered to return them.

Linlithgow Palace now remained roofless and untenanted. In 1832 the Commissioner of Woods and Forests, later the Ministry of Works, took it over, and in the 1890's considerable repairs were done to floors, wall heads and lintels. The Department of the Environment now maintains the palace, on behalf of the Secretary of State for Scotland.

On 11 July 1914, glory briefly returned to the palace of Linlithgow. King George V and Queen Mary, on a beautiful summer's day, held Court in the Lyon Chamber. **PMS**

124

LONDON HOUSES

17 Bruton Street

Two important royal occasions happened at 17 Bruton Street, the short road which connects Berkeley Square to Bond Street in London's fashionable Mayfair. This was the town house of the Earl and Countess of Strathmore, and from here their youngest daughter, Lady Elizabeth Bowes Lyon, set out for her wedding to Prince Albert, recently created Duke of York, the second son of King George V. Here also, three years later, was born their eldest daughter Princess Elizabeth, now the Queen.

On Thursday 26 April 1923, large crowds gathered on the pavement outside this house to watch the royal bride leave for her wedding at Westminster Abbey. This was the first occasion on which a British prince had been married there since Plantagenet days, and on which a son of a king had married a non-royal bride at a public ceremony since the advent of the Tudor dynasty; thus the event excited the greatest public interest.

To the sound of cheering, the bride left with her father punctually at 11.12 on that wet morning, in a state landau, escorted by four mounted Metropolitan policemen. As the bride was not yet a member of the Royal Family, it was not until after the wedding that the escort presented arms.

After their wedding the Duke and Duchess of York were granted White Lodge in Richmond Park, the home before her marriage of the Duke's mother Queen Mary, but before long they found that it was too far away for their many royal engagements in London. Accordingly they looked for a suitable house in the capital. Before they had settled on one, the Duchess was expecting her first child, and the King agreed that his first grandchild in the male line should be born at the London home of the Duchess's parents.

Sir William Joynson-Hicks, generally known as 'Jix', the Home Secretary, was present as the constitution then required, when, on 21 April 1926, Princess Elizabeth was born in a first floor room of 17 Bruton Street. A regular flow of messengers and boys brought flowers and telegrams on this auspicious day, and No 17 became one of the most important houses in London. That afternoon, King George and Queen Mary drove over from Windsor to see their new grandchild.

When Princess Elizabeth was a few weeks old the King told the Duke of York that he was required to represent the Crown at the first Parliament of the Commonwealth of Australia to take place in the new federal capital of Canberra. Reluctantly the Duke and Duchess had to accept this first major assignment, a royal tour, first of New Zealand and then of Australia. They would greatly have preferred

The Duke and Duchess of York leave 17 Bruton Street for their tour of New Zealand and Australia in January 1927. They never returned to the house, their entourage having moved to Piccadilly

to be at home with their baby daughter, superintending the interior of the new house in Piccadilly which they had found before they left, but now its redecoration would have to be done during their absence.

Life at Bruton Street was busy preparing for the tour, and weekends were often spent at St Paul's Walden Bury. There was so much to be done and little time for entertaining.

The Princess was aged eight and a half months when the Duke and Duchess had the wrench of saying goodbye to her at the very beginning of January 1927. When the Duchess got into her car in Bruton Street for Victoria Station she had to be driven twice round Grosvenor Gardens to give her time to prepare for the greeting of the crowds and the farewells at the station.

During the time the Duke and Duchess were away, the two grandmothers, Queen Mary and the Countess of Strathmore, were in charge of the baby, which was in the capable hands of Miss Clara Knight, the nanny who had once looked after the Duchess. Affectionately known as Alah (a name given by her charges who could not pronounce Clara),

she had come to Lady Strathmore when her youngest child, David Bowes Lyon, was one day old.

When the Duke and Duchess of York returned home, on 27 June 1927, they drove straight to their new house, where their fourteen month-old daughter was already installed. Bruton Street thus fades as a royal home, but its memory is retained by the Queen Mother with affection for the happy days she spent there.

17 Bruton Street was one of the most imposing houses there and was built, probably by Isaac Ware, in the classical style in 1742. Previous owners had been Lord Rosebery, Lord Ebrington and the Earl of Carnarvon. In 1937, the house, with others, was demolished to make way for a large block, Berkeley Square House. Today the ground and first floors of the Bruton Street frontage are occupied by a bank, Lombard North Central Limited. In the entrance hall there is a reminder that 'here was born on 21 April 1926 the Princess Elizabeth who was to become Queen Elizabeth II'. There is also a plaque on the outside, between the two entrance doors, telling the history of the house and the royal event which took place on this site in 1926.

145 Piccadilly

The first London home of the Duke and Duchess of York was 145 Piccadilly, where they lived for nearly ten years until they became King George VI and Queen Elizabeth. This was at Hyde Park Corner, half a mile up Constitution Hill from Buckingham Palace. Four doors away was Apsley House, popularly called 'Number One, London' the one-time home of the 'Iron Duke' and subsequent Dukes of Wellington.

Houses to the west of Hamilton Place were originally called Piccadilly Terrace. No 145, like its neighbours, was an elegant stone faced house of four storeys in a terrace, built about 1795 from designs by the Adam brothers, but as the Department of Woods and Forests required them to be refaced with stone when the leases fell in, the exterior lost traces of the original design.

The first owner was Sir John Smith-Burges, 30 years a director of the East India Company who had recently been created a baronet by George III. When his widow, then the Dowager Countess Poulett, died the lease was acquired by the first Marquess of Northampton, an eminent scientist who was President of the Royal Society. Three successive Lords Northampton made this their town house, and though later occupants were the brewer Sir William Bass and Albert von Goldschmidt-Rothschild, son-in-law of Baron Edmond James of the French branch of the Rothschild family, the name of Northampton House was continued. As late as 1947, Sir George Leveson-Gower, still referred to it as such in his *Mixed Grill.*

After a long hunt for a suitable London house, the Duke and Duchess of York had decided on 145 Piccadilly just before they left on their Australiasian tour early in January 1927. Having been empty for six years the house had become extremely delapidated. The owners, the Crown Estate Commissioners, had agreed to repair the fabric, and the Duke would pay for the lease on a yearly basis and add an extra bedroom that he required. While the Duke and Duchess were overseas the house was made ready so that they could take immediate possession on returning home.

Though the tall house with its narrow frontal looked rather austere from the front, the Duke and Duchess converted it into a comfortable home with exquisite taste. The size of their household was modest according to royal standards at that period.

The forecourt lay behind iron railings, and double black painted doors led into a short wide hall with light green pillars, with the dining room on the left. Beyond the hall, three wide steps led into the morning room which became the most frequently used room in the house. Here dinner parties were occasionally held, if too large for the dining room which could only seat twelve. A french window opened onto the private grounds at the rear, Hamilton Gardens, which contained a small lake where mallards nested, and from here a gate led onto Hyde Park. The drawing room was on the first floor, with the nurseries at the top of the house, which opened on to a circular gallery under a large glass dome. There was a first floor balustrade, stone balconies outside the second floor windows, and another balustrade concealing the roof.

On 21 August 1930, a younger daughter, Princess Margaret Rose, as she was then always called, was born to the

Opposite: 145 Piccadilly, where the Duke and Duchess of York were living at the time of the abdication

Duchess at her father's seat of Glamis Castle in Scotland. Miss Clara Knight concentrated most of her attentions on the new baby, leaving the under-nurse, the Scottish Miss Margaret MacDonald, known as Bobo, to look after Princess Elizabeth. Miss MacDonald's younger sister, Ruby was also recruited as a nursery maid. The two children played in Hamilton Gardens, and were taken for walks in Hyde Park until crowds made these expeditions difficult. Sightseers came to know that most afternoons a royal carriage, drawn by two bay horses, arrived to take the two princesses and their nannies for a two hour drive. Weekends were usually spent at the Royal Lodge, Windsor Great Park, which the King gave to the Duke and Duchess of York in 1931.

The Duke and Duchess did not entertain formally on a great scale. Most of their functions at 145 Piccadilly were connected with organisations with which they were involved. For example, the Duchess was Colonel-in-Chief of the King's Own Yorkshire Light Infantry, and the officers and their wives used to come to an annual tea party, at which the princesses were present.

This pleasant and relatively carefree life at 145 Piccadilly came to an abrupt end in December 1936 after the abdication crisis. On King George V's death that previous January, his eldest son Edward VIII became King, and his next son, the Duke of York, the heir presumptive. Tension over a possible abdication was rife when the Duke and Duchess returned from Scotland on Thursday morning, 3 December. Then, on the fateful day which followed, the King made his decision to abdicate in favour of his brother. On their return from the Royal Lodge, the Duchess was suffering from acute influenza, and could not be at her husband's side during the next few dramatic days.

The Duke, with endless visits to make to Windsor, 10 Downing Street, Marlborough House and others, returned late in the evening with his private secretary to Piccadilly, when he was chagrined to see the large crowds which had collected outside. Some shouted 'Long Live King Edward', but many more cheered the Duke. Next day, at 10 am Edward VIII signed his instrument of abdication in the drawing room of Fort Belvedere, witnessed by the Duke of York.

145 Piccadilly remained 'the King's palace' for the next two months, but for much of this time the Royal Family were at Sandringham during their Christmas holiday. When they returned to London on 17 February 1937, they moved straight into Buckingham Palace, which had been hastily prepared for them, for there was much to be done and the coronation to prepare. Stands along Piccadilly had already been erected for King Edward VIII, who was never crowned, and the same day, 12 May, was chosen for the coronation of the new King.

The Royal Family, particularly the two Princesses, missed the informal atmosphere of 145 Piccadilly when they moved into the grandeur of Buckingham Palace, but the same free and easy existence continued at weekends at the Royal Lodge. Princess Margaret, when told that no longer would her signature contain the words 'of York' is said to have exclaimed in disgust, "I'd only just learnt to write 'of York'."

145 Piccadilly received a direct hit on 7 October 1940, at 7.45 in the evening. Two people were hurt. The house remained in a derelict state until 1959, when it was demolished to make way for the new road which circles round Hyde Park Corner to link up with the underpass. **PMS**

NONSUCH PALACE

Of all England's vanished royal palaces none has so captured popular imagination as Nonsuch. One translation of Leland's Latin verse sums it up as:

that which no equal has in art or fame
Britons deservedly do Nonsuch name.

Henry VIII spent much of the last decade of his life in planning and executing the building of a palace which would be 'the pearl of the realm,' and would, moreover rival King Francis I of France's magnificent Chateau of Chambord as the wonder of Christendom.

Accordingly, in 1538, King Henry acquired the manor of Cuddington near Ewell in Surrey, by giving the owner a Suffolk manor in compulsory exchange. He then grandly swept away the village, manor and church to make way for his creation. Nonsuch was surrounded with the Great Park stretching northwards towards Malden, and the Little Park to the south. In all, 1,200 acres were enclosed and stocked with deer. Cartloads of thirteenth-century stone were brought over from the priory of Merton a few miles off, which, conveniently, had been dissolved and pulled down only a few days earlier.

520 workmen were engaged on the building, living in tents on the site. They were ordered to complete their work as expeditiously as possible. Not surprisingly many rumours spread around. A cowman in Oxfordshire was prosecuted for saying that workmen employed in other palaces would be dismissed since 'His Grace hath begun one other new work which shall be called None Such'.

Nonsuch was planned around two courts, the Inner and the Outward. The building of the Inner Court was completed about 1541, and work began on the elaborate decoration. Craftsmen from Italy and France working, it is said, under the direction of Toto del Nunziata, the King's Sergeant Painter, (although no documentary proof has been discovered that this was so) took at least four years to complete this intricate plan. King Henry's last wife, Catherine Parr, came over in September 1544, and in the following year, the King himself came to bully the supervisor of the plasterworkers for the slow rate of progress. Henry came back in June 1545 for his first royal progress to Nonsuch, when he stayed for three days. During his visit he watched hunting in progress from a 'standing' in the park, no doubt sighing that he could no longer participate. Up to 15 November 1545, the known expenditure on Nonsuch totalled £24,536 7s 7d.

Henry VIII died in 1547 without seeing the completed palace. Evelyn and many later writers have assumed that the Outward Court was built by Lord Arundel or Lord Lumley in a later age, but according to the researches of John Dent, in his *Quest for Nonsuch*, this was not so. What remained unfinished was relatively unimportant.

The palace was approached through the Bowling Green. The three-storeyed gatehouse of the Outward Court, 'very strong and graceful' was twice the height of the remainder of the buildings which surrounded it, which had only two storeys. Built of freestone, the court contained apartments on the first floor for courtiers, while below were those of the household servants. Flagged pathways crossed the cobbled courtyard, with an archway to the left leading to the kitchen court and another on the right to the stables. Ahead was the inner gatehouse 'which outdoes the first by one tower, a clock, a symphony, and six gilded horoscopes'. On each side of the building, which divided off the two courts, were chambers; to the left of the gateway the wine cellar, and to the right, probably the buttery.

The Inner Court, which contained the royal apartments, was decorated in white and gold with all the sumptuousness of the Renaissance. 'When you have greeted its threshold and seen with dazzled eyes, the shining lustre of the stone, glittering with purest gold,' wrote the Vicar of nearby Cheam, 'it is not surprising if it should hold you senseless.' The inner walls of the ground floor were of stone, and the walls of the upper floor timber. Between the studs of the main timbers were plaster models of classical gods and goddesses and below, a representation of the arts and virtues, which Cromwell's Commissioners were later to call 'a fair and very curious structure'. Engravings show us that this was also repeated on the outer walls of the court.

At the far corners of the Inner Court were two towers, 'the chief ornament of the whole house of Nonsuch,' stretching five storeys high, with oriels, heraldic beasts, cupolas, pennants and weather vanes. The south front is the most famous aspect of Nonsuch. It is portrayed by Speed in his map of Surrey published in 1610, and also in the earlier drawing by Hoefnagel, the original of which is in the Print and Drawings Department of the British Museum. There is a painting in the Fitzwilliam Museum at Cambridge, dated about 1620, with a view of the west wall, which was long thought to represent Richmond Palace, and another from the north-east at Berkeley Castle, painted by Danckerts, wrongly called 'St James's Palace.'

In the centre of the Inner Court was a white marble fountain, which a Swiss visitor, Thomas Platter, noted in

PALATIVM REGIVM IN ANGLIÆ REGNO APPELLATVM NONCIVTZ,
Hoc eft nufquam fimile .,

Effigiauit Georgius Houfnaglius Anno 1582.

Opposite: The south front of Nonsuch as drawn by Speed in his map of Surrey 1610
Above: Hoefnagel's drawing showing Queen Elizabeth I arriving at Nonsuch in 1582

1599, showed 'a griffin angrily spewing water with great violence'.

The exuberant Vicar of Cheam, Anthony Watson, takes us on a guided tour of the interior, graphically describing the scene:

> An archway leads, by the ascent of eight steps to the royal court. . . . Everywhere there are kings, Caesars, sciences, gods. Since the whole edifice is royal, it is divided into a king's side and a queen's side, on either side of the square. The King's way is guarded night and day by Scipio, clothed in bronze garments, and the Queen's way by warlike Penthesilia.
>
> Setting foot, with Scipio's permission, into the royal quarters you will first see the spacious chamber of the royal guard. From there the way goes up by generous winding steps, leading to the most glorious precincts of the royal presence. The precincts look out one way on the riches of the courtyard, and the other way on the perplexing twists of the maze and the scented beauty of the garden. From there, leaving the closets on the right, extends the dignified approach to the king's privy chamber. . . .
>
> A somewhat narrower room leads, to the right, to a lofty tower if you go right up, to a richly planted garden if you go down; while to the left it leads into two fine chambers exclusively reserved for the king. Adjoining these is the royal bedchamber. At the back is sited a gallery. From the king's quarters we go across to the queen's, which are accorded the unrestricted benefit and use of the gallery and are marked by the same spaciousness and ornamentation as the king's, as far as the gate of Penthesilia.
>
> . . . . The door which opens to the right of the king, leads into the garden. From there if you turn your gaze to the lofty towers, the turretted walls, the projecting windows, the plaster-work, the exquisite statues, you will wonder whether you are walking in courtyard or garden, for the face of each has the same splendour and majesty.
>
> Leaving the garden, we enter the wilderness, which is, in fact, neither wild nor deserted. The land, which is naturally somewhat hilly and plentifully watered, is set out with lofty and magnificent treelined walks to the south and west. At the end of the path to the south, the trees have been trimmed to form canopies.

Walking through the wilderness you would come upon the Grove of Diana, a glade with topiary, arches, walls and sandy walks, with a great marble fountain of the goddess. 300 yards to the west of the palace, was the Banqueting House decorated with the King's heraldic beasts.

After Henry VIII's death, his son the boy-king Edward VI, scarcely visited Nonsuch, although a few meetings of the Privy Council were held there. His half-sister and successor, Queen Mary, much preferred Oatlands, and contemplated demolishing Nonsuch. In 1556, her Lord Steward of the Household, the Earl of Arundel, persuaded her to sell him the palace and the Little Park. He then completed and embellished Nonsuch 'for the love and honour he bore to his old master and godfather'.

Two years later, Elizabeth I was on the throne, and

continued Lord Arundel's appointment. In the first summer of her reign, he invited her to Nonsuch for a week's festivities. For her entertainment there was a masque 'with drums and flutes, and all ye music that could be till midnight,' a play acted by the boys of St Paul's School, and a banquet which lasted until three o'clock in the morning. Bets were placed as to whether Lord Arundel would become the Queen's suitor despite the fact that he was twice a widower of nearly double her age.

When Lord Arundel first came to Nonsuch, he brought with him his son-in-law Lord Lumley, whose magnificent library, housed in the palace, was reputedly the best in private hands in England. Lord Lumley, like his father-in-law, was heavily burdened by debt, and in 1591 he offered the palace to his sovereign in recompense.

The most dramatic event at Nonsuch occurred at the end of September 1599. The Queen's erstwhile favourite, Robert Devereux, Earl of Essex, deserted his post as Lord Lieutenant of Ireland, where he had acted against the Queen's expressed orders and rode hotfoot to explain himself in a personal appeal to her. His pursuer, Lord Grey of Wilton, overtook him by ten minutes, and on his arrival was already informing the Queen's Secretary, Cecil, of what had occurred.

Rowland Whyte gives an eye-witness account:

Upon Michaelmas Eve, about 10 o'clock in the morning, my lord of Essex lighted at the court gate post, and made all haste to the presence, and so to the Privy Chamber, and stayed not till he came up to the Queen's bedchamber, where he found the Queen all newly up, the hair about her face; he kneeled unto her, kissed her hands, and had some private speech with her, which seemed to give him great contentment. . . .

'Tis much wondered at here that he went so boldly to her Majesty's presence, she being not ready, and he so full of dirt and mire that his very face was full of it.

The Queen wrinkled, without her red wig and with no rouge on her cheeks, politely asked Essex to return later that morning. Two interviews followed, and at ten that night Essex was ordered to be confined to his rooms. On Monday the Queen made her pleasure known; Essex was to leave Court, and be confined in London. Then followed Essex's madcap revolt and finally his execution in the Tower. The Queen never saw her Robin again.

James I had little regard for Nonsuch and made the palace over to his wife Anne of Denmark but he spent £5,600 on it and the estate was increased.

Charles I gave the palace to his wife, Henrietta Maria, and our knowledge of the domestic arrangements dates from this period. During the Civil War, Algernon Sidney was in residence and other prominent Roundheads, but on the Restoration the palace reverted to the Queen Dowager.

In the plague year of 1665, the Exchequer moved to 'the Queen's House' at Nonsuch, which shortly afterwards was visited both by Pepys and Evelyn. A year after the death in 1669 of Henrietta Maria, her son Charles II granted the palace to his grasping mistress, Barbara Villiers, Lady Castlemaine, whom he created Duchess of Cleveland and Baroness Nonsuch. He was already tiring of her, and these valuable gifts were probably by way of a sop.

Barbara Villiers was straight away plunged into a lengthy dispute with the Park Keeper, the first Earl of Berkeley, who himself was guilty of demolishing the Banqueting House, for which the notorious Barbara has often been blamed. In her attempt to rid herself of him, in 1682 she demolished the Inner Court and told him of her intention to dispark Nonsuch. Not only was disparking illegal, but Lord Berkeley had a 60 year lease on the Outward Court.

The dispute eventually led to an affray, when Barbara's son, the Duke of Grafton was accused of forcing an entry with swords, sticks and hammers. The case went before a court of law, but in 1687 the Duke was cleared on the technical point that his indictment had been wrongly worded. The Berkeleys then lost interest in Nonsuch.

As a palace, Nonsuch had been in existence for less than 150 years, and its demolition was a tragedy. The Great and Little Parks were mortgaged and eventually sold separately, the former becoming known as Worcester Park, after a former Keeper of the Park, the Earl of Worcester. A new mansion at Nonsuch was built on another site at the beginning of the nineteenth century. In 1935, what was left at Nonsuch Park, approximately one seventh of the original two parks, was purchased by the local authorities, and the London and Surrey County Councils. The palace and Banqueting House were successfully excavated in 1959 and 1960, but so far no markings have been made to show visitors the extent of the buildings of royal Nonsuch. **PMS**

Nonsuch from the west in about 1620. It is from this period that the records of the domestic arrangements have survived

OATLANDS

The large estate of Oatlands which stretched from the High Street, Walton to Thames Street, Weybridge, and from the River Thames southwards to St George's Hill, was first amalgamated by two brothers at the end of the fifteenth century. They were John Reed, a lawyer, and Bartholomew, a rich goldsmith of the City of London, who became Lord Mayor in 1502.

Henry VIII who used to hunt at Oatlands, when he became the master of Hampton Court, wished to take over this adjoining estate on the western extremity of his new deer park and in 1537 forced the Reeds to exchange with some property belonging to the suppressed Tandridge Priory. Immediately he demolished part of the house to ground level and constructed a new range of buildings and a gatehouse. Three years afterwards, he replaced the moat by a culvert.

At first the King enlarged Oatlands as a royal hunting lodge, but when his fourth marriage to Anne of Cleves was being negotiated he decided to convert the house into a palace to become the Queen's dower house. Materials were brought down the river: stone from Chertsey and Bisham Abbey, marble from Abingdon; and special red bricks were made at Woking. Anne quickly agreed to a divorce, and according to some accounts it was at Oatlands that the King married for the fifth time, to Catherine Howard (others said the ceremony was at Hampton Court). At all events it took place in secrecy on 28 July 1540 when the palace was

An engraving showing the view from the terrace at Oatlands with the River Wey winding into the distance

uncompleted. Then, after his sixth marriage (to Catherine Parr), he was busily occupied with his new brainchild, Nonsuch, and lost interest in Oatlands.

One approached the palace from the south-west from Monument Green, Weybridge, through the outer gate into the Outer Court. This was surrounded by a brick wall, of which a small part still exists on a council estate. On this side were the stables, and on the right a range of low buildings, some of which were constructed by Queen Elizabeth.

A broad and many-gabled principal front, with a turretted central gatehouse, led to the Middle Court, which was traversed by paths. Here were ranged the principal buildings, the Great Hall, Chapel and private apartments.

On the far side, a taller gatehouse with an octagonal turret led to buildings which formed an irregular triangle. The gatehouse led into the Inner Court, which contained a circular tower with projecting upper storey to the right, beyond which were the Privy Gardens, and a court of further buildings to the left. The apex of the triangle, overlooking the river, terminated with a tall turretted rectangular building.

The palace was depicted in the Wyngaerde sketches and Gough's engraving in the sixteenth century. The site was

excavated in 1968, when foundations of parts of Henry VIII's palace were revealed.

The interior was luxuriously furnished with tapestries, cloth of gold and 'carpets of Turque', and outside were terraces leading to the pleasance, then orchards, and onwards to the deer park. A new bridle way was constructed leading to Hampton Court, and another to Cobham.

Queen Elizabeth used to come in the summer to shoot deer, and some yew trees were termed 'Queen Elizabeth's Bowshot'. James I also came to hunt, and his wife Anne of Denmark constructed a brick built silkworm house in the middle of the mulberry gardens, at a cost of £600. The staircase in it was richly ornamented, and the windows contained the Queen's arms, but despite the surroundings it never prospered. There was also a large vineyard, and the gardens became famous.

In the first year of James I, reign in England, 1603, the Venetian, Scaramelli reported to his Doge a description of Prince Henry and one of his sisters:

> I have visited the Princes at Oatlands, to the great satisfaction of themselves, the King and Queen. The Prince is ten years old, little of body and quick of spirit. He is ceremonious beyond his years, and with great gravity he covered and bade me to be covered. Through an interpreter he gave me a long discourse on his exercises, dancing, tennis, the chase. He then himself conducted me down one flight of stairs and up another to meet the Princess. I found her surrounded by her Court under a canopy. They both said they mean to learn Italian.

Charles I's wife, Henrietta Maria, gave birth to her youngest son Henry, Duke of Gloucester, at Oatlands in 1640. He was to live for twenty years until just after the Restoration of his brother Charles II, when he died of smallpox. The last visit Charles I paid to Oatlands was in 1642, accompanied by his Royalist army, after they were repulsed in his unsuccessful attack on London.

On the orders of the Parliamentary Commissioners, Oatlands Palace was sold to Richard Turbridge, a Londoner, who demolished it between 1650 and 1652, and sold the bricks, timber, tiles and other materials. There remained a hunting lodge on the higher land about half a mile to the east of the palace, which was then sold.

On the Restoration, the estate was given back to the Queen Mother as part of her dower, and she leased it to her alleged lover and Master of the Horse, Lord Jermyn, newly created Earl of St Albans, whom Macaulay calls 'a dissolute lad'. Later the hunting lodge and lands were leased to the Herberts and in 1716 to Henry Clinton, seventh Earl of Lincoln, who rebuilt the house as his seat, where he died in 1728.

His son Henry, Earl of Lincoln, who was later created Duke of Newcastle, in 1791 sold the estate to George III's second son Frederick, 'the Grand old Duke of York', who became Commander-in-Chief of the Army. This was just prior to his marriage to the Prussian Princess Frederica, Frederick the Great's niece, and he vastly increased the parkland. Two years later, when away in Flanders, Oat-

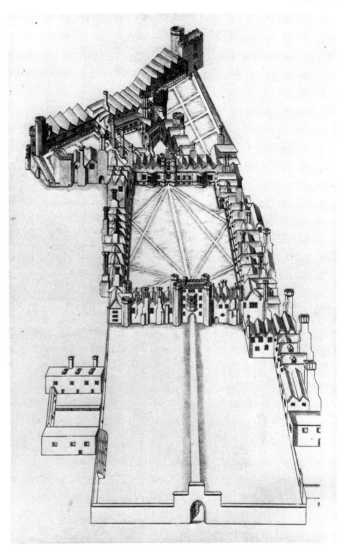

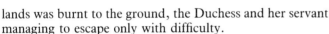

lands was burnt to the ground, the Duchess and her servant managing to escape only with difficulty.

In 1794 Henry Holland was commissioned to rebuild the house. It became a fine seat with views over the Broad Water at the bottom of the ridge, the Thames beyond to the north, and the North Downs to the south. Both the Yorks were eccentric characters. The Duchess, who was frequently alone at Oatlands, spent much of her time in the Grotto, which had been built in 1740 for Lord Lincoln by Lane of Tisbury at a cost of over £40,000. This contained four rooms. There was a subterranean gaming room, in which the Duke and Duchess spent long hours at play, a hall of stalactites, and another room with a pool, which Greville said was 'as clear as crystal and as cold as ice'. In the upper rooms the Duchess often had her meals and spent much of the night. Surrounding her were her 40 dogs, many monkeys, each with its own pole with a house on top, and several parrots. The Grotto survived until 1948, together with the statue of Venus which is now in the Weybridge Museum.

Outside the Grotto was the dogs' cemetery, with headstones containing names such as Grill, Grog and Gruel. Special favourites had memorial verses written by the Duchess. In 1871 Queen Victoria had the stones renovated. A few still survive.

The Duke of York, easily amused by the vulgarities of his friends, (as Greville noted, 'he has the feelings of an English gentleman'), was always in debt, like his brother

Above left: A drawing of a reconstruction of Oatlands Palace in Guildford Museum
Right: Richard Gough's engraving of the palace during the reign of Elizabeth I

and Prince Regent. When at dinner he once proposed the health of Mr Coutts as 'my banker for upwards of 30 years', Coutts was heard to say quietly 'it is your Royal Highness who has done *me* the honour to keep my money for 30 years'. In 1804 he obtained an Act of Parliament to give him the freehold instead of his Crown lease, thereby enabling him to raise a mortgage, but he agreed to keep Oatlands secure for the Duchess's lifetime.

When his brother became George IV in January 1820, the Duke became heir presumptive to the throne, and at his brother's flamboyant coronation, he was overhead exclaiming "By God, I'll have everything the same at mine", though this was not to be.

The Duchess died in August 1820, and four years later, the Duke sold Oatlands for £145,000 to Edward Hughes Ball-Hughes, who was nicknamed 'Golden Ball' from his wealth, which he quickly squandered. The Duke of York preceded his brother to the grave in 1827, and thus never realised his expensive dreams.

'Golden Ball' reconstructed the house, and all that remains of Holland's work are the fine gate piers. Oatlands was purchased by a syndicate, and converted into a hotel, Oatlands Park, which it is today. **PMS**

RICHMOND PALACE

When Henry VII erected Richmond Palace in 1501 it was the largest and most magnificent of his residences, covering ten acres of land. Today there is little left but the gatehouse and Wardrobe Court. Both the Palace of Richmond to the south-west of London and Greenwich, or Placentia, to the south-east, situated on the southern bank of the Thames, played a large part in the history of the Tudor dynasty.

In 1305 Edward I was King, and at Sheen he treated with the Scottish Commissioners after the execution of Sir William Wallace, when he forced them to accept his *Ordinances for the Establishment of Government*. Sheen was later made over to Isabella of Valois, the dissolute wife of Edward II, known as 'the she-wolf of France.'

After Isabella died in 1358, her son Edward III lost no time in carrying out extensive works at Sheen to make it one of his finest houses. The editor of *The King's Works* comments that this manor, together with Langley, Buckinghamshire, were to him what Osborne and Balmoral were to Queen Victoria, and Sandringham was to Edward VII. The manor then consisted of two courts, the upper, or Over, of farm buildings, and the lower, or Down, on the

river bank, approached by a bridge over the moat through a gatehouse. Edward III died in 1377 at Sheen a lonely old man, deserted even by his grasping mistress Alice Perrers, who we are told, had forced the rings off his fingers as he lay dying.

Richard II, who was devoted to Sheen no less than his grandfather, continued to beautify the manor. One of his improvements was to purchase from Katherine Lyghtfote, 2,000 painted tiles for the 'room set apart for the King's bath.' In 1384–8 he built for his adored wife, Anne of Bohemia, a new house on an island called *la Neyt* in the river, which was constructed of timber on stone foundations. This consisted of several chambers with fireplaces and a kitchen. At the same time he erected a paling round the island and bought a new barge to reach the river bank. Until 1394 Richard, with his new Queen and Court, came to Sheen whenever possible. In that year she became ill and soon afterwards died. Adam of Usk noted that the grief-stricken King then gave orders for Sheen to be 'utterly destroyed'. By a writ of the Privy Seal, John Gedney, Clerk of the Works, had orders to demolish 'the buildings in the court within the moat and the court without the moat,' including the house and buildings of *la Neyt*. Some of the materials were removed for use at the Tower of London.

When Henry V became King in 1413 he decided to rebuild Sheen, and in the following year the *Chronicles of London* stated that 'the King's great work was begun'. Materials were brought from the two houses of Sutton near Chiswick, and Byfleet near Weybridge which he no longer wanted, and two manors were erected at Sheen, where the name of Byfleet continued to be used. As the accounts show that the King spent £5,815 on 'Byfleet next to the manor

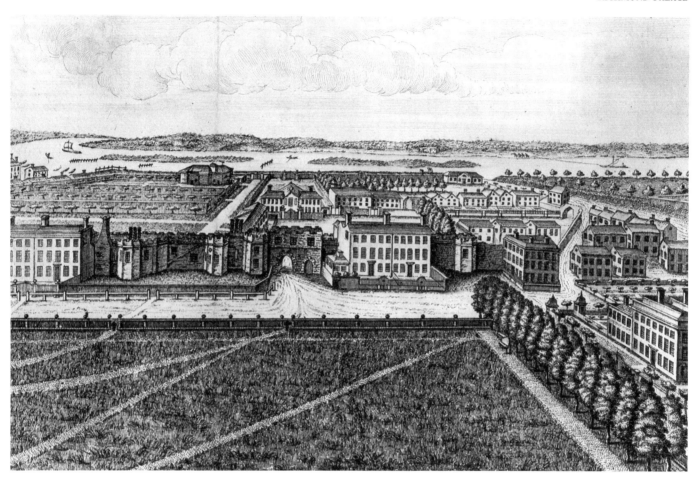

of Sheen,' and only £2,368 on the other manor, it seems probable that the former was his residence – it had a King's and a Queen's Ward – and the latter was used for lodgings and offices. Byfleet was a moated mansion of half-timber. The manor was surmounted by a great antelope, one of the King's heraldic beasts. White stone was brought from Caen and bricks from Calais, to make what the King's biographer, Thomas of Elmham, called 'a delightful mansion of skilful and costly architecture and becoming to the royal dignity'.

Work was uncompleted at Henry V's early death in 1422, and was continued in the minority of his son, Henry VI. In the years from 1436 to 1439 £1,015 was spent, and a great moat, 24 ft wide and 8 ft deep, was dug. Nevertheless much needed to be done when in 1445 the King married Margaret of Anjou. Nicholas says 'the Queen's lodgings were absolutely desolate and unfit for her reception'. New buildings were then erected by William Cleve, Clerk of Works.

Little was done to Sheen during the Wars of the Roses. William of Worcester came on a visit during Edward IV's reign and gave the dimensions of the Great Hall in paces. According to *The King's Works*, it measured about 77 ft by 40 ft, and the courtyard about 175 ft by 208 ft. In 1466 Edward IV gave the manor as part of her jointure to his Queen, Elizabeth Woodville, for life, and she held it until Richard III deprived her of her estates. The royal children were partly brought up at Sheen, including Elizabeth of York who married Henry VII.

When Henry VII, previously Earl of Richmond, acquired the throne, he again made Sheen a principal royal residence. Then, one day at the end of 1497 (some say 1499) disaster struck. The *Chronicles of London* record that: 'this year the

Opposite: The north-east front of Henry VII's palace showing the gateway on Richmond Green
Above: An engraving of 1742 showing the remains of the palace as it was then

King kept his Christmas at his manor of Sheen, and where upon St Thomas Day at night in the Christmas week about nine of the of the clock, began a great fire within the King's lodging'. As a result the manor was completely burnt out. The ashes were searched for treasures, and the Privy Purse accounted for £20 'for rewards given to them that found the King's jewels'.

King Henry decided to rebuild a palace which would impress everyone with the power of the Tudors. By 1501 work had been completed. In that year, according to the *Chronicles of London*, 'from this time forward it was commanded by the King that it should be called or named Richmount because his father and he were Earls of Rychemonde' in Yorkshire. Nevertheless, until it was swept away by George III the name of West Sheen continued to be used for the hamlet which clustered round the old Carthusian monastery, founded by Henry V in expiation of his father's murders of Richard II and Archbishop Scrope.

Although there is no existing plan of Richmond Palace, 'this earthly and second paradise of our region of England,' as it was called, we have a good idea of what the exterior looked like from Wyngaerde's drawings of the 1560's, now in the Bodleian Library, Oxford, and those of Hollar 80 years later. There are many descriptions by visitors, including that of the Richmond Herald when the palace was first erected, from a manuscript now in the College of Arms. Above all, there is an extensive survey made in 1649 by the Commissioners of Parliament.

Richmond Palace faced the river to the south, and was approached from Richmond Green to the north through two gateways. To the east it extended as far as Friar's Lane, beyond which, in Water Lane, was the Convent of Observant Friars, which Henry VII founded two years before the palace was built. The lower outer ranges which surrounded the approaches were built of brick, which in 1503 was noted 'to be vaned and bent with towers in each corner and angle, and also in his midway. His openings be strong gates of double timber and heart of ash stuck full of nails wrought and thick and crossed with bars of iron'.

The left hand gate led from the Green to the Royal Wine Cellar Court, with an open tennis court to its left. Beyond stretched the Privy Garden, surrounded by a brick wall, 12 ft high, with fruit trees and vines. In the garden, as well as flowers and yews were 'many marvellous beasts as lions, dragons and other of divers kind, properly fashioned and carved'. Behind was the Royal Orchard, which contained a turtle dove's cage, and a lengthy gallery which sloped diagonally to the right to join the Privy Lodging.

The main or outer gateway on the right, which still exists, has a four centred perpendicular arch, 18 ft high and 11 ft 3 ins wide. This has a stone plaque on which were sculptured Henry VII's arms and supporters, the Red Dragon of the Tudors and the Greyhound of York. This led into the Great Court, with an open gallery and the Wardrobe to the left. The paved courtyard, measuring 26 yards by 60 yards, was surrounded by a range of two-storeyed buildings for Gentlemen and Grooms of the Privy Chamber and Gentlemen of the Bedchamber.

To the south of the Great Court, through a turreted gatehouse, was the Middle Court. In the centre of the courtyard was a large ornamental fountain; 'in the upper part there are lions and red dragons and other goodly beasts, and in the midst certain branches of red roses out of which flowers and roses is evermore running, and course of clear and most purest water unto the cistern beneath'. To the left were ranged the Lord Chamberlain's lodgings and the Prince's Closet, and behind them, for the whole length of the court, the Chapel Royal, approached from the Middle Court by a flight of stairs. The Chapel, with 'handsome cathedral seats and pews,' then very unusual, 'a removable pulpit and a fair case of carved work for a pair of organs,' measured 96 ft by 30 ft. It was hung with arras and cloth of gold, and pictures of English kings who were saints. Below were two floors, one for the Yeoman of the Wine Cellar, and below it the wine cellar itself. On the far side of the Chapel, level with the Prince's Closet, was the Queen's Closet building of two storeys, with several rooms where lived the Queen, the princesses, and the Lady Margaret, the King's mother.

To the right of the Middle Court, parallel to the Chapel, was the Great Hall. This measured 100 ft by 40 ft, roofed with lead and supported on an undercroft, used for a buttery and other offices. Outside was the clock case, with a large bell and clock under it. Within, the Richmond Herald was impressed with the timber roof, neither beamed nor braced, and decorated with carved knots and hanging pendants. On the walls between the windows 'glazed right lightsome and goodly,' were pictures of warrior kings, 'in their harness and robes of gold', including that of King Henry himself. In the middle was a large brick hearth, the smoke from which was emitted through the domed turret called the *Louvre*. There was a large lantern in the roof, and a screen at the lower end, under a gallery.

A gateway from Middle Court led to the four-storeyed Canted Tower, 'the chief ornament unto the whole fabric,' containing 120 steps to the top, with a fine view over the palace. Everywhere were weather-vanes with the King's arms in rich gold and azure. Adjoining were the Privy Lodgings, the main residential part of the palace, three storeys high, built of brightly coloured stone, and having fourteen octagonal or cylindrical towers, capped with pinacles and cupolas. It ranged round a court of 24 ft by 40 ft, and had twelve rooms on each floor, including the principal rooms of state. On the middle floor were the Presence Chamber, the Privy Closet, the Withdrawing Chamber, and rooms known in the 1649 survey as 'the Duke of York's Bedchamber and the School Chamber'. Beyond the Privy Lodgings was the river.

The many kitchens, pantries and larders were situated to the right of the Great Hall. The Privy Kitchen had a large spired turret, and is to be seen in Wyngaerde's drawings to the west of the Great Hall. In a letter of 1554, one of Philip of Spain's household says that Queen Mary spent more than 3,000 ducats on victuals. 'From 80 to 100 sheep are usually consumed every day, a dozen head of cattle, a dozen and half of calves, to say nothing of what comes from the chase.'

Richmond was famous for its Library. In 1644, a French writer, Louis Jacob, said 'Henry VII, King of England, testified his regard for literature by the establishment of a Royal Library which he formed at Richmond.' The King's Privy Purse expenses show numerous purchases of books, manuscripts and elaborate bindings. Inigo Jones later carried out some repairs to the Library for Prince Henry, but as it was not mentioned in the 1649 survey, it is thought that the contents by then had been removed to Whitehall Palace.

A second fire broke out in 1506, when a gallery collapsed in flames, only a few minutes after the King and his family had walked along it, but repairs were completed within the year. Three years later the King died in the palace.

Henry VIII, was often at Richmond Palace, and participated in tilts and tourneys on Richmond Green. A son and heir, Henry, was born to Catherine of Aragon in the palace on New Year's Day 1611 with much rejoicing, but after a splendid christening, the boy died just over seven weeks later. Queen Catherine spent much time at Richmond, while her husband dallied in London with Anne Boleyn.

Queen Elizabeth I loved Richmond especially during the winter months. She called it 'a warm winter box to shelter her old age.' She was there for her last lingering illness when, piled on cushions, Cecil had to plead with her to go to bed. When, on 24 March 1603 she died at Richmond, the glories of this place departed for ever. The new King, James I, seldom came, but his athletic eldest son, Prince Henry, formed a picture gallery at the palace.

Though Charles I was seldom at Richmond, his children were here 'for the sweet air'. One of the last occasions he came was for a masque in 1636, which his son, the future Charles II took part in, as a boy and 'delighted everyone with his brightness and grace'.

In 1647 Parliament was anxious to take the King out of the army's hands and remove him to Richmond, but owing to the impeachment of the eleven members, the idea was abandoned. The palace fell into a ruinous state during the interregnum, and was sold to Thomas Rooksby and others, and later purchased for £10,000 by Sir Gregory Norton, one of the regicides, who refused to contribute to its upkeep.

In 1664 Charles II granted the manor, park and capital messuage to his younger brother James, Duke of York, afterwards James II. James contemplated rebuilding, and once asked Wren to do so, but nothing came of the idea. He also obtained a design from France. In June 1688, following the birth of an heir to his second wife, Mary of Modena, he had some parts restored as a nursery, and spent £1,800, principally in plastering, painting and glazing.

William III took no interest in the decayed palace, but some in the park, now the Old Deer Park and part of Kew Gardens, where he enlarged the lodge. Soon after his death in 1702, the park was acquired on a lease by the Ranger, the Duke of Ormonde, who partly rebuilt the lodge, which later was to become the home of George II when Prince of Wales.

The fragment of the palace on the left of the gateway is now known as the Old Palace. This and the gatehouse, until 1939, formed one house, but the Crown then partitioned walls in its passages, and converted the 30 rooms into two houses. The Old Court House, on the other side of the gateway, was built in the early eighteenth century, when the Wardrobe, in Old Palace Yard, once part of the Great Court, was reconstructed. On the south side of the yard, is the Trumpeters' House, confusingly known at one time as the Old Palace. It was built by Richard Hill, brother of Queen Anne's favourite Abigail Hill, and received its name from the two stone figures of boys blowing trumpets.

Also on the site of the palace is Maids of Honour Row, those fine houses built in 1724 for the maids to the Princess of Wales, and Lord Cholmondeley's house built in 1708, which became Queensberry House after the eccentric 'old Q', Lord Queensberry purchased it. Horace Walpole, in 1786, went round the house; this he found to be 'handsome and the views so rich, and the day was so fine that I could only have been more pleased if for half an hour I could have seen the real palace that once stood on that spot, and the persons represented walking about'. **PMS**

Two views of the reconstructed Richmond Palace. Above: An engraving showing the river front of the palace and (below) a 17th-century painting showing the whole scene

SOMERSET HOUSE

The present Somerset House stands between London's busy thoroughfare, the Strand and the River Thames, on the same site as the imposing Renaissance palace built by the Protector, Duke of Somerset, and afterwards the home of three Stuart queens.

When Jane Seymour became Henry VIII's third wife and mother of a king, her ambitious brother, Edward Seymour, climbed from being a mere Wiltshire squire to become Duke of Somerset and Protector of the Realm on behalf of his nephew, the boy-king Edward VI. To match his importance, he projected a great London palace in the most aristocratic part of the capital. These plans probably date from 1547, when he first became Protector after Henry's death. Accordingly the Duke cleared a large area of river frontage, 600 ft by some 500 ft, extending northwards to the Strand. He demolished the houses of three bishops, those of Chester, Worcester and Llandaff, the old church of St Mary-le-Strand (which he promised to rebuild, but this was not done until the eighteenth century) and several lesser buildings. An imposing entrance in the shape of a three-storey gatehouse was built on the Strand, with the main buildings ranged round an inner quadrangle, and the Great Hall to the south. Formal gardens extended to the river, which was reached through an ornate water gate.

Sir Nikolaus Pevsner comments that this palace 'marks the coming of a truer understanding of Franco-Italian Renaissance than existed in this Island before'. Nothing is known of the architectural details of the new palace nor the name of the designer. In John Thorpe's *Book of Drawings*, there is an elevation of the north front facing the Strand, which has such an affinity with Longleat, Wiltshire, as to make it seem likely that the same architect was responsible for both buildings. Sir John Thynne, the builder of Longleat, had been the secretary and steward of the Protector, and as such was largely responsible for the London palace. On the grounds of age alone, Thorpe himself could not have been the palace's designer.

As far as we know from his correspondence the Protector moved in while the house was still being constructed. Somerset Place, as it was called, was still far from being complete when Somerset's fall from power was engineered by his rival John Dudley, who made himself Duke of Northumberland. The Protector, Duke of Somerset, was beheaded on Tower Hill in January 1552, and his new palace declared forfeit to the Crown.

When Mary succeeded as Queen in the following year, she gave Somerset House to her half-sister Princes Elizabeth and it was hastily finished for about £900. Elizabeth seldom came to London in those dangerous times; in fact she spent three months in the Tower during her sister's reign. Somerset House must have had poignant memories for the Princess. As a young girl she was fascinated by the Protector's wild younger brother, Tom Seymour, who finished on the block. After Elizabeth I became Queen in 1558, she only visited Somerset House occasionally. At the beginning of her reign she travelled there by water 'with trumpets playing', from the Tower. She held several councils there before she moved just over a fortnight later, on 23 December, into Whitehall Palace in time for Christmas.

As there was then no permanent banqueting house at Whitehall, Somerset House was often used to impress vis-

Opposite: Two views of Somerset House (or Palace) as it was known in the 17th century. The upper one places it in context with other buildings

iting foreign princes and ambassadors. The Queen also came here prior to ceremonial visits to the city, as in 1571 for the opening of Sir Thomas Gresham's Royal Exchange, and in 1588 for the great thanksgiving service at St Paul's for the defeat of the Spanish Armada.

The house was used more after 1603 when the new King, James I, turned it over to his wife, Anne of Denmark, as part of her dower. Here Inigo Jones inaugurated several masques for this pleasure-loving Queen. More formal occasions included the famous Somerset House Conference of 1604. The famous scene with the English and Spanish commissioners ranged round the table is familiar from the picture by Marc Gheeraerts the younger, now in the National Portrait Gallery. In the Queen's honour, Somerset House was renamed Denmark House, by which name it was usually known until the Restoration.

The Queen employed Inigo Jones to carry out some alterations to the house, for apparently little had been done since Somerset's fall, beyond some patching up for Elizabeth and the carrying out of essential repairs. As late as 1603, Stow, in his *Survey of London*, merely mentioned that the palace was 'unfinished'. John Strype (1643–1737), in the *Survey of London*, 1720, stated that 'the palace was greatly improved and beautified by this Queen, who added much to it in the way of new buildings, Inigo Jones being called in to furnish the designs'.

Inigo Jones, who first enjoyed royal patronage in the Queen's service, originally became known for staging masques. Between 1605 and 1640 he arranged over 50, several of them at Somerset House, sometimes in the hall and sometimes outside in the Great Court. He later turned to architecture, and in 1610 he was appointed Surveyor to Henry, Prince of Wales. In 1615, a few years after the Prince's death, he became the King's Surveyor. His work at Somerset House included the Queen's private apartments, and in 1611–12 the Cross Gallery, which extended from the Lower Court to the east, with the flower garden to the south. A lantern over the hall was added in 1617–18.

Twice, Queen Anne's brother, Christian IV came here from Denmark to stay, and when the Queen died in 1619, her body was brought to the house to lie in state for over two months. This was only the first of many royal lyings in state, including that of James I himself in 1625.

When Anne died, Denmark House passed to her son, the future Charles I, who never lived there, though he did give a grand ball in 1620. The cost of this he wagered, and lost, over a game of tennis with the Duke of Buckingham, also at Denmark House. When Charles became King, he married the vivacious but spoilt French princess, Henrietta Maria, to whom he gave the house, and it is she who dominates its history as a royal palace.

As there was no Catholic chapel, the Queen had to say Mass in her closet. At length King Charles allowed her to have a chapel built at Denmark House. It was designed by Inigo Jones on the site of the tennis court, and though it was ordered in 1623, it was not built until 1630–35. Inigo stated that 'he ne'er presented a more curious piece in any of the masques at Whitehall' as his *Glory of Heaven*, portrayed over the high altar. The Chapel became a meeting place for London's Roman Catholics, a fact which did little for the Queen's popularity. Puritans termed her 'a wicked Jezebel'. Mobs outside the entrance in the Strand yelled 'death to the French papists'.

Apart from the Chapel, Henrietta Maria added the Queen's Cabinet Room in 1626, and the River Stairs between

1628 and 1631. The Cross Gallery was re-modelled in 1635 and a new Cabinet Room erected two years later. She then decided upon a new design for the palace, for which Inigo Jones drew up his plans in 1638. The great work was not started before the outbreak of the Civil War which resulted in the Queen's departure and the King's capture and execution. Inigo Jones was permitted to remain in the house, where he died in 1652, but the doors remained virtually closed for sixteen years. Oliver Cromwell's body was brought here to lie in state, complete with his wax effigy and the crown and sceptre which never were his.

In 1660 Charles II was restored to his kingdom, and his mother, Henrietta Maria, arrived in London that November. By then Somerset House, which had reverted to its original name, was undergoing restoration after severe delapidation. When the Queen Mother again returned from France in July 1662 she had to stay at Greenwich as Somerset House was still uncompleted. We do not know exactly what work was undertaken, but the plans prepared in 1638 by Inigo Jones, were brought out. As with Whitehall Palace, expense precluded their being fully implemented. As a result, the south front facing the river was extended by John Webb only to a length of 90 ft, instead of along the whole frontage. As well as this new gallery in pure classical style, other new chambers were added, a new gatehouse built and the Chapel splendidly restored. Accounts show that in 1663–64 payment was made for a new brick building erected at the end of the Cross Gallery 'in the Back Court of Somerset House', and a stone building facing the Thames.

Queen Henrietta Maria, adept at interior decoration, hung the chambers with silk and velvet, and filled them with the finest furniture and pictures that she could obtain. She laid out formal Italian gardens in front of both quadrangles, with straight paved walks leading to the water's edge. The river front can be seen in Johannes Kip's engraving of about 1690.

By November 1662, Somerset House was ready to receive the Queen Mother. People of fashion flocked here, and compared her excellent taste favourably to that of her son, Charles II. She invariably dressed elegantly in black, sitting in her favourite 'great black velvet chair' and sheltered from the draughts by an 'Indian screen of six leaves'. London winters were an anathema to her, however, and this life did not continue long. In 1664 Pepys visited the house and called its restoration 'mighty magnificent and costly'. Abraham Cowley wrote some poor verse *On the Queen's Repairing Somerset House*; while an anonymous poet, whom some said was Edmund Waller, wrote an effusion on *The Great Queen, Upon her Majesty's new Building at Somerset House*, of which the following is a specimen:

> This by the Queen herself designed
> Gives us a pattern of her mind;
> The state and order does proclaim
> The genius of that royal dame.

In the summer of 1665, the year of the Plague, the Queen left for her native France intending to return in the following year, but she never came back. She died four years later at her Chateau of Colombe.

On Henrietta Maria's departure, her son promised that the Chapel would remain carefully tended by her Capuchin monks. The palace was overhauled for Charles II's Queen, Catherine of Braganza, in 1671–72. The master carver took down the arms of France in the Queen's Great Bedchamber and put in its place those of Portugal. The Chapel was also re-decorated, for Catherine too was a devout Roman Catholic. In 1688 the sergeant painter was employed 'painting the clouds and cherubims between the Altar and Great Quire', and in 'mending the clouds in the ceiling'. When King Charles died in 1685, his Queen took up permanent

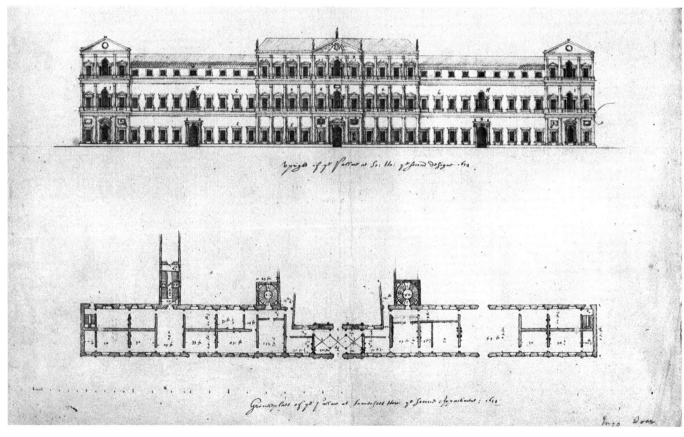

residence there. Masques and plays continued to be performed at Somerset House, and the Queen spent much of her time playing cards. Despite an involvement with the Popish Plot, Queen Catherine was left undisturbed until William III gained the throne in 1689. William however did his best to dislodge her, but she pleaded her title to the house and refused to budge. A move to restrict the number of her servants was thrown out by the House of Lords; but at length William's wife, Queen Mary, made Catherine's life so unpleasant that on 30 March 1692, she returned to Portugal for good.

With Queen Catherine's departure, Somerset House had no regular royal occupant, and soon fell into a shabby state. Part was given over to courtiers as a grace and favour house.

At present a mere lodging pen
or palace turned into a den

wrote the poet Churchill. Occasionally there was a masquerade or an ambassador was quartered here, as were the bridegrooms for George II's daughter, Princess Anne, and George III's daughter, Princess Augusta. Neither Queen Caroline, George II's wife, nor Queen Charlotte, married to George III, wanted this shabby house. The Strand had lost its pre-eminent position, and was swarming with footpads.

We can get an insight into the layout from an eighteenth- century plan referred to by Edward Walpole in his *Old and New London*, 1873. The main entrance from the Strand led to the Great Court, around which were ranged the principal buildings. The south side was occupied by a guard chamber, the Presence Chamber and the Privy Chamber. The west front, stretching from the Strand to the river, consisted of coach houses, stables and stores. Between them and the south west corner of the Great Court stood the Chapel. Stone stairs led to the gardens. On the east side, the back stairs led down to the Lower Court,

round which were the private apartments; to the east were the French Buildings, built by Henrietta Maria, later grace and favour lodgings, and the Cross Gallery. The Great Gallery led south, between the Lower Court and the flower garden.

In 1773, John Noorthouck commented on the neglect of Somerset House. Parts had then fallen into ruin, and part of the garden was used as a barracks and parade ground for soldiers. By an Act of Parliament in 1775, Buckingham House supplanted Somerset House as the Queen's house, and the old palace was demolished.

The first stone of the new building, designed by Sir William Chambers, was laid in 1776. No longer was Somerset House a royal palace.

Today the house has a number of different uses. The rooms in the north block for so long associated with the General Register Office of Births, Marriages and Deaths, have now been restored to their original ornate condition and have recently been used for several art exhibitions.

The south wing has been the home, for over 100 years, of the Probate Registry, which contains wills going back to 1382; while in the west wing is the Board of Inland Revenue, whose forerunner the Board of Taxes was one of the original offices in 1785.

Adjoining the east wing is King's College, London, which occupies part of the site of the original palace. This was founded in 1829, and was incorporated nearly 70 years later into the University of London. **PMS**

Opposite: John Webb's drawings for Somerset House which were based on those of Inigo Jones but which were never fully executed

Below: Johannes Kip's engraving of the river front in about 1690, showing Queen Henrietta's Italian formal gardens laid out in front of both quadrangles

THEOBALDS

Many palaces are particularly associated with one monarch. This is true of Theobalds, pronounced 'Tibbalds', near Cheshunt, Hertfordshire. It was James I's favourite English home from 1607 when he took possession until his death eighteen years later. Theobalds was not a royal palace for long.

Queen Elizabeth's great minister, William Cecil, later Lord Burghley, purchased Theobalds in 1564 so that he could pass the estate to his brilliant son by his second marriage. The hunch-backed Robert Cecil was every bit as astute as his father. Burghley, near Stamford was entailed to pass to the elder son, from whom the present Marquess of Exeter is descended.

When Cecil acquired Theobalds he found that it was a moated manor of moderate size which he immediately started to rebuild on a different site. The house was built round two great courtyards. In 1567 he added an outer court which became known as the Middle Court, and took six years to build. Entrance was from the Base Court, with the Dove House Court to the left, containing the brewhouse, bakery and laundry. The Green Gallery, which connected the Base Court with the Middle Court, was impressive, with walls 'excellently well painted round with all the several shires in England, and the arms of noblemen and gentlemen in the same'.

Queen Elizabeth, always anxious to see for herself the great houses of her subjects, came for a three day visit in September, 1571, before it was completed and was presented with a portrait of the house. She was duly impressed, but nevertheless suggested some alterations to her host. In Cecil's words, she found fault 'with the small measure of her chamber, which was in good measure for me'.

In fact this was the first of twelve visits the Queen was to make to Theobalds, resulting in the house becoming much larger and more magnificent than had been intended. Cecil said that the house was begun 'with mean measure, but increased by occasion of her Majesty's often coming'. It was indeed an expensive matter to put up the Queen and Court, each visit costing between £2–3000.

A year after the Queen first came, Cecil started to rebuild the original court, which became the Conduit Court, 84 ft square, pleasantly paved and containing a black and white fountain. On the east side was a cloister, 8 ft wide, with seven arches. According to the *Parliamentary Survey*, on the ground floor of this quadrangle was a spacious hall, paved with Purbeck marble, and the roof 'arched over the top with carved timbers of curious workmanship'. An even more impressive gallery, the Great Gallery, at the far end contained on the walls a genealogy of the sovereigns of England, to impress the Queen. Conduit Court took twelve years to complete, resulting in Theobalds becoming one of the three finest houses to be built during her reign.

The gardens were no less impressive than the house, with

flowering shrubs, an ornamental lake 'large enough', said Hentzner, 'for one to have the pleasure of going in a boat and viewing between the shrubs', a maze and a summer house with white marble statues of twelve Roman emperors. On one occasion when the Queen came, a special garden with a rock was prepared for picnics in 'the Queen's arbour'. Views to the south overlooked the wooded Enfield Chase.

In May 1591, shortly before Lord Burghley's death, the Queen and Court came to Theobalds for ten days. Lord Burghley dropped broad hints that Robert Cecil would be a suitable successor as Secretary. In this he was successful, but he little thought that Robert would soon part with his inheritance.

For years Robert Cecil had been engineering the peaceful succession of James VI of Scotland. Accordingly, in 1603, immediately after Elizabeth's death at Richmond Palace, he rode north to meet his new King, James I of England, on his way to London. Robert, soon to become Earl of Salisbury, greeted the King at York.

King James soon became enamoured of Theobalds, and before long made it known that he would like to receive the magnificent house in exchange for Hatfield, nine miles away. Lord Salisbury gave up possession in May 1607, on the occasion of a masque specially written by Ben Jonson.

Though the King was keen on hunting, he was an ungainly rider. Joseph Meade, writing to Sir Martin Stuteville in January, 1622, told that when he rode after dinner, his horse stumbled, and he fell headlong into the frozen New River. All that was visible were his boots. Fortunately for him, Sir Richard Young, riding at a distance saw the accident, alighted from his horse and ran to the rescue. The King's attendants were able to empty their master 'like an inverted cask' of river water, 'and a warm bed soon restored him to his pleasures and follies'.

King James enlarged the park by enclosing part of the chase, which he surrounded with a wall ten miles in circumference. When becoming gravely ill at Newmarket he insisted on being removed to his favourite house, and here died on 27 March 1625. His son, Charles, was sent for and arrived half an hour before becoming King.

Theobalds as a palace is described in 1650 by the Parliamentary Commissioners. The Presence Chamber, with carved wainscoting of oak, richly gilt, had a ceiling enriched with gilt pendants. Coats of arms were set in the large windows, which opened south on to the walk in the Great Garden. On the same floor were the Privy Chamber, the Withdrawing Chamber, and the King's Bedchamber. On an upper floor were the Lord Chamberlain's Lodgings, his Withdrawing Chamber and other apartments. Near these lodgings was a leaded walk, 62 ft in length, under an arch, which looked eastwards into the Middle Court. To the west was a similar leaded walk of the same length to Fountain

Court. At each corner of these walks stood four lofty towers with lions and vanes. Over the hall, was a lantern tower, with pinnacles at each corner, twelve bells and a chiming clock.

King Charles I did not come to Theobalds much. His last visit was in March, 1642, on the way to Nottingham. The Commissioners later reported that the palace was an excellent building, in very good repair, 'by no means fit to be demolished', and that it was worth £2,000 per annum, exclusive of the park. Yet should Parliament think proper to demolish the house, they estimated the materials were worth £8,275.11s. As it was decided to sell the palace, the greater part was taken down, and the proceeds divided among the army. At the Restoration the manor was granted to the Duke of Albemarle. Today, a few rooms and some original windows are incorporated in the house, known as the Old Palace, built in 1768. A stairway was taken to Herstmonceux Castle.

When Temple Bar archway was removed from Fleet Street in 1878, Sir Christopher Wren's masterpiece stood in pieces in a builder's yard until Sir Henry Meux, ten years later, decided to move it to his estate at Theobalds as the gateway, where it stands today.   **PMS**

Above: An interior of Theobalds
Below: The exterior of James I's favourite palace

WHITEHALL PALACE

From 1529 until 1698 Whitehall Palace was the official London residence of our kings and queens. It was then burnt to the ground in a fire which was the greatest to befall a palace in our history. An onlooker then wrote, 'It is a dismal sight to behold such a glorious, famous and most renowned Palace reduced to a heap of rubbish and ashes, which the day before might justly contend with any Palace in the world for riches, honour, nobility and grandeur'.

In 1233 Hubert de Burgh, King John's Justiciar, purchased these lands from Westminster Abbey, and a few years later his trustees sold them to the Archbishop of York, Walter de Gray. Through a private transaction, in 1245 they were transferred to the See of York, and 'our houses in the street of Westminster' became York Place, the London residence of the Archbishops of York.

Thomas Wolsey who, in 1514, became Archbishop of York, and in the following year a Cardinal, lavishly decorated and enlarged York Place so that it became the envy of the King. York Place had a long river frontage just to the north of Westminster Abbey, where the Thames flows northwards. The eastern boundary followed the parallel street, now known as Parliament Street and Whitehall, which connects Westminster with Charing Cross. The southern end was the exceedingly narrow King Street. The central portion, also narrow, was known just as 'the Street', and the northern portion, from the present Banqueting House to Charing Cross, was to become Whitehall subsequently taking its name from the palace.

In medieval times the riverline was approximately 100 yards west of the present bank of the Victoria Embankment, and on a line where the present Horse Guards Avenue turns off Whitehall was the palace entrance. A right of way led to the busy Whitehall Stairs. This formed the northern boundary, and close by these stairs was the Chapel which the Cardinal adorned and also renovated. Immediately behind he built the Great Hall which was completed in 1528. This was a 40 ft wide and 70 ft long, and had a high pitched roof, surmounted by a huge lantern at the southern end. Both these buildings stretched across the present Horse Guards Avenue, at its junction with Whitehall Court. The Cardinal also built on his newly acquired land of Scotland Yard to the north, near Charing Cross.

Slightly to the south-west of the new Great Hall, Wolsey built his wine cellar. One of the main features of his palace was a great gallery, which extended from across the Great Court, parallel to the river, to the southern boundary, which was in line with the present Downing Street.

Henry VIII was a frequent guest, and he must have compared it to his own badly damaged old fashioned palace at Westminster, which he had abandoned apart from ceremonies held in the Great Hall. Then, in 1529, Wolsey fell

The interior of Inigo Jones's great Banqueting House at Whitehall

into disgrace and was compelled to leave York Place. Ten days later, on 2 November, the King moved in, though the formal transfer from the See of York, had to wait until the following year.

The King's first action was to give his acquisition a new name. Shakespeare, in his *Henry VIII*, refers to this:

"Sir, You must no more call it York Place; that's past;
For since the Cardinal fell, that title's lost;
'Tis now the King's and called Whitehall."

Why the name Whitehall was chosen is a matter of speculation. There is no evidence that white stone was used instead of Tudor bricks. Perhaps there was some association with the White Hall in the Palace of Westminster.

As there was no room at Whitehall Palace for his sporting activities, Henry bought some land across 'the Street' on the St James's Park side. Here he built a turretted closed tennis court, bowling alley, tiltyard and cockpit. It was under the general name of 'the Cockpit' that this part of the palace became known.

Now that Henry's palace straddled both sides of the Street, in 1531 he started to build two imposing gates from one side to the other; Holbein Gate to the north, which was at the southern tip of the present Banqueting House, and King Street Gate on the palace boundary to the south.

Holbein Gate, long a London landmark with its two octagonal turrets, was built in three storeys of chequered stone and flint, tessellated in two colours. The second gate was less elaborate, being constructed of stone in two storeys, with circular turrets having domed roofs. Both had a central arch for vehicles and small archways on either side for pedestrians.

Though traditionally Holbein designed the gate which bears his name, this was not so, though the painter may have lodged in an upper chamber when working for the King, and painting the ceiling of the Long (or Matted) Gallery, the first floor of Wolsey's gallery. Henry VIII, himself, seems to have had a study in an upper chamber of the gate, called the Chair House.

About the same time, Henry rebuilt the main palace gate, known as Whitehall (or Court) Gate. This led into the Great Court, which later was known as Whalebone Court because of a great skeleton on view there in James I's reign. Above Wolsey's wine cellar he built the King's Guard Chamber (or Great Chamber), sometimes used for dissolutions of Parliament, which communicated both with the Chapel Royal and the Presence (or Audience) Chamber.

Henry VIII commandeered Wolsey's great gallery from Esher, which he brought in pieces and re-assembled in St James's Park. This was called the Privy Gallery in distinction from the original Stone Gallery. The Privy Gallery was erected at right angles to the Stone Gallery, and extended to the far side of Holbein Gate, over the Street. The rectangular space between the two galleries and the Street, at first the Orchard, was laid out as one of his two Privy Gardens, also known as the Great Garden. The other one, to the north gate of the Privy Gallery, was the Inward Garden, later paved.

The Count of Belgrade who, in 1531, made a visit to Whitehall Palace, tells of:

Long porticoes or halls, without chambers, with windows on each side looking on to gardens or rivers, the ceilings being marvellously wrought in stone and gold, and the wainscot of carved wood representing a thousand beautiful figures; and round about there are chambers and very large halls, all hung with tapestries.

On 28 January 1547, Henry VIII died at Whitehall Palace, holding the hand of Archbishop Cranmer. He left the palace in fine order, including the construction of a river wall with six semi-circular bastions, 50 ft in front of the earlier wall.

The Inward Garden came to be used for outside preaching. Bishop Latimer once preached a sermon from a pulpit before the young King Edward VI and 'four times as many people as could have stood in the King's Chapel'. As a result of these many addresses, this became known as the Sermon Court.

Queen Elizabeth gave many stately receptions and banquets in Whitehall Palace, including a banquet in the Stone Gallery in 1559 for the visiting Duke of Montmorency, when the gallery 'was all hung with gold and silver brocade and divided into three apartments . . . The whole gallery was closed in with wreaths of very sweet odour and were marvellous to behold.' Nevertheless the critical Venetian ambassador said that 'the delicacies and cleanliness customary in Italy were wanting', and owing to the size of the ladies' farthingales, some had to eat their dinner sitting on the rushes on the floor.

Elizabeth hastily built a banqueting house in 1581 to receive the Duke of Alencon who came to propose marriage. One of the celebrations was a tournament held in great magnificence in the tiltyard. The Duke arrived in May 1581, but he appeared far more interested in raising loans from London merchants for his Netherlands schemes, and showed no signs of departing. Finally he left in the following February, to everyone's relief.

The Stuarts made far more use of Whitehall Palace than the Tudors. James I had the 'old rotten, slight building', the banqueting house demolished, which he replaced by another 'strongly builded with brick and stone', which was opened in January 1608 with a performance of Ben Jonson's *Masque of Beauty*. This building, however, was burnt down in 1619 by two workmen sweeping up after a masque. Their candles caught some oily clothes used in the performance.

Within two months, Inigo Jones presented his plans for a new banqueting house, which still stands today, the first great Renaissance building in England. This fine Palladian building of Portland stone was erected from 1619 to 1622 and immediately excited an interest throughout Europe. A visiting French architect later called it 'the most finished of the modern buildings on this side the Alps'. Measuring 110 ft long and 55 ft both broad and high, it forms a perfect double cube.

The King's private apartments were situated near the Privy Gallery. Where this met the Stone Gallery was the King's Withdrawing Room, which became known as the Vane Room, as above it was the principal weathercock in the palace. Next to this, in the Long Gallery, was the Old

Bedchamber, and beyond, the Lesser Withdrawing Room or Horn Room. On the other side of the gallery was the Stone Table Chamber, leading into the Council Chamber. Access from the Privy Garden was via the Adam and Eve Staircase, so called from a picture at the head of the stairs.

Charles I erected a cabinet room where he kept many of his art treasures. The position is uncertain but it was probably near his private apartments. The King left Whitehall to raise troops in January 1642, and it became 'a palace without a possessor' according to a pamphleteer at the time. He only returned for his execution on 30 January 1649, the most dramatic occasion in Whitehall's history.

The King was brought from St James's Palace, across the park, through the stairs to the Tiltyard Gallery and then to Holbein Gate, where he was allowed to rest awhile. Then through the Gallery to the Green Chamber, between the King's Closet and his Bedchamber, where he sought solace in prayer. Finally he was led to the Banqueting House, where a scaffold was erected on first-floor level in the street outside, which he approached through a hole cut in the wall. After donning an extra shirt, so that the intense cold would not make him shudder and appear frightened, he was beheaded, maintaining throughout great dignity.

Charles I had converted the Cockpit into a theatre, which Parliament now closed, although Cromwell once entertained members of the House of Commons there 'with rare music, both of voices and instruments'. Cromwell had lodgings there, but when he became Lord Protector he moved into the main palace to live in state, though his wife complained that the state rooms were too far from the kitchens. Here at Whitehall, Cromwell died in 1658.

At the Restoration, Charles II entered Whitehall on 29 May 1660, riding in procession from Charing Cross. He established a brilliant Court, and obtained his pleasures to the full. He was keen on drama, so the theatre was reopened. He built a new closed tennis court, and was delighted when, in 1667, the weighing machine he installed there showed that he had lost 4½ lbs after a game. He erected a fine new library, visited by Evelyn, and a laboratory, where the King's Drops were invented to cure a number of ills. Meanwhile, at the tiltyard, bear-baiting took place and there were one or two guard houses as well. In 1664 barracks were built, covering the whole area, to house the Horse Guards and some Foot Guards, which began the Army's association with Whitehall.

As no sermons had been preached since 1630, Sermon Court was now known as Pebble Court from that particular form of paving. In 1668 and 1669 the wooden terrace, which divided it from the Great Court, was replaced by the brick built New Gallery. This extended from the Whitehall Gate to the Guard (or Great) Chamber.

After five years the theatre was closed at the Cockpit and moved into the Great Hall. There were lodgings for the King's mistresses, the Duchesses of Cleveland and Portsmouth, in Whitehall Palace, and much of his dallyings with them, and with Nell Gwynn, occurred within its walls. When he died in 1685, they and their brood came to say goodbye.

In James II's short reign, he made considerable alterations to Whitehall Palace. He pulled down the old Privy Gallery, and the apartments connected with it. Only two months after his accession, Wren was busy preparing in its place, new apartments for the Queen, Mary of Modena. The new block, 200 ft long, contained a fine Portland stone staircase with iron balustrading. The Queen's Great Bed-

chamber had a ceiling painted by Verrio and a chimney piece with carving by Grinling Gibbons. He also built a new Council Chamber and Treasury Office next to the Banqueting House.

The Chapel Royal was now overshadowed by the new Catholic Chapel which was opened on Christmas Day, 1686, its western end fronting the Street. This too was richly decorated by Verrio and Grinling Gibbons. William III later took down Gibbons' splendid altar piece which was stored at Hampton Court. Today it is in Burnham Church, Somerset.

The last great ceremony in the palace occurred in the Banqueting House, when on 13 February 1689, in the present of the assembled Lords and Commons, the Prince and Princess of Orange were declared King William III and Queen Mary II, to reign jointly. York Herald proclaimed them sovereigns at Whitehall Gate.

In deference to his wife, a daughter of the dethroned James II, the statue of that King in the garb of a Roman Emperor by Grinling Gibbons, remained in Pebble Court. Today the statue stands in front of the National Gallery.

William III, who disliked Whitehall Palace, because it was bad for his asthma, nevertheless considered the rebuilding of part of it from Wren's designs. A fire in 1691 resulted in several buildings between the Stone Gallery and the river being destroyed. All that was built was the Queen's Riverside Terrace, completed in 1693. The Privy Stairs, erected by Henry VIII to the south of the public Whitehall Stairs, were demolished to make room for the terrace in front of the Queen's Withdrawing Room. The terrace was 280 ft long and 70 ft wide, with curved flights of steps to the waterside at each end.

A 17th-century engraving of Whitehall Palace from the Thames, showing the Privy Stairs and Landing Place

Between 3 and 4 o'clock in the afternoon of 4 January 1698 the fire began which was to consume all the Palace of Whitehall on the river side, with the exception of the Banqueting House, although even this was damaged. A Dutchwoman in Colonel Stanley's lodgings was drying some linen in an upper storey before a charcoal fire when she was called away and the clothes caught fire. The flames quickly spread through the Great Hall, the Chapel Royal, the private apartments, including all the new buildings of James II, which became ashes. The Dutchwoman lost her life. William III came to view the ruins, and Sir Christopher Wren prepared designs, but Whitehall was never rebuilt.

Most of the buildings on the Cockpit side were demolished in the eighteenth century. The last to survive was Henry VIII's four-turretted tennis court, which remained until 1846. Kip's view of Whitehall from St James Park of 1720 shows what was left of Whitehall Palace, 22 years after the fire.

Due to congestion of traffic, King Street Gate was demolished in 1723, and Holbein Gate in 1759. The materials from the latter were given to the Duke of Cumberland who was to re-assemble the gate at the end of the Great Walk of Windsor, but he never did so.

The sole survivor of Whitehall Palace, the Banqueting House, was long used as a chapel, and here distribution of the Royal Maundy took place until 1890. Sir John Soane began his restoration work in 1829. In 1895 the Banqueting House was opened as the Museum of the Royal United Service Institution. **PMS**

WOODSTOCK PALACE

The grandeur of Vanbrugh's great Blenheim Palace in Oxfordshire, built by the grateful Queen Anne for the Duke of Marlborough after his victory at Blenheim, has disguised the fact that this had been the site of the royal palace and manor of Woodstock since the days of the pre-Conquest kings.

Woodstock had royal associations even before the Norman Conquest, for King Ethelred the Unready held a council there. In the *Domesday Survey* there are references to the King's forests of Woodstock, Cornbury and Wychwood, and there is evidence that Woodstock became a favourite home of Henry I. In 1109 or 1110 he surrounded the park with strong stone walls, seven miles in circumference. William of Malmesbury tells us that he collected a menagerie of what were then strange beasts:

> He was extremely fond of the wonders of distant countries, begging with great delight from foreign kings, lions, leopards, lynxes or camels, animals which England does not produce. He had a park called Woodstock, in which he used to foster favourites of this kind. He had placed there also a creature called a porcupine, sent to him by William of Montpelier.

Henry I's grandson, Henry II, was also a frequent visitor to Woodstock, where in July 1163 he had angry words with Thomas Becket. But Woodstock is chiefly remembered for the bower of Henry's mistress, Rosamond Clifford, 'cunningly contrived that no stranger could find the way in, yet Queen Eleanor did, being guided by a thread'.

Rosamond was a daughter of a Welsh marcher baron, Walter de Clifford from whom the powerful baronial line descended. His stronghold was Clifford's Castle near Hay. When Rosamond became the King's concubine is uncertain, but it probably dated from 1166. That year the King spent £26 9s 4d on making a spring called Everswell, which was later called Rosamond's Well. This now lies under the lake in Blenheim Park, made for the Duke of Marlborough by Capability Brown.

There are so many legends and ballads about Henry II and Rosamond Clifford that it is difficult to obtain the truth, but all these point to the murder of Rosamond by Queen Eleanor, for which there is not the slightest evidence. In a fourteenth-century French *Chronicle of London*, the Queen catches Rosamond in her bower at Woodstock, strips off her clothes and roasts her between two fires. The girl was then bled to death in a hot bath. Later versions say that she was given the choice of drinking poison or being stabbed to death with a dagger. Most of these say she took the poison. The Queen is said to have discovered her secret bower by following a trail of silk leading to a casket which King Henry had given her.

Presumably when the Queen returned to her native Aquitaine in 1165, the King dallied with Rosamond. The following year Eleanor returned to England and gave birth to her youngest son, John, at Oxford Castle on Christmas Eve.

Ten years later Henry tried to obtain a divorce from her, and Cardinal Uguccione of St Angelo came to England as Legate, but left without even hearing the case.

So frequently did Henry II come down to Woodstock that, in order to find lodging for his courtiers, he founded the borough of New Woodstock, half a mile north east of the house. His palace, one of the most splendid in medieval times, crowned a small hill above the River Glyme, close to the north end of the bridge across the lake which was constructed in the eighteenth century. The 'spacious church-like hall, with two fair aisles with six pillars, white and large, parting either aisle', noted in 1634, would have been built by Henry II or his grandfather. At one end of the hall was the 'King's high chamber,' approached from the courtyard by a flight of steps.

Henry built a water palace at Everswell, a few hundred yards to the east. In the seventeenth century John Aubrey drew a plan of its remains, which shows three baths or pools. A large one was surrounded by 'the great cloisters', and there were two smaller ones below it.

Rosamond fell ill in 1176 and entered the convent of Godstow near Oxford, and she died that year. Benedict of Peterborough said that the King gave the nunnery many large gifts for her sake. According to tradition, Henry himself composed the epitaph:

> Hic iacet in tumba Rosa mundi, non rosa munda;
> Non redolet, sed olet, quae redolere solet.

which was usually translated:

> Rose of, not to the world, here Rosamond lies;
> Since once she was, but now 'tis otherwise.

Philip Howard, in his *The Royal Palaces*, translates it thus:

> Here lies the Rose of the world, not a clean rose;
> She no longer smells rosy, so hold your nose.

Roger of Hovenden, in his sixteenth-century chronicle, records that when Bishop Hugh of Lincoln called at Godstow about 1191 he was shocked to find Rosamond's tomb standing in the middle of the choir being venerated by the nuns who constantly kept the candles burning, and ordered her remains to be moved out of consecrated ground to the chapter house.

According to Leland, writing in the reign of Henry VIII, 'Rosamond's tomb was taken up of late. It (had) a stone, with this inscription 'Tumba Rosamundae' her bones were closed in lead . . .' and when Agnes Strickland visited it to write her *Queens of England* in the 1841, part of the convent ruins were used as a cowhouse.

Henry II did not desert Woodstock after Rosamond's end, for he knighted his son Geoffrey there in 1178, and eight years later entertained King William the Lion of Scotland when he gave him his kinswoman, Ermengarde de Beaumont, in marriage.

In 1238 Henry III was nearly murdered at Woodstock by a madman. According to the chronicler Matthew Paris, he accosted the King, shouting "Resign to me the kingdom which you have unjustly usurped". Royal servants ejected him, but that night he stole through a window into the King's bedchamber carrying a dagger, but 'by God's providence', King Henry was then with his Queen. One of her ladies, Margaret Bisset, quietly reading her psalter by candlelight, saw the man searching every corner, swearing wildly, and raised the alarm. This, or her screams, woke up servants who overpowered him. The would-be assassin was executed, being 'torn assunder by wild beasts'.

Henry gave immediate orders for iron bars to be added to the windows of his own and the Queen's chambers. Her apartments are first mentioned soon after their marriage in 1236. The chamber was vaulted, and was immediately beneath the King's. Later there are references to the 'Queen's new chamber' whose location is not known.

Henry III, a religious man, added five more chapels to his palace at Woodstock. These included a round chapel, still existing in 1599 when a foreign visitor was taken to see it, a chapel for the King's private use, separated from his chamber by a vaulted vestibule, and one for the Queen stood on an undercroft, with a passage way specially constructed so that she should not get her feet wet.

At the time of Henry III, Woodstock Palace contained a chamber for the Lord Edward, afterwards Edward I, the King's and Queen's wardrobes, the kitchen, buttery, spencery, larder, wine-cellar, almonry, stables, smithy, knights' chamber, stewards' chamber and clerks' chamber. The main gateway was on the west side, being approached by a causeway which crossed the valley of the Glyme between the King's fishponds.

Woodstock was in its heyday in the next few reigns. Edmund, Earl of Kent, Edward I's son by his second Queen, Margaret of Valois, was born there, as were two sons of Edward III, the eldest, the Black Prince, (who married Kent's daughter Joan, the Fair Maid of Kent) and the youngest, Thomas, Duke of Gloucester. Edward III gave orders for 'the house beyond the gate in the new wall' to be rebuilt. Edward IV and Henry VII were often at Woodstock, and King Henry considerably enlarged the palace and rebuilt the gatehouse, which contained a rhyme with his name.

Elizabeth was confined in Woodstock for eleven months in 1554 by her half-sister Queen Mary, when she was lodged in the more recent gatehouse. Her gaoler, Sir Henry Bedingfield, reported that 'in the whole house there was but three doors only that were able to be locked and barred, to the great disquiet and trouble of mind of the persons commanded to attend upon her grace in so large a house and unacquainted country'. Elizabeth herself compared her imprisonment as 'in worse case than the worse prisoner of Newgate'. When she became Queen she seldom came back to this decaying palace.

There is a brief description of the palace in *A Topographical Excursion* 1634, when it was described as 'that famous Court and Palace which as I found it ancient, strong, large and magnificent, so it was sweet, delightful and sumptuous and situated on a fair hill'. There was 'a spacious Court, the large strong and fair Gatehouse, the spacious church-like Hall with aisles and pillars and rich tapestry hanging wrought with 'the story of the Wild Bore', then the stately rich chapel with seven round arches, curious font, windows and admirably wrought roof'. Passing on, we come 'to the Guard Chamber, the Presence Chamber, the Privy Chamber, which looks over the Tennis Court into the town, the Withdrawing Chamber and the Bedchamber, both which have their sweet prospect into the Privy Gardens'. Next is the Queen's Bedchamber, 'where our late virtuous and renowned Queen was kept prisoner in,' and a neat chapel 'where our Queen (1634) heard mass'. Then, from the gateway appears the prospect of the walled park and its handsome lodges, and 'the Labyrinth where the fair Lady and great Monarch's concubine was surprised by a claw of silk'. 'I found nothing in this bower but ruins, but many strong and strange winding walls and turnings, and a dainty clear square paned well, knee deep, wherein this beautiful creature sometimes did wash and bathe herself.'

Woodstock never recovered from the twenty-day siege in 1646, during the Civil War. In 1649 the Parliamentary Commissioners came to take stock and found it barely habitable. They turned the King's bedroom into a kitchen amd the Privy Council room into a brewhouse. Most of the buildings were demolished for the stone, leaving only the gatehouse where Elizabeth was imprisoned and a few adjacent rooms.

At the Restoration the manor reverted to the Crown. Lord Lovelace was appointed Ranger, and made a new house out of the surviving fragments, where he died in 1670. Then came the witty and licentious Lord Rochester, who penned the famous words on Charles II:

> Here lies our sovereign lord the King
> Whose word no one relies on;
> He never says a foolish thing
> Nor ever does a wise one.

The manor and park were granted by Act of Parliament in 1705 to John Churchill, Duke of Marlborough, the year Vanbrugh started on the monumental Blenheim. Four years later Vanbrugh argued that Woodstock should be preserved, not for 'magnificence or curious workmanship' but 'because they move more lively and pleasing reflections (than history without their aid can do) on the persons who have inhabited them'. The architect spent some £2,000 on repairs to what remained, but when the Treasurer, Godolphin, was staying at the unfinished Blenheim in 1714, he remarked to the Duchess that it was a pity the view was spoilt by a pile of ruins. The end came in about 1718. Not a stone of Woodstock remains, except a few with chevron ornamentation which were found in the rubble filling of the eighteenth-century bridge in the park.   **PMS**

An engraving of Woodstock from a drawing by W Westall

BRIGHTON PAVILION

'It is as though St Paul's had gone down to the sea and pupped', said Sydney Smith, himself a Canon of the cathedral, about George IV's multi-domed vision of the gorgeous East at Brighton. People had started flocking to the sea in the middle of the eighteenth century when the beneficial effects of salt water were bruited around. The fishing village of Brighthelmstone in Sussex, conveniently close to London, suddenly became a fashionable resort where society sought to heal themselves with the particularly good local sea-water – either to be 'cur'd like tongues by dipping into brine' or by actually imbibing the stuff.

Among those who took houses near the Steine, the fashionable promenade in the village, was George III's brother the Duke of Cumberland and in 1783 the 21 year-old Prince of Wales came to stay here with his reprobate old uncle. The pleasure-loving Prince, enchanted by the place and its frivolous atmosphere, returned the following summer to a rented house of his own. The year after that he secretly married Mrs Fitzherbert, a Catholic widow two years his senior, and leased 'a superior farmhouse', dreaming of the simple life.

'Prinny' was not, however, a simple man. His tastes ran to something considerably more lavish. First, in 1787, Henry Holland transformed the farmhouse into a Palladian villa topped with a cupola and with a central rotunda between two wings. Bow windows and balconies relieved the classical severity. Then an oval room was added at each corner of the front by Holland's pupil, Robinson, and later William Porden completed the remarkable glass-domed stables in the Indian style next door to the 'Marine Pavilion', as it was known.

The Prince Regent had considered a Chinese-style pavilion; now he toyed with the Indian taste. In the year of Waterloo he commissioned John Nash to proceed with a design that is at once Chinese and Hindu, with a saucy dash of Tartar. Inside the onion-shaped domes and tent-like roofs, developed a riot of red and gold, of dragons and bamboos, pagodas and banana foliage.

Mrs Fitzherbert never actually lived in the pavilion herself, maintaining a separate establishment nearby having regard to the secrecy of their marriage. The Prince Regent finally ditched her in 1811 after which she never visited the pavilion again in his lifetime. She was, in her own words, 'drove by Lady Hertford', one of the massive middle-aged Marchionesses with whom the Prince chose to spend his time. The other was Lady Conyngham who very much ruled the roost at the pavilion, though she did not care for

Opposite: The breathtaking splendour of the oriental Dining Room with its table laid for a banquet
Top left: The instantly recognisable exterior of the pavilion and (right) the beautiful domed Music Room

Brighton and eventually, under her influence, George IV stopped coming here.

In his Regency heyday the entertainment at the pavilion had been on a truly princely scale, with elaborate dinner-parties twice a week, music and other jollifications. Princess Lieven, the wife of the Russian ambassador, did not believe that 'since the days of Heliogabalus, there has been such magnificence and such luxury', but others found life at the pavilion not quite so sybaritic as it was cracked out to be, and even surprisingly formal despite the King's wishes to the contrary. It was stuffy in more senses than one, thanks to the patent stoves and the innovatory gas-lighting.

The next monarch, William IV, an old salt, enjoyed his visits to Brighton and he entertained there frequently, being particularly hospitable to poor Mrs Fitzherbert. Queen Victoria, however, found the people of Brighton 'very indiscreet and troublesome'; seeking more privacy for her seaside holidays, she and Albert made for the respectable Isle of Wight. The Queen was also out of sympathy with the pavilion's architecture and at one stage there was even a plan to raze it to the ground. As it was, the interior was dismantled in the 1840s. However, in 1849, the town of Brighton bought it for £50,000 and since then the pavilion has been carefully restored to much of its original splendour.

The spacious corridor, or Long Gallery, with its pink halls and cornucopia of bamboo, was where the guests assembled before dinner. Then the Prince Regent, with the lady of the highest rank on his arm, would lead the company into the most brilliant of the state apartments, the Banqueting Room, with its domed ceiling 45 ft high, giant gasolier and ubiquitous dragons. William IV was nervous of the gasolier causing 'some dreadful accident' by falling down, so he temporarily removed it. The excellent Regency suite of 'dolphin' furniture in the South Drawing Room was presented, appropriately enough, by a naval widow called Mrs Fish. The Central Saloon dates from Holland's building, though the oriental decoration is by Nash. Sadly Nash's richly decorated Music Room was badly damaged by a fire a few years ago and is still being restored. The oriental flavour of this exotic pleasure-dome is even carried into the kitchen which has cast-iron and copper columns in the shape of palm trees. Carême, who invented caramel, worked as the chef in this highly efficient and practical temple of the culinary arts where the Prince himself occasionally dined with his servants.

The Royal Pavilion at Brighton was a fantastic personal triumph for the Prince Regent. There remains nothing quite like it anywhere. For all his profligacy and spoilt behaviour, the man had style, wit and imagination. Hardly any of his contemporaries, save possibly the Duke of Wellington, appreciated the fact that he contributed more to the splendour of the scene than any other sovereign. They merely worried about money; but, just as it can be argued that the pathetic Ludwig of Bavaria (the 'Dream King' declared mad because of his reckless extravagance) actually laid the foundations of the booming Bavarian tourist industry, so George IV's debts came from his desire to give the monarchy a suitably magnificent background which has proved an inestimable addition to our cultural heritage. What is more, the pavilion is fun.   **HMM**

These three pictures show the designs for the Pavilion gardens, conceived by Humphry Repton but never fully implemented

BROADLANDS

The royal connection with Broadlands came about through the marriage of Edwina Ashley, who inherited the place in 1939 from her father, Lord Mount Temple, to Admiral of the Fleet Earl Mountbatten of Burma. The late Earl, a great-grandson of Queen Victoria and uncle of the present Duke of Edinburgh, was a member of what can formally be described as the Royal Family, though his descendants, who include the current owner of Broadlands, Lord Romsey, are not. The Queen and Prince Philip spent their honeymoon here in 1947 and ten years later, planted some mulberry trees during the celebrations of the 350th anniversary of the grant of a charter to the Borough of Romsey. As his father has done 34 years earlier, Prince Charles brought his new bride to Broadlands at the start of their honeymoon in the summer of 1981.

Broadlands originally formed part of the Romsey Abbey estate but after the Dissolution of the Monasteries, it eventually passed to the St Barbe family. Sir John St Barbe left it in 1723 to his cousin Humphrey Sydenham who in turn sold to Henry Temple, first Viscount Palmerston, in 1736. The first Viscount commissioned Kent to do some landscaping which involved changing the course of the River Test. 'Capability' Brown carried out more landscape work for the second Viscount in the late 1760's as well as transforming the earlier house into the imposing white brick Palladian mansion we see today. Later Brown's son-in-law, Henry Holland added the east portico and the Sculpture Hall, decorating the main state rooms in the style of Robert Adam. Angelica Kauffmann helped design the Saloon and was responsible for the oval paintings on the Drawing Room ceiling. The octagonal domed Entrance Hall and the Doric-screened Sculpture Hall beyond, contain sculptures collected by the second Viscount on his Grand Tour. He also started the Wedgwood collection at Broadlands. The Dining Room contains four splendid Van Dyck portraits and the Drawing Room family portraits of the Palmerstons include works by Reynolds and Lawrence.

The third Viscount was the famous Victorian statesman. 'He had very many valuable qualities', wrote Queen Victoria of the breezy haw-hawing 'Pam', 'though many bad ones, and we had, God knows! terrible trouble with him about foreign affairs. Still, as Prime Minister he managed affairs at home well, and behaved to me well. But I never liked him.' Following his death in 1865 (the Palmerstons were noted for their longevity), Broadlands passed from his widow to his stepson William Cowper, later Lord Mount Temple, whose brother owned Sandringham. Then from Lord Mount Temple the estate passed to a nephew, Evelyn Ashley, a younger son of the Earl of Shaftesbury, whose other properties included Classiebawn in County Sligo near where Lord Mountbatten was assassinated. Ashley's son, the Lord Mount Temple of the later creation, married the daughter of the rich Jewish financier Sir Ernest Cassel; they were the parents of Edwina.

A few months before the Earl's murder in 1979, the Prince of Wales officially opened Broadlands to the public. It has proved a most popular attraction. Apart from the richly decorated interior and many notable works of art, there is a special exhibition on the life and times of Lord Mountbatten. On 9 May 1981 the Prince of Wales and Lady Diana Spencer came to the house to open the exhibition. **HMM**

Opposite: The south front of Broadlands
Above: The west front with the lawn and River Test

Below: The Saloon, designed by Robert Adam and Angelica Kauffmann

CLAREMONT

By his disastrous official marriage to Caroline of Brunswick, George IV had an only child, Princess Charlotte, who would one day have been Queen but for her early death. She was a good-looking, intelligent and popular princess and her husband, Prince Leopold of Saxe-Coburg and Gotha later proved to be a great European statesman. They lived briefly together at Claremont in Surrey before her death here following the birth of a stillborn son in 1817. Leopold stayed on in this idyllic spot until accepting the throne of Belgium when he nominally retained Claremont as his English home.

Claremont takes its name from the politician Thomas Pelham, Earl of Clare and afterwards Duke of Newcastle, who bought the estate from Sir John Vanbrugh, the architect and dramatist. Vanbrugh had acquired the property in 1708, building a crenellated house for himself, but seven years later he was remodelling it for the new owner. By the time Clive of India bought the place in 1769 the house was pedimented and wide-spreading with a park that had been transformed by William Kent into a glorious landscape of lakes, wooded hills and gently rolling sward, adorned with temples, lodges and a castellated belvedere.

Because of its damp, low-lying site, Clive promptly pulled the old house down and replaced it with a compact white brick block of two storeys on an unusually high basement with a giant Corinthian portico to the design of Lancelot 'Capability' Brown and his partner Henry Holland. Holland's pupil John Soane also worked here from 1772. The finest room is the hall with red scagliola columns

and an oval ceiling. The Great Drawing Room (now the Assembly Hall of the school there) also has a fine plaster ceiling and the original fireplace with two termini caryatids.

Clive raised the park fence to keep in his extraordinary menagerie, though on one occasion a nylghau jumped out and got as far as Cobham before it was caught; while a female of the same species suffered a worse fate, being killed, as Clive put it, 'by the amorous violence of Dr Hunter'. Clive's widow sold Claremont twelve years after his death.

A Gothic teahouse designed by Papworth and A C Pugin built for Princess Charlotte became a shrine to her memory; Papworth also built the Camellia Terrace with a greenhouse (now demolished) for Prince Leopold. Parliament voted the King of Belgians £10,000 a year for the upkeep of Claremont and in 1848 Leopold lent the place to his new father-in-law Louis Philippe, the exiled King of France, who died here two years later. His widow lived on, despite nearly drowning on one occasion in Clive's marble bath, at Claremont until her death in 1866. Queen Victoria later bought the reversion; she was very fond the place but found the drive from Windsor, followed by the 22 steps up to the house, rather exhausting. In 1881 she presented Claremont to her youngest son Prince Leopold when he became Duke of Albany. His widow was the last of the royal occupiers.

The estate was later infringed by stockbroker-belt developments and the gardens became overgrown. Happily, however, the National Trust has recently restored the latter to much of their former glory. So now one can enjoy such delights as the amphitheatre, a spectacular earthwork which is the only surviving example of its kind in Europe, the grotto, the belvedere and bowling green. The amphitheatre was originally designed by Charles Bridgeman in about 1725 as a dramatic eye-catching feature to complement a round pond formed in the valley below. It was never actually intended for theatrical performances, covering some three acres. Kent left it well alone but 'Capability' Brown planted it up in the 1770's so that it lay hidden and forgotten until the Trust's restoration 200 years later. The belvedere and the house itself are now owned by Claremont Fan Court School.

The final royal link with Claremont was broken with the death in 1981 of the Duke of Albany's 96 year-old daughter Princess Alice, Countess of Athlone (the oldest ever member of the Royal Family), who recalls her childhood there in her engaging memoirs, *For My Grandchildren*. **HMM**

Opposite top: Claremont today; the house is run as a girls' boarding school
Bottom: The Gallery in 1848 at the time of Louis Philippe, exiled King of France
Below: A plan of Claremont in 1738 showing the house and several features such as the amphitheatre, the bowling green and the belvedere

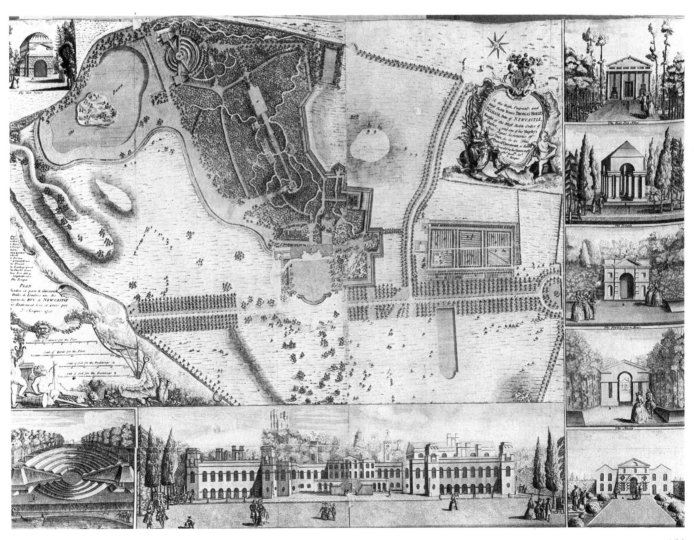

EDINBURGH CASTLE

The Castle is to Edinburgh rather what the Tower is to London. Perched on the top of its famous rock, Edinburgh Castle enjoys the advantage of a supremely defensible site, not to mention a magnificent view. The action of glaciers in the Ice Ages left near-vertical faces to the rock on the north and south sides, with a more gradual slope on the west and a gently descending ridge on the east. The earliest evidence of occupation dates from the sixth century, though it is not until the eleventh century that the castle is clearly established from records as a favourite residence of the kings of Scotland. It was here that St Margaret died in 1093, shortly after hearing of the death of her husband Malcolm III and her eldest son. The most venerable sur-

viving building in the castle complex, the tiny Chapel, is dedicated to her memory, though it may not have been actually built until after her youngest son David I came to the throne in 1124.

In the next 200 years the castle changed hands several times in the course of Scotland's bitter struggle for independence of English domination. The Scots themselves demolished the castle's defences in 1313 so the place could not be held against them by the English, and it was only when David II started major rebuilding after his return from English captivity that the castle walls began to take their present shape. He and his successor added notable towers.

James IV, who established Edinburgh as Scotland's capital early in the sixteenth century, built a great hall and was probably responsible for the southern part of the palace building. After being attacked by an English force in 1544 the castle defences were augmented, an Italian engineer building an artillery bastion in front of the cross-wall. From this period the Scottish kings tended to prefer to lodge at the less spartan Holyroodhouse and the use of the castle as a royal residence took second place to its military and political significance. However, in times of emergency it continued to be a secure refuge.

The birth of the future James I of England which took place at the castle in 1566 can be seen as a tribute to the symbolic importance of the place by his mother, Mary Queen of Scots, rather than a choice made on account of the convenience of its royal apartment. For James's brief homecoming in 1617 the palace block was extended to provide more suitable accommodation for the King. In the seventeenth century the castle itself was still confined to the highest part of the rock, with the palace and hall around two sides of a courtyard and a munition house (originally a church) on the third. The Chapel (then in use as a powder magazine), some distance to the north, and the Half Moon Battery, bristling with guns, overlooked the approaches from the town.

By now the castle's residual royal connection had largely come to an end, though part of the palace was fitted up in 1672 for the Duke of Lauderdale, Commissioner to the Scottish Parliament. Cromwell had begun to convert the other royal buildings into barracks and the castle settled back into its primary role as a fortress. There were brief flurries of Jacobitism and the last action the castle saw was rather a half-hearted effort by Bonnie Prince Charlie at capture in 1745.

Happily, some nineteenth-century antiquarianism stepped in to prevent the castle from becoming just a barracks, and restoration work was carried out on the Great Hall and the Portcullis Gate in the 1880s, whilst a new entrance front was built on the east side overlooking the Esplanade where the Tattoo is held. The Scottish National War Memorial was added in the 1920s. The Scottish regalia, 'rediscovered' in the nineteenth century by Sir Walter Scott and others, are on show in the Crown Room which adjoins the royal apartments. **HMM**

The two upper pictures show the way in which the castle dominates Edinburgh from its impregnable position atop the famous rock
Below left: St Margaret's Chapel, restored during the 19th century. This is now known as the Armoury and contains exhibits of great antiquity
Right: The Great Hall of the castle which was built in the 12th century

GLAMIS CASTLE

For over 600 years Glamis has been the historic seat of the Bowes Lyon family, Earls of Strathmore, and before them, the kings of Scotland. The castle has had a turbulent history, quite unlike the quiet pastoral charm of St Paul's Walden Bury, the other home of Queen Elizabeth the Queen Mother before her marriage. Rising from the hollow of a plain between the Grampian Mountains to the north and the gentler Sidlaw Hills in the county of Angus, Glamis is everything a castle should be: many towers and battlements, allusions in Shakespeare's *Macbeth*, several blood-curdling ghost stories, a secret room, the deathbed of a king many centuries ago and the birthplace of a princess a few years before World War II started.

Shakespeare wrote:

> This castle hath a pleasant seat; the air
> Nimbly and sweetly recommends itself
> Unto our gentle senses.

Though the visit of King Duncan to Macbeth at Glamis is only legendary, there is good authority that Duncan's grandfather and his predecessor on the throne, King Malcolm II (1005–1034) met his death at Glamis. In the ancient Scottish Regnal Lists, it is recorded:

> *Malcolm MacKinath rex victoriosissimus 30 an.*
> *Mortuus in Glamis, et sep. in Iona insula.*

The ancient royal lands of Glamis were given by Malcolm's descendant, Robert II, (the first Stewart to be King of the Scots) to his Chamberlain, Sir John Lyon in 1376 on his marriage to his daughter Jean. With this royal alliance, the Lyons received the double tressure to their coat of arms

of a lion rampant azure, and, it is said, their crest of 'a lady to the girdle', holding the thistle of Scotland was granted because of their royal descent.

Their grandson, Patrick Lyon of Glamis, Master of the Household to James II, became the first Lord Glamis, and died in 1459. The oldest part of the castle, the crypt and the lower part of the great central tower, probably date from the 25 years of widowhood of Isabel Ogilvy of Lintraten, the first Lady Glamis. A 1641 manuscript at Glamis says that she completed the rebuilding. The aisle in the church, now called the Mortuary or Chantry Chapel, beneath which is the family burial vault, with her husband's altar tomb, is also her work.

James V, long a prisoner of his stepfather, the Earl of Angus, whom he despised, vented some of his anger on the Earl's sister Janet Douglas, widow of the sixth Lord Glamis. She and her second husband, Archibald Campbell of Skipnish, were accused of plotting the King's death by poison and witchcraft and were sentenced to death. In 1537 the innocent Lady Glamis was consigned to the flames on Castle Hill, Edinburgh, while sympathetic crowds stood helplessly by. The day after her trial, her husband, attempted to escape from Edinburgh Castle and was dashed to pieces by falling rocks. On the day following his mother's burning, John, seventh Lord Glamis was taken to Edinburgh Castle and sentenced to death when he became of age, and Glamis was declared forfeit to the Crown.

From that year until his death in 1542, James V and his Queen were frequently at Glamis. There are several entries in the Lord Treasurer's accounts, such as that in 1547 showing the royal consumption of 54 capons, 90 poultry

and 24 geese. Several writs were passed at Glamis under the Great Seal during this period. Some of the family possessions were removed, and the Exchequer Rolls show that twelve great silver flagons were melted down to supply silver for the royal mint.

As soon as James V was dead, Patrick was restored as seventh Lord Glamis, and during the time of his son, the eighth Lord, James V's daughter, Mary Queen of Scots, in 'weather foul and cold' came to the castle on her first progress to the Highlands to quell the 1562 rebellion of Lord Huntly. She brought with her, her half-brother the Earl of Moray, the four Maries, her ladies, and many others. Her menu is still at Glamis. When here, she presented a watch made in Rouen by Etienne the elder, to Lord Glamis' sister, later Marchioness of Hamilton, which was preserved by her family for many generations.

The castle then consisted of the main keep in the familiar 'L' design, surrounded by a towered wall, with outbuildings. In about 1600 the keep was altered by Patrick, ninth Lord Glamis, whom six years later, James VI created Earl of Kinghorne (by a later charter this was altered to Strathmore and Kinghorne). He began the Banqueting Hall, where his and his wife's initials, with the date 1606, appear above the window. James VI was often at Glamis, and Lord Kinghorne and Lady Anna Murray had married at the royal palace of Linlithgow in the presence of the King and his Danish Queen.

John, second Earl, continued his father's rebuilding. His and his wife's initials, with the date 1621 appear on the fine arched ceiling of the Banqueting Hall. This, the most splendid room in the castle, measures 60 ft by 22 ft. His son,

Opposite: The 19th-century engraving shows the additions made to the castle since the engraving (above) of 1790

Earl Patrick, in his *Book of Record*, speaks of 'my great Hall, which is a room that I ever loved'.

Patrick became the third Earl in 1647. In his time, Cromwellian soldiers came to occupy Glamis, when he and his family left. When they returned in 1670, the castle was bare of furniture. He then carried out a thorough restoration of the castle which continued until 1689. He built the west wing, put up a new roof on the east wing and built the central tower. This, containing the great staircase, projects in front of the main building, part of the walls of which were removed to receive it.

At the foot of the tower, over the outer door of oak, the royal arms are sculptured in stone, and the immense iron door-knocker bears the date 1689 when Lord Strathmore's work was completed. Behind the door is a heavily grated iron gate, which probably guarded the fifteenth-century castle. The spiral staircase to the summit of the tower, contains 143 steps, 6 ft 2 inches wide, each of one stone.

Leading from the Banqueting Hall is the Chapel, whose area is 30 ft by 20 ft, which was dedicated in 1688. Earl Patrick engaged de Wet, who executed for him a series of paintings on the life of Christ and the Apostles for the walls and ceiling. The contract of *Mr de Vite Limner*, is still in the Charter Room.

The crypt and lower portion of the tower are formed of large rough blocks of old red standstone. This is a low vaulted chamber of stone with seven windows, some of which are cut out of the thickness of the walls, suggesting

it was once used for sleeping. A passage leads to King Duncan's Hall, where that king was alleged to have been murdered. Earl Patrick also rebuilt the castle walls, erected gateways and planted trees.

His son, John, fourth Earl of Strathmore, called by a contemporary 'well bred and good natured. . . He hath two of the finest seats in Scotland, Glamis and Castle Lyon; is tall, fair and towards fifty years old'. He was a Jacobite supporter, and only saved himself from trial for treason by obtaining a certificate saying that he could not leave Glamis without danger to his life.

His son, John, the fifth Earl, raised a regiment to support James II's son, Prince James Edward, the old Chevalier, and was killed fighting for him at the battle of Sheriffmuir on 13 November 1715, at the age of nineteen. The Old Chevalier came to Glamis in the following year, when his host was Charles, the sixth Earl, a sixteen year-old boy. The royal visitor touched for the King's Evil in the Chapel, and it was said 'all the patients recovered'. He slept in a high chamber in the tower, and left behind him his sword

inscribed 'God save King James VIII, prosperitie to Scotland, and no union', and his silver watch under his pillow. This was appropriated by a servant, but many generations later a descendant restored it to Glamis.

In another room below in the tower, Sir Walter Scott, as a young man, came in 1793, and was duly impressed with the castle.

After a very hospitable reception. . .I was conducted to my apartments in a distant part of the building. I must own that when I heard door after door shut, after my conductor had retired, I began to consider myself too far from the living, and somewhat too near the dead. . . The heavy pile contains much in its appearance, and in the tradition connected with it, impressive to the imagination. It was the scene of the murder of a Scottish King of great antiquity, not indeed the gracious Duncan, with whom the name naturally associates itself, but Malcolm II. The extreme antiquity of the building is vouched by the thickness of the walls, and the wild straggling arrangement of the accommodation within doors. . .

In spite of the truth of history, the whole night scene in Macbeth's Castle rushed at once upon me and struck my mind more

forcibly than even when I have seen its terrors represented by John Kemble and his inimitable sister (Mrs Siddons).

Scott drank to his absent host from the famous 'Lion of Glamis', a seventeenth-century beaker of silver double gilt, formed in the shape of a lion, with the Augsburg mark and the letter 'E'.

Glamis underwent structural changes in 1811 by the tenth Earl, and again in 1849 by the twelfth Earl, after the west wing was burnt down. In 1891 the east wing was added in the Baronial style.

When the Duke and Duchess of York were on their honeymoon in 1923 after staying at Polesden Lacey in Surrey, they went to the bride's old home, Glamis Castle. Her father, who became the fourteenth Earl in 1904, and mother, the former Cecilia Cavendish-Bentinck, provided for them a suite of first floor rooms in one of the original wings, overlooking the Angles Park. To these rooms they were often to return in the future.

Princess Margaret, their younger daughter, was born on 21 August 1930, in Lady Strathmore's bedroom overlook-

Opposite: A spectacular view of the castle from the south showing the additional east and west wings which were built in the 19th century
Above: The Queen Mother's sitting room

ing the private garden. This was the first birth in the immediate Royal Family on Scottish soil since 1602, when Charles I's youngest brother Robert, was born at Dunfermline.

The event was celebrated by the Glamis pipe band in full dress, who piped the villagers to the top of Hunter's Hill, two miles away, for the lighting of a beacon by two girls from the village. Two large barrels of beer were taken to drink the Princess's health.

Meanwhile, in the grounds, the Duke of York and his parents-in-law watched the ceremony, of which the four year-old Princess Elizabeth was allowed to catch a glimpse from her window.

The present owner of the castle is the seventeenth Earl of Strathmore and Kinghorne, nephew of Queen Elizabeth the Queen Mother. **PMS**

LEEDS CASTLE

Surrounded by a lake this splendid group of buildings near Maidstone in Kent represents a fairytale vision of a castle. In fact much of what one sees in the way of medieval defences were put up in the nineteenth century, but Leeds Castle played a significant part in royal history.

Originally an earthwork enclosure on the site may have been converted to stone and given two towers along the perimeter in the reign of King Stephen, the Conqueror's grandson. In about 1138 Robert, Earl of Gloucester, had held the castle for his sister Matilda, Stephen's rival for the Crown, but Stephen was able to wrest it from him without too much trouble by the end of that year. Traces of arches in a vault thought to be Norman were discovered at the beginning of this century.

In about 1278 the owner of the castle, William of Leybourne (or Leyburn), who was in financial difficulties, made it over to Edward I by way of part payment of some debts. The King rebuilt much of the castle, providing an outer stone curtain wall round the edge of the largest of the islands, with flanking towers and a watergate in the south-east. The gatehouse on the south-west was also improved. This led out across a drawbridge to a smaller island on which was built the '*Gloriette*' (or keep), a 'D'-plan tower complex, containing other buildings such as the hall, Chapel and so forth, which was much altered later on. Edward I established the elaborate water defences and the lake was created by damming the River Len.

Traditionally, Leeds became a sort of dower castle for medieval queens after Edward I installed a chantry in memory of his beloved Queen, Eleanor of Castile. But when the castellan of the rebellious Bartholomew of Badlesmere, who was holding Leeds as a gift of Edward II, declined to admit Queen Isabella, the King had to recapture the castle. One of the romantic stories attached to the castle is that Henry V's widow, Catherine of Valois, fell in love with her Clerk of the Wardrobe, Owen Tudor, while living at Leeds. Their great-grandson Henry VIII was apparently a regular visitor to the castle and is credited with the transformation of a fortress into a palace. The 75 ft long banqueting hall is named after him.

After Henry's death the castle passed out of royal ownership when it was granted to Sir Anthony St Leger, Lord Deputy of Ireland, who died while being prosecuted for falsifying accounts. Leeds later went through several ownerships passing from the Culpepers to the Fairfaxes and then to the Wykeham-Martins who carried out much of the nineteenth-century medievalist reconstruction.

In 1926 the castle was purchased by the late Lady Baillie (daughter of Lord Queenborough by his American wife Pauline Whitney), who renovated the stone work and redecorated the interior with notable collections of furniture, tapestries and paintings.

Between the wars Lady Baillie entertained several members of the Royal Family here. Before her death in 1974, she set up a charitable trust, the Leeds Castle Foundation, to maintain it for the nation and latterly it has achieved a new fame as an international conference centre. The attractions for the public include a museum of dog collars, though no canine visitors are allowed on account of the duckery and aviary in the romantic grounds which were landscaped by Russell Page. **HMM**

Opposite: The castle today and as it was in 1784 (above); by then the castle had passed out of royal ownership

OSBORNE

When Queen Victoria came to the throne in 1837 she inherited Windsor Castle, Buckingham Palace and the Royal Pavilion, Brighton. She longed to have a retreat away from the formality of the first two, and Brighton she disliked, with its crowds and lack of a private garden by the sea. After her marriage in 1840 to Prince Albert, and the subsequent arrival of their first children the matter became urgent. Sir Robert Peel, the Prime Minister, was encouraging, and her thoughts turned to the Isle of Wight which she had first visited as a child with her mother.

Before Christmas 1843 there were negotiations to take Osborne on a lease from Lady Isabella Blachford (sister of the Duke of Grafton), with an option to purchase. Situated a mile from East Cowes on high ground, with a sweeping view from its windows of the Solent and Spithead and with a private beach, this was just what the Queen and Prince Albert wanted. He was an out of door person and had come up against the Department of Woods and Forests when

Osborne, a square eighteenth-century house built by Robert Pope Blachford, proved too small to take the Royal Family and the royal household as it only contained sixteen bedrooms. The Queen and the Prince called in Thomas Cubitt, the successful builder who had already developed most of Belgravia, to rebuild the house from Prince Albert's designs. He favoured an Italianate style, likening the view across the Solent to the Bay of Naples. The house was to have two *campaniles*, a courtyard, balconies, a gaily tiled corridor and an Italian garden. But as Sir Nikolaus Pevsner and David Lloyd point out in their *Hampshire and the Isle of Wight*, it is not like any Italian *palazzo* or villa. Its inspiration lies in the paintings of Claude Lorraine.

It was decided to build the house in two separate parts. First, a pavilion for the Royal Family, adjacent to the old house, and when that was completed the original house would be demolished, and the Main Block, containing the household wing, erected in its place.

The Queen and her husband came to the island to lay the foundation stone in June 1845. Charles Greville, however, was not impressed. At a Privy Council held at the old house, he commented that it was:

> a miserable place and such a vile house that the Lords of the Council had no place to remain in but the Entrance Hall, so we walked about looking at the new house the Queen is building; it is very ugly and the whole concern wretched enough. They will spend first to last a great deal of money there, but it is her own money and not the nation's.

The new owners were delighted with the pavilion, and on 15 September 1846 they spent their first night there. The Main Block was now started, which at Victoria's request contained the wall of the old manor. The block was completed in 1851. Eventually, long after the Prince's death, the Durbar Block was added.

Osborne House is built round an open courtyard facing the drive. The Pavilion Block is in the middle, and to the right of the courtyard is the Main Block which formed an 'L' with the pavilion, until the Durbar Block was erected to the left of the courtyard.

The pavilion contains the state rooms, of which there are three, though structurally the Billiard Room is one with the Drawing Room, which is at right angles. This gives the advantage that though the household were technically present with the Queen, they were out of sight and did not have to stand. The two rooms were connected with a screen of imitation marble columns. The Drawing Room contains a large central bow, like the garden front of Buckingham Palace. These rooms all open into each other round three sides of the staircase. On the first floor were Queen Victoria's private apartments, with her sitting room behind the bow, and the second floor contained the nurseries.

The three blocks are joined by a large and spacious Grand Corridor which runs right round the courtyard. Statues in alcoves and gay Minton tiles give an Italian flavour, emphasised by the open loggia on the right (or east) side of the first floor.

A prominent feature of Osborne are the two *campaniles*. The square Flag Tower, of 107 ft rises above the Pavilion Block, and on the opposite side of the Main Block is the slightly different Clock Tower, 90 ft high.

Beyond the north front of the house, facing the Solent, formal gardens were made on two levels, with stone balus-

attempting to alter the gardens at Windsor and Buckingham Palace.

Prince Albert went to inspect the property in the following March, and the Queen did so herself that August, after the birth of their fourth child. She wrote:

> I am delighted with the house . . . which is complete and snug. The rooms are small, looked very nice, and the offices and stabling very good. With some alterations for the children it might be made an excellent house.

After a certain amount of haggling about the price, Lady Isabella accepted £26,000 for about 1,000 acres, and in May 1845 Osborne became Queen Victoria's private property. She wrote enthusiastically to her uncle Leopold, King of the Belgians, that it was:

> nice to have a place of <u>one's own</u>, quiet and retired, and free from all Woods and Forests, and other charming Departments who really are the plague of one's life.

trades, and adorned by fountains, including the *Andromeda*, brought from the Great Exhibition of 1851. Beyond were oaks, elms and beech, many of which were planted by Prince Albert himself, to ensure privacy.

A half mile south-east from the house is the charming Swiss Cottage, a chalet bought in sections from Switzerland, and erected in 1853. Here the royal children learnt cooking, carpentry and gardening, and often used to entertain their parents to tea and to sample their cooking. The thatched shed holds their garden tools and wheelbarrows, each marked with the owners' initials, like 'P W' and 'Pss A'. A second Swiss Cottage was built in 1862 to house some of the children's collections, and nearby is the miniature fort built by the ten year-old Prince Arthur, later Duke of Connaught.

The Queen and Prince Albert came to Osborne twice a year – after Christmas to the end of January, and again in the summer from July to August. Queen Victoria bathed from her elegant horse-drawn machine, still to be seen. When she first used this on 30 July 1847, she noted in her diary:

> Drove down to the beach with my maids and went into the bathing machine where I undressed and bathed in the sea (for the first time in my life), a very nice bathing woman attending me. I thought it delightful till I put my head under the water, when I thought I should be stifled.

She never again let her head get wet.

When the adjacent estate of Barton Manor was up for sale, the Queen purchased this rather gloomy house, which was inhabited by her equerries.

With the Prince Consort's death in 1861, everything changed. Five days afterwards, his distraught widow returned from Windsor to the island where he had been at his happiest. Everything of his was left exactly as it was, and as it still remains to this day.

After Queen Victoria was declared Empress of India in 1876, she had an intense interest in the sub-continent, and in 1890 started to build a two-storey wing containing the Durbar Room, with apartments for ministers above. This was erected on the site of a lawn where a marquee had sometimes stood for receptions which were too large for the dining room. The designs were drawn up by Rudyard Kipling's father, who was Curator of the Lahore Central Museum, and Bhai Ram Singh an expert in Indian decorative work. The exterior matched the rest of the house, but inside was 60 ft of heavily carved teak, surmounted by plaster walls, and above the chimney piece was a plaster peacock.

A difficult situation arose with the household when a successor to John Brown, the Munshi, became the Queen's confidant. John Brown, himself, was often at Osborne to the chagrin of the household. When he died in 1883, the Queen wrote 'he had become my best and truest friend as I was his,' and she filled half a column of the Court Circular in tribute to him. There is a memorial granite seat dedicated to him below a terrace, which is one of the few remaining memorials to survive. The Queen's son, Edward VII, obliterated most of them, and was said to have smashed some plaster statuettes with his own hands.

Abdul Karim joined the Queen's service in 1887 as one of the two Indian servants then engaged. He was an ambitious young Moslem of 24 years, and in 1889 became the Munshi (teacher) to teach his mistress the elements of Hindustani. So devoted did she become that she was about to show him confidential papers from India, until Prince Louis of Battenberg, Lord Mountbatten's father, pointed out that this might result in dangerous consequences, for the Hindu population would resent his position as adviser. She gave way, but made him her Indian Secretary.

The Munshi tried to push forward a disreputable friend, and when in the spring of 1897 the Queen decided to take the Munshi with her to Cimiez, the household 'put their feet down', for he would have had to dine with them. A Lady-in-Waiting, Harriet Phipps, had the task of giving the Queen an ultimatum: either no Munshi or no household. Victoria flew into a rage and swept everything on her desk onto the floor. Lord Salisbury, the Prime Minister, was summoned and persuaded her, diplomatically, that the French were 'too old' to understand the Munshi's position and might be rude to him. She then dropped the idea, but the Munshi and his friend came to Cimiez uninvited.

The Queen was not to be browbeaten and had her last ministerial row over the Munshi. It is strange that this old lady had challenged on his behalf, two Viceroys of India, two Prime Ministers and two Secretaries of State, beyond many lesser fry. As late as 1899, Marie Mallet, also of the household, wrote 'I am forever meeting him in passages or the garden, or face to face on the stairs, and each time I shudder more.' It was not until after Queen Victoria's death that the Munshi returned to India.

Osborne was the scene of many Victorian events. Gladstone tended his resignation in the Audience Room when he told the Queen, "I am old and weary, Ma'am, and in need of rest", and the classic remark "We are not amused", was addressed to Alec Yorke, her Groom-in-Waiting, when he was ordered to repeat to her a slightly *risqué* story told at the table.

Queen Victoria died at Osborne on the evening of 22 January 1901, surrounded by her family, in the arms of her grandson the Kaiser. Here she remained lying in state in the Dining Room, commemorated by a brass plate in the floor, before being taken for burial at the Mausoleum at Frogmore.

Edward VII did not want Osborne, for he was devoted to his Norfolk estate of Sandringham, and neither did his son, the future George V. The King offered Osborne to the nation, and the public were to be admitted to the state apartments with the exception of his mother's private suite. The Queen's bedroom became a kind of shrine to her family, especially during Cowes Week, when they came to meditate in the room where she died.

The Main Block became a Convalescent Home for Officers, to which the public is not admitted, and until 1921 the Royal Naval College was housed in the grounds. Here the three brothers, Edward VIII, George VI and the Duke of Kent, and also Lord Mountbatten and his brother, were cadets. The car park is now on the site of the RNC.

In 1954 the Queen consented to the opening of Queen Victoria's private apartments to the public. Osborne was the home she loved best. She wrote to the Princess Royal in 1858, 'Osborne is really too lovely. Charming, romantic and wild as Balmoral is – there is not that peaceful enjoyment that one has here of dear Osborne – the deep blue sea, myriads of brilliant flowers – the perfume of the orange- blossom, magnolias, honeysuckles, roses . . .' **PMS**

Top left: The Swiss Cottage, a hideaway for the royal children. Right: The royal kitchens and (bottom) Queen Victoria's Drawing Room in 1875

ST PAUL'S WALDEN BURY

The first fourteen years of Queen Elizabeth the Queen Mother's life were spent at St Paul's Walden Bury, near Hitchin, the Hertfordshire home of her parents, the Earl and Countess of Strathmore. Her father, as Lord Glamis, had been granted this estate by his father on retiring from the Brigade of Guards. When his youngest daughter, Lady Elizabeth Bowes Lyon, was aged three, he became the Earl of Strathmore.

The Bury, as the house is known locally, came into the Strathmore family through the Bowes, who had inherited it from the Gilberts. Edward Gilbert, the Hertfordshire forebear of the Queen Mother, built the house about 1730, and laid out the formal garden in the French style, with three main radiating rides. Both Edward Gilbert, and his wife Mary, lie buried in St Paul's Walden churchyard, half a mile from the house. He died in 1762, aged 81, and she in 1742, aged 46.

The Gilberts only had one daughter and heiress, Mary, who married George Bowes of Streatlam Castle, Co Durham. James Paine, a *protégé* of Mr Bowes, about 1767 rebuilt the three-storeyed red brick house for his patron's widow, Mrs Mary Bowes. Her daughter, Mary Eleanor Bowes, heiress of that family, married the ninth Earl of Strathmore. The house was restored in 1887.

The Queen Mother's parents, Lord and Lady Strathmore, spent most of their time at the Bury, going to Glamis Castle in Scotland in the summer and autumn. Thus, when their youngest daughter, Lady Elizabeth Bowes Lyon, was born on 4 August 1900, the Bury meant home, Glamis a place for holidays, and Streatlam Castle, which was later demolished, was merely a house to visit. She was christened in the old church at St Paul's Walden. Walden has a long history, being mentioned in the Domesday Book. The name of St Paul's was added when the Dean and Chapter of St Paul's Cathedral were granted the parish by Henry VIII. Previously it had been known as Abbot's Walden, belonging to the suppressed St Albans Abbey.

Here, in this delightful estate in the depths of the country, with magnolias and honeysuckles climbing the walls, the future queen grew up. Two years later, a brother, David, was born, and these two became known in the family as 'the Benjamins', being so much younger than their brothers and sisters. There was a close bond of affection between them. Like their mother, Lady Elizabeth and David Bowes Lyon became enthusiastic gardeners. He later became President of the Royal Horticultural Society.

In their happy childhood, they played games in the

Top: The lawn outside the Bury with one of its renowned statues
Bottom: An elegant inglenook fireplace, partially covered by a screen of blue tiles

grounds and woods. They had their dogs, cats and tortoises, but their favourite pet was her Shetland pony, Bobs, who used to follow her in and out of the house and even up and downstairs. One of their haunts was 'the Flea House', a disused old brew house, to which the only form of approach was a rotten wooden staircase, not strong enough to bear the weight of an adult. Here they laid in rations, and here too were multitudes of kittens. Then there was the harness room. Picnics took place by the statues of *Diana* or the *Discus Thrower*.

When the Great War came in 1914, the usual pattern of life was changed. An army convalescent home was opened at Glamis, and all the family at home helped to run it. With this responsibility Lady Elizabeth changed from a child into an adult.

On 13 January 1923, the 27 year-old Duke of York came for the weekend in his sports car to stay with Lord and Lady Strathmore. He had often come down before because he was a close friend of their sons, with whom he shot and of their daughter Lady Elizabeth, with whom he played tennis.

That Sunday morning he and the 23 year-old Lady Elizabeth did not accompany her family to church as usual, but instead they went for a long walk in the wood. Before luncheon they returned to the house, engaged to be married. Before this particular visit he had broached the subject to his parents, King George V and Queen Mary, at Sandringham during their Christmas stay. "You'll be a very lucky fellow if she says yes," said the King. Now a telegram was despatched from the Bury reading 'All right. Bertie.' Just over three months later, Lady Elizabeth Bowes Lyon became Duchess of York, and thirteen years later, Queen.

When, in 1937, King George VI and Queen Elizabeth were crowned in Westminster Abbey, a plaque commemorating her baptism and coronation was unveiled at the parish church, and she planted two oak trees in the grounds of the manor house, the Bury.

One of the favourite statues at the Bury was *Charity* by Sir Henry Cheere (1703–1781), portraying a mother protectively bending over her three children. As a gift from a friend, the statue was copied and placed in the Wilderness Wood at the Royal Lodge, Windsor. When, as Duke and Duchess of York, George V gave them the lodge, and they came to lay out the long-neglected gardens, those at St Paul's Walden Bury were an inspiration to them.

When King George VI and Queen Elizabeth were living in London, at Bruton Street and Piccadilly, and subsequently at Buckingham Palace, they loved to come down to their country home of the Bury. The death in 1961 of the Queen Mother's brother, Sir David Bowes Lyon, who inherited the Bury, proved a great loss. His widow, Lady Bowes Lyon, still lives there. **PMS**

WHITE LODGE
RICHMOND

Richmond Park contains three houses of historic interest; Thatched House Lodge, Pembroke Lodge and White Lodge. Today only the first has royal residents, but White Lodge has most links with the Crown. Having been built by George II, the lodge became the home, until her marriage, of Queen Mary, and was the birthplace of her eldest son, King Edward VIII, later Duke of Windsor.

The lodge which Lord Pembroke and Roger Morris erected for the King was a fine three-storied house of Portland Stone, standing in a commanding position on rising ground, not far from Sheen Gate. Sir Nikolaus Pevsner notes that White Lodge 'is a very early monument to the Palladian revival, much influenced by Lord Burlington'. Work was started in 1727 as it was on the lesser lodge, now called Thatched House Lodge, but two years later it was noted that 'flooring and fitments of the Great Room were still under construction'.

Lord Pembroke's lodge, now the central block, is a rectangular building, with ground floor, state floor and basement, the long facades having five bays, and the sides three. The house faces west, with views over the mile long Queen's Ride, named after Queen Caroline and stretching as far as Richmond. This west-facing side is the handsome garden front, with a pediment and four Tuscan columns attached to the portico, to which a large open staircase leads up from the garden. The main entrance is at the east front, and from this side the views extend over Beverley Brook to Wimbledon Common. Inside there is the large Banqueting Room or Great Drawing Room, in which King George and Queen Caroline liked to entertain their friends. The fine staircase

has wrought-iron balustrading.

The house was first called the Stone Lodge, but soon became generally known as the New Lodge in distinction to the Old Lodge, (the Ranger's home which Walpole had extended); finally it became known simply as White Lodge. The first mention of this name occurs in 1768 in *The Letters and Journals of Lady Mary Coke*, but over a 100 years later many maps still marked it as New Lodge. The Ordnance Survey first showed 'White Lodge' in 1867–69.

In 1751, George II granted the office of Ranger of Richmond Park to his daughter Princess Amelia who, like her parents, had a passion for hunting. She had succeeded on the death of Robert Walpole, Earl of Orford, son of the great Prime Minister. Though the Princess normally lived in the Old Lodge, her father's house White Lodge, became her occasional residence. In the late 1750s towards the end of her tenure, she began to erect two pavilions of brick designed by Thomas Wright and Robert Morris, to flank the entrance court on the south-east front, linking them to the main block with a passage at basement level.

As White Lodge had been neglected for many years, George III carried out repairs at his own expense before handing over the lodge. By employing James Wyatt, Deputy Surveyor of Woods and Forests, he erected quadrant corridors to link the two pavilions to the main block, and built the entrance porch. The King rode over from Kew to mark out an area of 60 acres of parkland as grounds for the house, (of which none then existed), but Addington refused to accept more than five acres.

Addington resigned office as Prime Minister in 1804 and

also offered to give up his house and place in Richmond Park. The King said, "No! No! That was an act of private friendship." Pitt, his successor, obtained for him the title of Viscount Sidmouth, and as such he is remembered in Richmond from Sidmouth Wood, planted in 1823, now a bird sanctuary.

Humphry Repton laid out the grounds at White Lodge. When he first visited the spot in 1805, he commented that 'a small quantity of land had recently been allotted to the park, without which indeed the house was hardly habitable, although it was surrounded on every side with various landscapes and scenery of a forest rather than that of a park. . . the deer and cattle of the forest had access to the doors and windows, and were only kept from the corridors by a chain or hurdle put across the arches.'

Many of the leading men of the era visited Lord Sidmouth at White Lodge, including his great friend Sheridan, who frequently dined with him, Pitt, Scott, and most famous of all, Lord Nelson. The latter dined at the lodge barely five weeks before he met his death at Trafalgar, and dipped his finger into his port glass and traced his plan to break the enemy lines on the table, which now has a bronze plaque, and is still preserved by the Sidmouth family. In 1844 Lord Sidmouth died at White Lodge, having survived two wives.

In May 1858 Queen Victoria and the Prince Consort decided that their sixteen year-old son and heir, the Prince of Wales, later Edward VII, should have a separate residence and establishment at White Lodge. In fact, the intention was to isolate the boy from all outside influences, and as the Prince Consort wrote to Baron Stockmar, for him 'to only associate with those who are good and pure'. Occasionally he rowed up the river from Mortlake or Richmond to see the Cambridges at Kew, mooring his boat alongside the landing stage at Brentford Ferry. In later days King Edward VII told Lord Esher that he hated the memory of White Lodge, where he had been 'bored to death in his youth', surrounded by middle-aged men, and cut off from young companionship.

Princess Mary Adelaide, of whom the Duchess of Cambridge was so fond, married in 1866, Prince Teck, later the Duke of Teck, and in 1869, Queen Victoria granted them White Lodge in addition to apartments at Kensington Palace. Here their three sons and their only daughter Princess May, later Queen Mary, spent much of their early days.

Life for this semi-royal couple (the Duke of Teck was a son of a morganatically born Württemberg prince) was exceedingly empty, and the handsome but penniless Duke spent his time gardening, collecting Chinese porcelain, wallpapers and brocades. The Duchess, an ample and extravagant lady, full of good works, was highly delighted when their daughter Princess May, married in 1893 Prince George, Duke of York.

In the early summer of 1894, the Princess went on a long visit to her parents at White Lodge, where on 23 June, their eldest child, Prince Edward, was born – the first great-grandson in the direct line to the throne. A few weeks later, on 16 July, his christening by the Archbishop of Canterbury took place in the Great Drawing Room. Queen Victoria travelled by train to Richmond Station, the route through the town being decorated, and she was escorted to White Lodge in the rain by her Hussars.

The Duchess of Teck was known for her unpunctuality.

White Lodge, its shutters closed against the sun, is now the home of the Royal Ballet School

No more royal children were born at the lodge, because the Duke of York found it a trying time staying there. Writing to his wife, he said 'I am very fond of dear Maria (as he called the Duchess), but I assure you I wouldn't go through the six weeks I spent at White Lodge again for anything. She used to come in and disturb us and then her unpunctuality used to annoy me too dreadfully. She was always most kind to me and therefore it made it impossible for me to say anything.'

It was Queen Mary's idea that after her second son, the Duke of York, married in Lady Elizabeth Bowes Lyon in 1923, that their first home should be White Lodge, and she personally supervised its organisation and decoration. They moved in at the beginning of June, and invited his parents to luncheon during Ascot week. 'I had better warn you,' wrote the Duke to his mother, 'that our cook is not very good, but she can do the plain dishes well, and I know you like that sort.' The King and Queen were delighted with their visit, but it soon transpired that White Lodge was not a suitable home for the busy programme which the Duke and Duchess had to carry out. In the spring of 1924 the Duke's sister Princess Mary and her husband lent them Chesterfield House, and eventually they acquired a house in Piccadilly.

Lord Lee of Fareham, Lloyd George's First Lord of the Admiralty, who presented Chequers to the nation as a home for our Prime Ministers, was granted White Lodge in 1926, but soon afterwards he decided to move to Gloucestershire, and an auction of the contents took place at White Lodge.

The Royal Ballet School, which had been founded by Dame Ninette de Valois, moved into White Lodge in October 1955. Dame Margot Fonteyn formally opened the school, and appropriately enough, there is a bronze statue of her by Maurice Lambert, in the entrance hall, lent by the trustees of the Chantrey Bequest. Happily, the school is still at White Lodge, and the doors were opened for the first time to the public in 1957.

Though the interior of George II's Lodge has been altered several times by successive residents, some of the original work is still to be seen. The largest and most imposing room of the house, the Great Drawing Room, rising through two storeys, has the original fireplace, door frames and panelled dado. The room to the left, historically known as the Blue Room, was the Duchess of Teck's sitting room, and the room leading off was the Dining Room. These all have eighteenth-century plaster ceilings and panelling. To the right of the entrance, was the Duke of Teck's sitting room, with its original fine arched screen. On the other side of the Great Drawing Room was the Library.

The wing to the left of the main block from the entrance portico is known as the Prince of Wales' Wing, called after its occupant, the future Edward VII. Here, in the central room on the east front was born a later Prince of Wales, his grandson, who became Edward VIII, then Duke of Windsor. On the other side, in the Queen's Wing, were the apartments used by Queen Victoria and the Prince Consort, and Queen Mary's Boudoir, which opened on to a balcony overlooking the garden.

In the Green Corridor, connecting the Prince of Wales' Wing with the main block, both the Duchess of Teck and Mrs Albertini used to receive their friends, with Queen Mary's favourite seat in the recess. The corresponding corridor to the Queen's Wing was used by the Teck children. The five acres of grounds, too, have undergone many changes since they were laid out by Repton. **PMS**

175

Bibliography

Archaeology of the City of London (1980)
Bates, L M *Somerset House* (1967)
Blunt, Wilfrid *In for a Penny, a Prospect of Kew Gardens* (1978)
Cecil, Lord David *The Cecils of Hatfield* (1973)
Chancellor, E Beresford *History and Antiquities of Richmond, Kew, Petersham and Ham* (1894)
Collenette, C L *A History of Richmond Park* (1937)
Cook, Alan *Oatlands Palace Excavation* (Interim Report 1968)
Courlander, Kathleen *Richmond* (1953)
Dent, John *The Quest for Nonsuch* (1962)
Dugdale, G S *Whitehall through the Centuries* (1950)
Dunbar, Janet *A Prospect of Richmond* (1966)
Fletcher, Benton *Royal Homes near London* (1930)
Girouard, Mark *Victorian Country Houses* (1971)
Hastings, Maurice *Parliament House* (1950)
Hedley, Olwen *Kensington Palace* (1976)
Hedley, Olwen *Royal Palaces* (1972)
Hibbert, Christopher *George IV, Prince of Wales (1761–1811)* (1972)
HMSO *Caernarfon Castle and Town Walls* (1953)
HMSO *Linlithgow Palace* (1953)
HMSO *Osborne House* (1960)
Howard, Philip *Royal Palaces* (1970)
Hudson, Derek *Kensington Palace* (1968)
Lee, Alfred T *The Town and Parish of Tetbury* (1857)
Marshall, Edward *The Early History of Woodstock Manor* (1875)
Matson, John *Dear Osborne* (1978)
Moncreiffe of that Ilk, Sir Iain, Bart *The Palace of Falkland* (1973)
Morshead, Sir Owen *Windsor Castle*
Pevsner, Sir Nikolaus – Editor-in-Chief *The Buildings of England* and *The Buildings of Scotland* (series)
Plumptre, George *Royal Gardens* (1981)
Pyne, W H *Royal Residences* (1829)
Stirton, Rev John *Glamis Castle* (1938)
Summerson, John *Georgian London* (1945)
The King's Works
Wheldon, Huw and Plumb, J H *Royal Heritage* (1977)
Whittle, Tyler *Victoria and Albert at Home* (1980)
Williams, Neville *The Royal Residences of Great Britain* (1960)

Picture acknowledgements

Antler Books Ltd 12, 47
BBC Publications 63
Michael Braid 52, 53
Brighton Corporation 152, 153
British Library 138
Camera Press 96, 97
Colour Library International 153
Country Life 31, 33, 58, 77, 85, 118, 158, 159
Department of the Environment 60, 67
Mary Evans Picture Library 12, 24, 66, 110, 114, 143, 163
Fitzwilliam Museum 130
Keith Gibson 112, 122
Tim Graham 24, 25, 81
Hamlyn Picture Library 18, 27, 35, 38, 44, 45, 54, 56, 76, 83, 125, 164, 173, 174
Peter Jackson 22, 99, 103, 108, 111
Jarrold Colour Publications 21, 29, 64, 68, 80, 104, 121, 144, 161
Keystone 90, 95
Mansell Collection 9, 18, 19, 22, 28, 50, 54, 62, 105, 106, 109, 119, 128, 131, 137, 138, 141, 147, 149, 154, 155, 162, 167, 168
Museum of London 102
National Portrait Gallery 57
Radio Times Hulton Picture Library 126
Scottish Development Department 161
Scottish Tourist Board 113, 160
Trustees of Sir John Soane's Museum 22
John Stidolph 21, 41, 101, 103
Tony Stone Associates 49, 165
Syndication International 25, 36, 63, 75, 79, 84, 94, 156, 157, 166
Reproduced by gracious permission of HM the Queen Frontispiece, 7, 10, 12, 13, 14, 15, 17, 20, 22, 29, 30, 33, 34, 36, 37, 39, 40, 41, 42, 43, 55, 58, 72, 74, 75, 88, 89, 91, 92, 100, 106, 107, 116, 117, 132, 133, 134, 135, 137, 143, 158, 171